> "Thirty-five seconds to go.
> This is the one.
> It's coming back for Jonny Wilkinson.
> He drops for World Cup glory.
> It's up! It's over! He's done it!
> Jonny Wilkinson is England's hero
> yet again. "

Tackling Life

Jonny Wilkinson

Tackling Life
Striving for Perfection

with Steve Black

headline

First published in 2008 by
HEADLINE PUBLISHING GROUP

1

Cataloguing in Publication Data is available from the British Library

Hardback ISBN 978 0 7553 1843 8

Typeset in Bliss by Avon DataSet Ltd, Bidford on Avon, Warwickshire

Printed in the UK by CPI Mackays, Chatham, ME5 8TD

Headline's policy is to use papers that are natural, renewable and recyclable
products and made from wood grown in sustainable forests. The logging and
manufacturing processes are expected to conform to the environmental
regulations of the country of origin.

HEADLINE PUBLISHING GROUP
An Hachette Livre UK Company
338 Euston Road
London NW1 3BH

www.headline.co.uk
www.hachettelivre.co.uk

I dedicate this book to the challenges that make
life so worthwhile.

Jonny

I'd like to dedicate this work to my daughter, Emma,
who I have thoroughly enjoyed working with on this project
and whose assistance kept my focus.

Blackie

Contents

Acknowledgements   ix

Introduction   1

A Note from Blackie   5

Then and Now   7

1 The Winning Habit   19

2 Anxious Moments   41

3 A No-fear Environment   61

4 No Pain, No Gain   77

5 Mountain Climbing   91

6 Beginnings   105

7 The Road Back from Hell   125

8 Injury Time   139

9 Nervous Energy   153

10 Playing the Game   169

11 Fighting to Recover   179

12 Grappling with Fitness   195

13 The Main Attraction   211

14 Ringing Changes   233

15 New Game Plan   245

16 Relative Values   265
17 Gathering Momentum   283
18 Final Progress   299
19 In a Perfect World   309

    Bibliography/Further Reading   317
    Picture Credits   323

Acknowledgements

I would like to thank my mum, my dad, my brother and my girlfriend for their never-ending unconditional support in everything I choose to do and obsess over. I would like to express my gratitude to all the people in my life who have helped me to become who I am and to inhabit such an incredible journey as this one. There are a few other people I'd like to mention – Dudley Colbrook for all his photocopying and faxing, Mum again and Blackie's daughter, Emma, for all their typing work and of course not forgetting Blackie himself for just being Blackie. Finally, to David, Rhea and all at Headline for affording me the opportunity to take on a special project like this. I hope it is something you all can gain from too.

'For all that has been, thanks. For all that will be, yes.'
Dag Hammarskjold

Jonny

I'd like to thank my wife Julie, sons Stephen and Mark, and my mother for their help and support throughout this project. I'd especially like to thank my daughter Emma for her hard work in managing this project for me and liaising so well with Philippa Wilkinson to bring it to a fruitful conclusion. To the entire Team Wilkinson for their support and camaraderie throughout, I thank you all. Special thanks to Jonny for allowing me to support him through all these years. Also, not forgetting all the hard work from David Wilson, Rhea Halford and all the team at Headline.

God Bless,

Blackie

Introduction

❝ *Lessons always arrive when you are ready, and if you can read the signs, you will learn everything you need to know in order to take the next step* ❞

Paulo Coelho, *The Zahir*

Writing this book has been a pretty big deal for me. I have never been the most expressive person. I have the habit of hiding the revealing stuff inside, and just telling people what I think they want to hear.

I have been in professional rugby now for approaching twelve years, from the day I left school. That was when I first met Steve Black, Blackie. The first thing I remember, apart from his ridiculous beard and the fact that I couldn't understand anything he was saying due to his Newcastle accent, was the aura which surrounded him. When he spoke, I saw respect in the eyes of the senior players, all of them established internationals. It was, I later learned, an admiration born half from a state of worship and the other half from a state of absolute fear. It didn't take me long to understand that doing what he told me, when he told me to do it, and staying on his good side, were all superb ideas!

For every day of those twelve seasons we have worked with great enthusiasm to find the true potential inside the both of us. We have trained hard in the gym, on the field and off the field, focusing on the body, the mind and never forgetting the spirit. Over our time together we have built a strong bond and shared some truly wonderful experiences, many of them in the highly intense world of elite sport among some of today's most awesome competitors.

The lessons we have learned, and the messages and techniques they have inspired, are presented here. The crazy period which encompassed the two most recent Rugby World Cups, and the four years in-between, are what I have chosen to focus upon. It is then that the life I knew so well changed for me – over and over again. The kind of pandemonium I endured inside my head was something I am glad I experienced, but would certainly never welcome back anytime soon.

During this time though, I made a significant personal discovery, probably the most important of my life so far. It forms the central theme of this book. I realised that the way I interpreted what was happening around me was actually damaging me, and yet despite the obvious pain, I dared not challenge how I was looking at life. I chose instead to fight what were inevitably futile struggles; I just didn't know that then. Today, all I want to feel is that I'm being the best I can be, and in pursuing a goal like that there can be no right or wrong beliefs, only helpful and unhelpful ones.

I came to the conclusion that the way I perceive my life right now will definitely determine the quality of the rest of it. That's what this book is about: a different way to look at experiences and emotions which might just help you to uncover more of the brilliance inside you.

Every word attributed to me is my own, from my imaginings, thoughts and memories, originally penned by hand. In tandem with my story, in shaded boxes throughout the chapters, Blackie has pulled together his years of knowledge and wisdom to produce insightful, objective and practical commentary on what he perceives to be the key issues in teamwork, learning and living – to name but a handful of the topics he covers. Blackie's approach to life and living has energised me for years. I very much hope that, in the same way, you find something that works for you in the following pages.

Together, Blackie and I have wanted to take absolute ownership of this project. It is not a comprehensive life-teaching manual – heaven forbid – it is just our contribution to the subject. In staying true to the core concept of the book, I would say it is not what you read but what it makes you think about that actually counts. I really hope these stories inspire something deep inside you, the way my experiences did – in real time – inside me.

I learned that to turn anything around in my world, I have only to make a change inside of myself. It was a big relief. It isn't anyone else's responsibility but my own. For me, it was empowering to learn that and when I did, I began to feel a little more in control of my life and dreams.

I know there's more to come, more excitement to be had along this path of ours, and suddenly, that future looks very bright indeed.

Jonny Wilkinson

29 August 2008

A Note from Blackie

In 2006 I was the proud recipient of the prestigious Wilkinson Sword Award given for services to North East sport. I felt humbled by the honour as it had been won by many of my heroes including 'Wor' Jackie Milburn and Sir Bobby Robson, so I was in exalted company. I really wanted to do justice to the occasion during my acceptance speech. I thought long and hard about what I could say. The best I could come up with, which also explains the philosophy behind my embracing this project so readily, as well as my relationship with Jonny was this . . .

'I'd like to thank all the people who've helped me through the years . . . and all those people who have allowed me to help them. Without both sets of people I wouldn't be receiving this wonderful award tonight.'

This book with Jonny incorporates some of the lessons I've learned from both relationships. I sincerely hope they are of interest and may be of use to you as you continue your journey through life. Please take up the hope that drives and underwrites my coaching career: Help Other People Excel.

Please enjoy.

Steve Black
29 August 2008

Then and Now

> ❝*What is defeat? Nothing but education; nothing but the first step towards something better*❞
>
> Wendell Phillips

I find it incredible how, with the seemingly random nature of the world, we can conjure up elaborate dreams then use our abilities, and our strengths, to bring those dreams towards reality. It is almost impossible to fathom that, even with the individual desires and action of billions of others also in play, life can still find a way of balancing everything up and allowing us each to have an influence.

We do not exist as isolated individuals. All our actions and decisions are interrelated with those of others around us, who unknowingly work with and not against each other. If we hold a mental picture of what we want to achieve, and how we want to achieve it, we have the ability to take a potentially unpredictable future and organise it into something pretty wonderful.

As Einstein said, imagination is 'a preview of life's coming attractions'.

What we'll never know though, is how the process works in full. But we need to keep faith that it does. Sometimes, often in fact, things don't go perfectly to plan. When that happens, it can make us want to cave in.

I remember the three consecutive Six Nations international rugby competitions (the first was actually when it was the Five Nations) which ended in disaster for England. On all three occasions I was playing and we were unbeaten, in full flow leading up to the Grand Slam decider. I will give you a short account of each of them.

1999

England played Wales away at Wembley. Blackie was coaching Wales at the time but, despite that, it was a game we weren't about to lose. With five minutes to go we decided to kick for the corner rather than for goal. It was not an irrational decision when you consider that, although Welsh goal-kicking had kept them in touch with us, we had outscored them three tries to nil. But Wales stopped our lineout, worked their way to our try line and scored on the final whistle. We fell victim to our own indiscipline – giving up all those penalties – but even then, the whole thing seemed grossly unfair.

> **We coughed and spluttered our way to another shock horror defeat**

2000

England played Scotland away at Murrayfield. We travelled to the game in the early afternoon and the weather had been fairly reasonable. When we came out of the changing room for the match, however, there was a touch of rain in the air. That didn't bother us. Midway through the first half we were looking fairly solid and in control with a small lead. But the 'touch of rain' soon became a downpour, so vicious and so cold that I couldn't speak, let alone see. It was maybe the strangest weather conditions I have ever seen, definitely the most ridiculous I have ever played in – or tried to play under. As a team England had destroyed a few defences by moving the ball and in this situation we needed to play the conditions more effectively, as our opponents did. To a man we didn't and we coughed and spluttered our way to another shock horror defeat.

2001

England played Ireland away at Lansdowne Road. Easily my favourite season, with the new addition of Jason Robinson in the back line, we were electric throughout the tournament. The momentum was building and building – it can't have been far from unstoppable. Ireland are always tough opposition, even more so in Dublin, but the confidence among the boys was infectious. With the two lessons from the previous years' shenanigans stored firmly under our belt, we could not, would not, let this opportunity slide. But we didn't get the chance to prove to ourselves, and to the public, that we had become a winning team. An outbreak of Foot and Mouth put the game back five months. In that period players from all four home nations teamed together to represent the Lions. It was a great experience but the different agenda broke our rhythm and when we reconvened, ready to finish the competition, in October, we were too slow to find our stride. Ireland, and their better teamwork, took the spoils and, in doing so, took a small part of my will to live. Third time unlucky. This was ridiculous.

I was fed up with failure after failure, I really was. My belief in my own set of principles, how I thought life should be conducted, how it worked, was being severely tested.

That was then. Now, when I look at these events, I do not see failure. And with the benefit of hindsight, which allows me to factor into the equation what happened for that England team shortly afterwards, I know why. With these defeats ingrained in all our minds, the England squad was now well and truly armed for anything. We had learned from them. More specifically we were ready for an uncompromising Grand Slam, a completely unbeaten season and, of course, a first ever Rugby World Cup victory.

Blackie: Wales lend a helping hand

'Failure is an event, never a person.'
William D. Brown

I have this romantic thought that England's Wembley loss to our Welsh team in 1999 taught a lesson that became an integral part of the strategy behind their eventual World Cup victory. We beat an England team who were better than we were on the day in all areas, other than our out-and-out passionate belief that we were destined to win. I also think that the England team didn't think of us as a real threat. We were an 'easy touch', an undisciplined, fragmented group who hadn't proven consistent ability. What the media didn't realise was that the spirit in our camp had moved to a new high after our victory in Paris against the French and an outstanding performance of flowing rugby against the Italians in Treviso. Subconscious or not, there was a definite air of inevitability emanating from the media leading up to the game, and some of the England camp probably lowered their guard accordingly.

The press didn't ask who would win, instead they asked if we could give them a game; could we keep it competitive? Did the game matter more to England? On the surface, perhaps. A victory for them would have given them the championship whereas a victory for us would give Scotland the championship. But Wembley that day became a mini-Wales as thousands of Welshmen and women, including Max Boyce, Tom Jones and all, descended on the English capital. We were convinced that England would underestimate Wales's desire and collective resolve to overcome her greatest sporting enemy.

Watching the game again, it was actually closer than I remember. I thought England were by far the stronger, better team. But on reflection, they were better, but not out-of-sight better. Neil Jenkins kept us in the game. Kick after kick. We had known that during the eighty minutes we would have chances, and when we got those chances we had resolved to take them. Eventually that's what happened; we took our chances and they didn't.

To be fair to Sir Clive, he and his team learned from the experience and undoubtedly continued the journey better equipped to deal with the tournament pressures of an Australian-based World Cup. The team and its support off the field became more streetwise and better able to deal with an emotionally charged opponent. That type of opposition always poses a challenge but if your mental focus doesn't waver, the right team will probably win.

There are epiphany moments in all sports – games and results which serve as a massive learning tool for the future. A couple of years ago in the soccer world, Chelsea were once again leading the charge for the Premiership, but Manchester United were coming up fast on the rails. They'd won nine in a row in the league and their week ahead was, and would prove to be, vital to the eventual outcome that season. They would play bottom-of-the-table Sunderland (where I had not long been coaching alongside my pal Kevin Ball, the manager) midweek then their arch rivals Chelsea in the game after next. This was a huge test of focus for that Manchester United team. They had the two opposite ends of the league to negotiate in the space of little over a week.

So the scene was set, almost a cup final for our Sunderland team, who had already been relegated and would be playing for professional pride, and for the wonderful fans who had stuck behind the team in so difficult a season. For United, it was the chance to keep their winning run going leading into what people thought would be 'The Championship' game against Chelsea. Subsequently, that United team of Ronaldo, Rooney, Ferdinand vintage has matured and swept away all before them. Sir Alex Ferguson has stated that they are probably Manchester United's best ever team. But at that time they were on their way there. They were still on their journey to that higher level. Well, that night we were Rocky Balboa from the Hollywood movies and against all the odds with nothing to play for but personal integrity (is there any greater cause?) we got a 0–0 draw before 72,000 Old Trafford fans.

United went on to lose 3–0 to Chelsea and I am certain the psychological blow they were dealt by not securing all three points against us was a contributing factor. So, just as England learned from their Welsh defeat, so Manchester learned from their draw with the Black Cats. Both events were hugely disappointing for the teams, but because the players and the management had been brought together on such strong foundations and a belief in teamwork and team ethics, I believe they were able to turn the results into something positive. They didn't crumble. Instead, they grew and both sides went on to become world class.

The interrelated nature of life was showing its hand in those Grand Slam defeats. I didn't see it at the time of course, as I was way, way too upset, too disappointed, too insecure and too self-absorbed to learn anything from the losses. But those three defeats certainly made us stronger as a team. They helped us. They laid the path to victory in Sydney in November 2003.

> **With these defeats in-grained in all our minds, the England squad was now well and truly armed for any-thing**

I can see that now. We hated the taste that had been left in our mouths and we were determined to do everything we possibly could, as individuals and as a unit, to savour something far sweeter.

Of course, you've got to recognise that you can take something from such upsets; that there is a way to make your world better as you go forward. But you don't always realise exactly what that is at the time. Yet somehow you respond. If you allow yourself to, that is. To me, instances such as those three matches are like the seemingly random coming together of events and people that happen to us all and actually shape our lives.

If I stop to consider how any one of the many factors that make up my life today came into being, I will find its path littered with coincidences and chance. If I trace my life back far enough I will notice some nonsensical and, to be honest, unfeasibly ridiculous moments when my path crossed with someone or something at just the right time.

At other times important people appeared from nowhere and stepped into my life and made it better. There were also, of course, instances when my world was turned upside-down, my trust tested and my ego crushed. I know now some of these moments actually saved my career in so many ways, and others somehow managed to make me a better and stronger-performing person. They prepared me and empowered me, ready to go on.

> " *If I hadn't worried so much, I would have made more of my time* "

Back then I was blind and deaf to all this. Nowadays I try to listen to what my experiences are telling me – I truly believe the world has my best interests at heart – provided I am prepared to fight for those interests in the right way. I realise now I shouldn't be afraid when some new, unexpected (and probably unwelcome at the time) avenue suddenly opens up in front of me. I am on my way down a new road now, but my dreams and hopes are still the same as when I set off. As long as I never stop trying to achieve more, and to follow my dreams, then the route will be OK. It might not look exactly like the perfect map I envisioned at the beginning; I believe, instead, that it will in fact turn out to be going somewhere far better.

That all makes sense to me now. Sort of, at least. But it certainly didn't for a very long time and I suffered because of it. If I hadn't worried so much, I would have made more of my time. And if I'd done that, I would have enjoyed life to a far greater extent and I might even have got to more or less where I was wanting to be a lot quicker.

I am still trying to make sense of all this. I probably never will. But I don't think that's a problem in the least. What I do know is that I feel a lot better in myself and I enjoy life and success a lot more now. A lot more. And that's important. How can I explain what I mean? About how we can take in what is happening around us, the people, places and things, the good and the bad, and utilise them to move forward? It is a bit like creating a painting.

How we physically influence the outcome and mentally perceive what happens in front of our eyes determines the kind of picture of life that we will paint. Without our perceptions there is no real world out there. Our interpretations of what we see, taste, hear, touch and smell give us our attitudes, our limits, our successes and our failures. They give us the memories of our pasts and the dreams of our futures. These and all the emotions which go hand in hand with them become the colours from which we can choose when we want to begin the painting process. Our actions, which are driven by our feelings, offer us the opportunity to live; they let us go out and leave a mark, they put the brush in our hands. Actions cause things to happen and from those outcomes we learn, we improve and we find the best path for an amazing existence. We make our own masterpiece. And it all starts from a blank canvas.

I base my perceptions and beliefs on a natural desire for peace and the desire to experience exciting opportunities. The quality of how I see things determines how much of my zest for doing good stuff, for being brilliant if you like, manages to shine through. We can all shuffle our views and interpretations around a bit to make a better life. Just look at the way we are able to put the past behind us and reinvent ourselves, if we so choose. We can throw away yesterday's painting and begin afresh tomorrow.

To make the best of life, sometimes you need to run into a few dead-ends and sometimes you have to be prepared to drop back and look at your painting from different angles. Once or twice we may be required to go back to the start before the realisation of the helpful or unhelpful really sink in. That's certainly my story. Feeling devastated at throwing away those Grand Slams – what good could come of that? I may as well just jack it all in. That was me. But if I'd listened more carefully to what my experiences were trying to tell me, I would have seen that these little (or not so little – the mud and rain of Murrayfield felt anything but minor) unexpected excursions were there to point me towards the good stuff, physically and mentally.

The events of my own life in the strange world of professional sport, and what they have shown me, are what I want to share with you because I strongly believe they relate to almost every walk of life.

That's what this book is all about. Trying to explain where I felt I went wrong in my decision-making and my attitude and how it hurt me. How I wasted time and didn't achieve all that I now believe I was capable of. How I could have extracted more enjoyment from the journey which at times did get me exactly where I was aiming, and how I might have arrived there a little sooner. I hope it makes interesting reading.

The Winning Habit

> *"As a hyperactive nine-year-old I had already drawn up my first list of goals for my future. Clearly outlined at the top was playing for England and winning a World Cup"*

2003 was a great year for the English rugby team. Success didn't just appear out of thin air though. We had been working hard for it long before the previous World Cup in 1999. It hadn't been plain sailing either – that's for sure.

During this period we won many games, we lost a few big ones, learned a lot and refined our plans daily. By the end of it there were a little over thirty players from a wide range of Premiership clubs working hard together in a very tight squad. We became good friends through our journey, getting to know each other so well, and began operating pretty much on the same wavelength.

> **When people combine to pull in the same direction, with a will to give unselfishly to the cause, there can only be one outcome**

The enormous positivity which became our driving force generated self-belief and momentum. This in turn created an air of inevitability about the quality of our performance, which began to take care of our preparation, and ultimately our results.

Our enthusiasm and desire didn't just encourage us to get out there, do our best and last the full eighty minutes. Although that is important, it went deeper than that. The team held inspirational energy in spades. Every attitude, thought, feeling and intention had a boosting effect on the group. We had learned to support, drive and push each other every day to be better than we ever thought we could be. We all wanted exactly the same thing and we wanted it more for one another – I think – than we did for ourselves.

When people combine to pull in the same direction, with a will to give unselfishly to the cause, there can only be one outcome. We developed a reassuring self-confidence in the final stages of tight games.

Winning was becoming a bit of a habit. By keeping each others' feet on the floor, however, we were able to maintain our focus and use it to improve our individual contributions and our collective strength.

What gets rewarded, gets done!

Winning is always a great feeling – we treasured it and celebrated it. We were not willing to give it up.

* * *

There is such a thing as a Law of Attraction. We have the ability to acquire whatever it is that we want as long as we go about it the right way. It is what turns our dreams into reality. The Law of Attraction has been brought to wide public attention by Rhonda Byrne's book, *The Secret*, but I'm not sure if any of us knew much about it back then. Not that that mattered, as we were definitely using it well.

'Don't panic! There is no need to panic. We still have plenty of time. We will win this game.' *World Cup final, one minute, thirty-five seconds to go. Martin Johnson (as I remember it) under our own posts as Australia level the scores.*

What we focus our minds on is more often than not what we end up with — well, pretty much what we end up with. There is a slight difference. In my head I can hit the ideal kick over and over again. In real life I probably can't but I reckon with the right preparation, understanding and conditions, like the ones in my mind, I could get damn close. Practising flawlessly in the mind without even venturing anywhere near a field can actually improve my physical skills and begin to close the gap between imagination and reality. There is no harm in striving for perfection, there is only good. With my thoughts and imagination I am drawing the experience towards myself. With great actions I can finally receive it.

* * *

Blackie: The Law of Attraction

'As a man thinketh in his heart, so is he.' Proverbs 23:7

Our Newcastle Falcons league-winning team in 1997 is a great example of the Law of Attraction in action. We knew we had a good team of people working together who all felt they'd been hand-picked for success. Rob Andrew, Dean Ryan, Steve Bates, Jonny, Inga Tuigamala, Pat Lam, John Bentley, Tony Underwood, Doddie Weir, Gary Armstrong, Garath Archer, Alan Tait, Nick Popplewell, Tim Stimpson . . . the list is long. They were household names and all expected to win consistently. We felt we couldn't get beaten and when we were, on the few occasions, we ignored it. We had the inner team confidence and collective belief to keep doing the same things in training in order to embark on a new winning run. It was the collective confidence that drove our team performances. Just looking around the dressing room lifted expectations and heightened our faith, knowing that each of us fully supported the man next to us. That effect is priceless.

When Graham Henry and I arrived in Wales in 1998 we found a team full of talent but lacking enormously in expectation and confidence. I remember my first collective address to the lads. The essence of the message was that we'd now follow what are known as Nordstrom Rules – each of us would be expected to use our own good judgment at all times. We'd train with great energy and enthusiasm. The team would effectively play a brand of rugby that suited this 'new' squad of highly talented individuals. They would reinvent themselves, not necessarily with regard to the outside world, but more so within themselves. And that is what they all did. But that wasn't where the X-factor lay – that was in their total belief in their ability to win each game that they played, to the extent that Wales won ten international games in a row, a record for the national team. During that run we beat England, France twice, won a tour in Argentina and beat the then-current World Champions South Africa at the opening of the new Millennium Stadium in 1999. We then lost a fluke game in the 1999 World Cup during the opening round matches, but since we had over seventy per cent of play (possession and territory), we probably had *deserved* to win.

Looking back, the only good things to come out of that defeat were that we'd still qualified for the quarter-finals, and the Samoan team that had beaten us contained Inga Tuigamala and Pat Lam, two great friends of mine. Although I hasten to add that, at the time, that was no consolation! I suppose it's the beauty of hindsight which affords me the ability to draw some positives from these experiences, given the bigger picture.

We had developed the habit of winning and we genuinely believed we were going to win the tournament. The quarter-final threw up a good Australian team (is there ever any other?) and for the first time since early in our winning run, we were playing a team whose expectation of victory was as great as ours, if not greater. The game was close, very close in fact, and at seventy minutes we were 10–9 down, still very much in it. There was a stoppage and I ran on to give the players a drink. I became aware of a strange feeling I had not felt from within this team since we'd lost against Scotland at

Murrayfield back in February, which was a dozen games ago. I sensed that the team did not really believe that they could win in the last ten minutes. My journal entry that evening, as I considered our 24–9 exit from the World Cup, told of that collective lack of confidence I felt as I ran on to the pitch.

I feel I must also quantify something about the Law of Attraction. There are some things that you simply can't attract into your life. If you don't have the necessary talents to star in a leading Hollywood movie, then no matter how you try, you'll never get that role. However, you can, and almost definitely should, apply the Law of Attraction in the areas where you *know* you are capable and set into motion the possibility of making your dreams come true from the belief and knowledge in your ability to achieve.

Your dreams are incredibly powerful and wonderful things in this sense. They can be a potent stimulus to guide you towards taking the action which will turn them into reality. Frank Sinatra was once asked in a TV interview if he preferred his life as it was, with all the luxuries and excesses that his position brought him, or his fantasy life. Unhesitatingly, and not so tongue-in-cheek, he answered, 'Dreams, without doubt. You meet a far better class of people.' What an answer!

Your dreams can really act as a powerful magnet which draws you towards your ambition. And fortunately, our dreams tend to filter out things that are wildly and truly unrealistic, a waste of time and thought. I believe the filter process stops me, for example, believing I could play the lead role in a West End or Broadway musical because no matter how I try to convince myself that I'm capable of that, I know I'm not!

The *knowing* is the thing. The things you *know* you can do, you can pursue with a chance of making them come true. I dream of an opportunity to develop a club from scratch again as we did at the Newcastle Falcons from 1995; to put processes and structures in place that optimally support the right group of players, recruited in order to grow and maintain success. It can and will happen.

'Whether you think you can or you can't, you're right.' Henry Ford

The autumn series 2002–03 season was, I believe, a turning point for us. We faced New Zealand, Australia and South Africa, the superpowers of modern-day rugby union. In the latter stages of two of the games the scores were incredibly tight. Against the All Blacks we had to hold on to a slender three-point lead. They were running hot when it mattered – at the end of the game. The pressure was ours to deal with. In situations like these, with very little separating winning and losing, every bit of energy from the execution of your belief, decisions and skill becomes hugely important. A few thoughts out of sync, or a few fears, can decide the game, either directly or indirectly, in the way it touches your team-mates. Do you make the choice to inspire or do you make the choice to limit the future? Do you respond to the call of circumstance or do you hide – leaving everyone out to dry?

In all teams every member has a big contribution to make. This will include a technical side – calls to understand, specific moves and skills (for instance, lineout throws, kicking) to perform etc. But it is a great deal more simple than that for me. A true team player is someone whose every behaviour feeds positive energy into everyone else's efforts. The biggest problem always lies in those whose actions sap energy from everyone else. The kind of people around whom you find it difficult to be yourself and feel good. This is the only benchmark I need for evaluating my daily contribution. Does what I say, feel or do make it easier or harder for myself and the team to be at their best? It's all about my intentions – are they decent and honest? Do I prefer to look after myself first and judge others? Or am I unselfish and supportive, first to put my body on the line?

'Drop goal routine. Drop goal routine.' *World Cup final, one minute fifteen seconds to go. The call heard and understood by every member of the team including Ben Kay, who then demanded that Steve Thompson, under pressure, hit Lewis Mood at the back of the lineout.*

It is impossible to over-emphasise the impact the slightest negative imbalance can have, even if it occurs inside just one member of the team. Is someone unsure of a play call they just heard or concerned about an injury? Is someone else still stewing on an earlier error or busy shouting blame at his team-mates? It can and does happen all the time when you let it. In a rugby game it can be disastrous.

In both of the tight Tests we needed every ounce of every

> " *Does what I say, feel or do make it easier or harder for myself and the team to be at their best?* "

player's focus to be right on the money. We were exhausted and facing the big defeats which could have changed everything that year.

With two minutes ticking away on the Twickenham digital display, New Zealand set themselves for a lineout fifteen metres from our try line. They had the momentum in their favour and the last two scores too. The stage was set perfectly for them to cap off a great second-half comeback with a last gasp win.

Ben Kay read the movement of their lineout jumpers and their lifters and worked with his own to rise up and steal possession. I cleared the ball back towards halfway. We grabbed ourselves a piece of the upper hand and it was enough; the final whistle blew. It was the first time we had beaten them in nine years.

Without all our self-belief and the inclination to attack the situation with ambition, we might have tried instead to soak up ten or so phases waiting for the sort of mistake that New Zealand teams just don't make.

Blackie: The power of optimism

'I became an optimist when I discovered I wasn't going to win any more games by being anything else.' Earl Weaver

Being in an optimistic state of mind will ensure that when opportunity presents itself, you are ready to take it. It is very difficult to be in this mindset if you are fearful, restrained or just trying to survive. Ambition opens doors that conservatism can't possibly, but you have to maintain your concentration so that the chances that come along don't pass you by. This is hugely important in general, but especially at elite level where opportunities to win games are at a premium.

In the second match of that autumn series, Australia deserved the nine-point lead they held in the final stages of the game. To pull back two scores within less than ten minutes is a big thing to ask by anyone's standards, but against probably the best team in the world it is damn near unheard of. In any field of life some demands can seem like way too much. The key for us that sunny November afternoon was to break down this ten-minute challenge into single seconds.

Clive Woodward, our coach at the time, enjoyed reminding us all after our 1999 Grand Slam Wembley disaster against Wales, in which they snatched victory at the death: 'It only takes twenty seconds to score.'

> *'I don't want to lose' is not the same sort of thought as 'I want to win.' The message that this focus emits is totally different*

To win this one we had to forget the past – leave the 'what ifs' well alone. We had to get into the very here and now of the present. Bit by bit was how we were going to claw our way back. Johnno asked me to shoot for goal instead of kicking for the corner with five minutes to go, so he obviously felt the same. We were going to have to go the length of the field to win this game now, with the patience to remain composed. One step at a time, we advanced down the field. With a clearly defined vision of what was needed from every player we managed to keep our eyes off the clock and on the ball, waiting to pounce on the first sniff of an opening. Ben Cohen found that opening and, as he so often does, found the try line shortly afterwards.

'I don't want to lose' is not the same sort of thought as 'I want to win.' The message that this focus emits is totally different. The first is almost a plea for mercy which gives away any power you have as you cry out to be spared by chance. The latter is an eminently stronger, more proactive intention which forces you to look inside and uncover the innate strength we all possess for making things happen. As a member of an underdog team I have been pipped at the post too many times because when potential glory loomed, the grip of fear was stronger than the liberating effect of ambition. Fear is negative and inhibiting; ambition is positive and motivating. The effect is manifested clearly in the team as a whole. We had got rid of fear and were embracing ambition. We were getting that bit right.

Blackie: Believe you can run the four-minute mile

'Faith is a passionate intuition.' William Wordsworth

You've got to believe in what it is you are trying to achieve. Without that belief you've little chance of accomplishing anything of worth. The winners in life have a feeling of certainty that they are going to achieve what they set out to achieve. They want to win, they set out to win, and they do just that – they win.

They don't actually consider in much depth, if at all, the prospect of failing. Even if they don't succeed in a particular task, they are likely to consider that the circumstances which engulfed this task were beyond their control and therefore their loss – the failure in their eyes – can be dismissed as the result of these external influences. I am not suggesting they'd openly voice this reasoning though. In fact, I'd go as far as to suggest the contrary, as in many situations they would appear humble, self-effacing and absolutely accountable to the outside world. But they'd probably also be saying something rather different to themselves, repeating the message that they will win the next time out so as to recharge their confidence. They have to believe that the loss they have encountered does not represent or reflect the true extent of their abilities. Such winning individuals let the experience go and move on. This is because most successful people don't subscribe, or dwell upon, excuses. You can't make excuses and be a high-achiever. You can only do one or be the other. It's a choice.

Your actions are driven by your beliefs which, over a period of time, become your habits – your recognised behaviour and reputation. A strong belief in your ability to get the job done will allow you to be assertive, decisive, patient, reflective, supportive and optimally pro-active. You will play above yourself. Your thinking will be empowered and you will find yourself in a very positive position to move forward. On the other hand, if your belief system is weak then you'll be in a negative mindset which will hinder your progress. People with this personality trait more often than not want proof that something can be done before they'll confidently embrace the belief that they can do it. High-achievers adopt a very different approach – they have a faith that the best of life yet to come.

One of the best examples of this is the world mile record set by Roger Bannister in 1954. There were medical experts who told the world that there was no way a man could run the mile in four minutes or less and, if a person did, their heart might explode. Here was the 'proof' that stopped others believing they could do it. Yet with Bannister it was different, he knew he could do it. He'd hit the mark often in training and knew that it wasn't *if* he was going to break the four-minute mark but rather *when*. So he had the belief from his training stats to support his intuitive feel that breaking the record was inevitable. Of course once Bannister broke the record in 1954, thirty-seven did it in 1955 and over two hundred in 1956! Breaking the four-minute mile is now commonplace among senior school and college athletes. People now believe they can run the mile inside four minutes – so they do it.

One great strategy to help nudge you towards the habit of expectancy and inevitable success is to imagine you've already reached what you set as your 'ballpark destination' – picture that you have accomplished your goal, you've won your World Cup. Act as if you've already achieved what you wanted to achieve. Behave how you'd expect yourself to if you met this particular goal; consider how you'd walk, talk, sit, listen, show patience, be controlled and exude confidence.

Become relentless in forging the habit that drives you to behave in that winning way. If you do this, the strength and unstoppable momentum of your mindset will deliver. It's got to.

'Catty, it's yours mate. Get us going forward. You know what to do!' *World Cup final, one minute ten seconds to go. Me passing the ball and the buck to inside centre Mike Catt.*

In the 2003 Rugby World Cup the big game in our pool group, which everyone had earmarked as the crucial Test, was the match between England and South Africa. It was going to be massive, the atmosphere, the build up, the nerves. It wasn't going to disappoint.

When I looked around the fairly tight changing room at the faces of my team-mates I smiled on the inside. They were going about their last-minute preparations; putting on shoulder pads, stretching, talking to physios or just sitting down staring deep into a potentially great performance and towards an ideal outcome. As they did, I saw looks of quiet confidence and controlled self-assurance shaped by years of experience and decisions taken to face up to big questions and challenges. The energy was infectious, and the whole team was feeding on that energy.

I saw Neil Back and Will Greenwood, players who, as far as I was concerned, did it right every time. Their values were spot on when it came to team play and individual performance. I saw Jason Robinson, a man who had already spent ten years at the very top and yet still managed to create a sense of awe in a packed stadium. He was hungrier than ever, a hero of mine in rugby league and now union too. I heard Lewis Moody's unique form of laughter down the corridor. Here was a guy who gave the expression 'putting your body on the line' a brand-new meaning. Phil Vickery and Martin Johnson walked by me and grinned. 'You all right, Wilko?' They had a way of making me feel like a million dollars, at ease yet raring to go. With these characters around me I always felt ready for the challenge.

Blackie: The worth of mutually beneficial relationships

> 'Set high goals, and be positive so others who share your goals will work together to attain them.' Jody Conradt

Recognition and affection from a respected source who is universally acknowledged as a master of their craft is worth its weight in gold. The same words and gestures from someone who has failed or who has yet to gain your respect are rendered almost inconsequential. The lesson here is to surround yourself with substantial and worthy team-mates, colleagues and supporters with whom you can form mutually beneficial relationships – you gain from their promptings and they gain from giving someone of your perceived stature their support.

The energy of every thought, fear, intention, nervous feeling and belief emanating from us all in that changing room prior to the South Africa match created a tension that was so thick and intense that I was struggling even to walk through it, let alone cut it with a knife. It was the result of a building process which had taken place not just over our time together but over our whole lives. This game was to be another step on that journey of self and collective discovery, one step closer to the big finale and it felt great – as did the 25–6 scoreline when the referee blew his whistle eighty or so minutes later.

'Wilkinson right back in the pocket . . . And Dawson suddenly gets away.' *World Cup final, fifty seconds to go.*

The quarter-final stage was where we exited the previous World Cup in 1999. Thanks to a very professional performance by South Africa and five drop goals from Jannie de Beer. Four years later and we were back in the same position and desperate to stay at least a couple of weeks longer.

I'm guessing that the majority of the England fans might have been pleased to see that Wales were probably going to be standing in our path, as likely runners-up in their pool to New Zealand. We were OK with that, considering we had beaten them in the Six Nations already that year. But could we repeat the feat on a bigger stage? We thought so.

In the bus on the journey back from our final pool game against Uruguay, someone asked the driver to turn the radio on so that we could listen to the end of the Wales versus New Zealand game. Incredibly, against all expectations, Wales were winning with just five minutes to go. For me the next few miles were adrenalin filled. With each team's score I tried to calculate what it all meant for our future. Eventually I realised that whichever way it turned out we were in for one hell of a challenge. You see New Zealand really are that good and well, Wales, did you see the way they played? They drew gasps from our team room as we analysed the game the next day. Despite that, in the end New Zealand's finishing class brought them through, so we were back where

> **We entered the dressing room in a disrupted state, quiet and fatigued. We left it together as one**

we began. Wales versus England in Brisbane on 9 November; 60,000 capacity – a sell out.

Wales had been on fire and a week later they hadn't cooled down at all. We were played off the park in the first half. I seemed to be chasing shadows. I ran until I could no longer breathe, making last-ditch tackles before lifting my head to see the Welsh players fly off somewhere else at breakneck speed. We were poor by our own standards; we seemed to be playing like individuals rather than a team. Too often we lost our shape because we lost our nerve under pressure. At the half-time break, 10–3 down and lucky to still be in it, it was time for the coaching staff to show that they could keep their heads.

This was crisis management. Five years of everyone's hard work was slowly leaking out of the changing room via the back door.

Clive and the guys combined composure with controlled urgency to deliver detailed, deliberate and easy-to-understand messages. Tactically they kept it simple but they made big decisions. Mike Catt was coming on to do what he does best – take the game by the scruff of the neck. We needed to slow their ball down and inject our own pace into the game. We were asked to put them under more pressure, to squeeze them into making mistakes from which we could feed. In attack we needed more width in our alignment, more space and big runners to take us forward. We also needed more kicking options. Dave Reddin, Dave Alred and Phil Larder all did the rounds, reassuring and calming the players, covering their specialist areas but also doing the small things like handing out water and encouragement.

We entered the dressing room in a disrupted state, quiet and fatigued. We left it together as one, with a fire burning in our stomachs, a fire which you could see in our eyes.

Blackie: Keeping check of your emotions

'To see a man beaten not by a better opponent but by himself is a tragedy.' Cus D'Amato

Leaders must always seem to be in control and to have the solution to any situation or problem that presents itself. They must not panic. Instead, their role should be to pull together, succinctly and clearly, the squad's focus, directing it towards overcoming any obstacles that may appear to stand in the way of progress. Being confident and exuding control in this situation in an assertive, authoritative and expectant manner can, in my experience, turn the tide and win games that may otherwise have hung in the balance. Of course, some coaches and managers overreact. At half time they will scream and shout and let their emotions get the better of them. And guess what? There are times when that team then goes back out and wins the match. But I don't put that down to the rant the players received. I believe that teams in these circumstances win in spite of the ranting and raving, and not because of it.

The next forty minutes were just a blur. Jason Robinson, I remember, made a classic Jason Robinson break and offloaded to Will for a classic Greenwood poacher's try. Catty did his thing and we did what we could to help him. With an eight-point lead at the end I dropped my favourite goal of the whole tournament right on the final whistle. Thank God that was all over.

What our coaching staff did that day, and on so many others, was a perfect example of what, I believe, we should all do to inspire us towards our goals in life – they focused us on going back out there and doing what was required to get the job done. There is nothing to be gained from just sitting back and hoping for the best, you've got to make the best happen.

Everything I have ever wanted in my world has been and will be achieved by someone else at some stage. One team *will* win the next World Cup, certain players *will* be picked for certain teams, someone *will* get the job which you want and earn the money which you feel you could really use, buy the house you like and enjoy the life of which you dream. Such experiences already exist around us. In order to grab hold of them and be that special someone, we need to find a way to fall in line with these experiences and make sure our paths cross with them.

It is my job to become who I need to be. I have to acquire the right skills sets, execute them to the best standards I can to demonstrate the dedication I believe is required to get what I want. If I equip myself in the best fashion possible then, with all this, I can draw my prize, bit by bit, closer towards me. What my immediate efforts provide, be they successful or not, are opportunities to learn on the way to achieving my ultimate goal. They show me ways in which I can perform better and highlight new skills I will need, so that as I move nearer to where I want to be, I am wiser and better informed as to what is required.

Through the team's missed opportunities and lost Grand Slams, I believe we all, to a man, had learned more or less the optimal way to find the World Cup victory we wanted so badly. But without the enormous guidance of the coaches throughout we couldn't have done it. They really came up trumps for us.

It is astounding when I think about the power we all possess to determine our futures. We can decide that we want to achieve something and despite the number of variables, the obscene odds, the sheer volume of competition and even the absurdity of the request, we can still fashion our own path towards it.

As a hyperactive nine-year-old I had already drawn up my first list of goals for my future. Clearly outlined at the top was playing for England and winning a World Cup. And here I was, hundreds of ups and downs later, a short life already full of challenging lessons, the victim of thousands of exhausting weights, skills, fitness and speed sessions, and what must have been nearly a million different kicks in my memory bank, entering the semi-final – fifteen years on.

Blackie has already mentioned a great piece of advice I was given to help me realise my dreams – it is simply, in my mind and my actions, to become the sort of person who already has what he wants. That way, if the world is to settle into the proper rhythm of cause and effect with my lifestyle, then it is going to have to fall in line with me sooner or later.

When I have an honest and deep-rooted confidence in something it is normally because I am channelling my thoughts and intentions effectively. I am so focused, it is almost as if I am consumed by what I am doing. The concentration of energy becomes a very effective and powerful tool (a bit like a laser, I suppose). When I allow myself to feel great, letting in only the most positive and optimistic thoughts, then great things start to happen. When I decide to let instinct and compassion drive me instead of judgment, then good people seem to appear in my life and nice things begin to occur for them too.

What helped me to notice this first, however, was in fact the flip side of the coin. It was the impact of my negative and self-pitying moods. The mornings when I got out of bed the wrong side or woke up feeling a little off were so often followed by awful 'why me?' days when everything just seemed to go wrong. Have you ever stepped back to look at the damage you cause in other people's lives when you are concerned only with moaning about your own misfortune or taking out your frustrations on them? I did, and I started to look at how all those bad days could easily have been great for me and those around me if only I'd shaken off the ill feeling. If I open my eyes and I feel a little low, with a touch of anger now, I take a bit of time to drive the negativity away. I concentrate on how lucky I am to be in the position I am, with the friends I have around me. I inspire myself by concentrating on thoughts of what might happen in my life if I really pull out all the stops and how I could help others to achieve their goals too. I retain a memory of something which makes me laugh out loud and I make sure I leave my front door with a smile on my face. I choose to have a great day and in doing so I choose to help my colleagues at least have the option of a good one too.

Over the five-year stretch, which comprised two World Cups and countless other events, players and coaches alike had been working desperately hard to achieve success based on good values. We sprinted out on to the field for the second half against Wales wearing our hearts, desires and passion on our sleeves, full of positivity and belief again. It may have been perhaps the single most important moment of the whole competition for us.

Anxious Moments

> **❝***As we walked around the field in our celebratory lap of honour I could feel my dream beginning to slip away. The brightness was already fading and with each second that passed so was my happiness***❞**

The top table for our post-quarter-final World Cup press conference was a daunting place. I was experienced enough by now to know that it was going to be a 'right old grilling'. 'Did we really feel we were good enough to win it after that performance?' 'Is there unrest in the camp?' 'Is our confidence lagging?'

'Surely France must be favourites now?'

I was about to reach into my tracksuit trouser pocket and hit the imaginary autopilot button: straight answers only, just be calm, polite and respectful. I wanted to get out of there as soon as possible. These guys were dragging me down. Clive then woke me out of my act and got the pens scribbling among the journalists.

'We will beat France – I've no doubt about that.'

Such an outwardly certain response as that was brand new to me. Sure we were always full of confidence – every ambitious team should be. We had faith in our ability but to put it out there in the media was a big play and not our usual style.

A thin line separates self-belief from arrogance. I have never been able to condone arrogant behaviour. In sport, nothing fires up opposition teams more than when they can sense disrespect expressed in terms of hugely over-assured and brash views. The difference between confidence and arrogance is often only evident in how you express your intentions or in the value you give to other teams.

Clive was not being remotely arrogant; it's not his way. He wasn't playing games either. What I heard was the voice of belief and conviction in his team's potential. It was a statement of ambition born out of being with them day in and day out, through thick and thin. It came from a deep personal knowledge of every player. It inspired me, sitting next to him, to feel that kind of decisiveness from a guy who always made a point of respecting, praising and learning from all opposition. He is a very honest man who, I believe, follows his intuition because it serves him well. If it felt right to him to say what he said then it was fine with me. I suddenly sat up straight in my chair and started looking forward to the semi-final and away from the disappointment of our Wales performance. Maybe that was the effect he knew it would have, on all the players and media too.

Perhaps getting this belief out in the open reinforced it for us. It was a coaching move as well. We were re-invigorated and beginning to turn the corner. Clive, on this occasion, also happened to be correct. After a week in the Brisbane sunshine spent preparing to play elaborate, open rugby against a mercurial French side, it rained on game night. So instead, after recovering from an early setback in the form of Serge Betsen's try, we ended up playing uncompromising rugby in wet conditions. The forwards were ruthless, powerful and precise.

At twenty-four points to seven, with five minutes to go, we had put three scores between France and ourselves. This would normally be one of my favourite situations, knowing that the game was effectively over result-wise but not yet time-wise – a chance to relax and enjoy the sense of security and invincibility. Not this time though because this was the semi-final of the Rugby World Cup and

> **We were re-invigorated and beginning to turn the corner. Clive, on this occasion, also happened to be correct**

every moment was now in some way relevant to the outcome of the final.

The three drop goals I was involved in during that game and the manner in which the team presented me with the opportunities was for us a payback of sorts for the way we all took on, responded to and endured the Welsh experience, and indeed the earlier group trial against the incredibly tough, lightening fast Samoans. With twenty minutes to go in that match we were still behind. At that stage the World Cup final seemed a long way off. So I wasn't about to change my routine now. I had chosen to suffer heavily during the last two weeks, mainly by letting nerves and the intensity of the media attacks stress me out. I would take another instalment of it all if it meant winning the cup.

When the semi-final ended I commiserated with the French boys then tried to jog straight from the field to the quiet changing room where I could start working it all out in my mind. I felt that I couldn't be concerning myself with celebrating, high fives and all. I needed to reflect and start planning immediately for what needed doing in seven days' time.

It seems strange at this point, when we were so close to achieving something fabulous, which we had been striving towards for our entire lives, that I could still have questions and hesitations holding me back. But that – I guess – seems to be the nature of the human mind. Mine was trying to protect me from the inevitable fear and potential disappointment which occur when you actually have to live an event which you have been dreaming of for a long time and is never likely to come round again: a do-or-die situation. I was telling myself that I'd done well whatever happened; that it was OK even if I performed poorly in the final. It wouldn't matter that much, would it? In fact, I was sinking back into my shell when it mattered most to be at my best. It wasn't my voice I was hearing, it was the voice of my comfort zone drawing me back in trying to wrap me in cotton wool.

Nothing that I truly want ever seems to come easy. Maybe getting it wouldn't feel so great if it did. I find, as tough as it seems, in order to be rewarded I need to step out of my comfort zone and leave myself open to failure. And that's not going to be an easy place. The higher I set my goals the greater the possibility of taking a fall. That's just the way it is. You have to allow yourself the possibility of success, to be prepared to leave behind the good stuff and go in search of great stuff, whatever it is that you are hoping to achieve. But if you don't put yourself there, you have no chance of taking the big prize. There is no point in hiding from it and claiming later that it wasn't your fault. That you were unlucky. That's no way to live. So you have to be there – away from the norm. But stepping out of the comfort zone doesn't have to be that uncomfortable. It is challenging when you face your fears but it broadens personal horizons and can liberate you from a kind of prison environment.

It can also have a real driving effect too. I have tried to create an ethos wherein I actually choose to give myself more to lose than just a rugby game on the weekend. I try to commit a great deal more of myself than just trying hard for eighty minutes then going home. I am not afraid of sticking my dreams in there along with hope and a lot of my time. That's what the crazy kicking practice, the early mornings, the gut-wrenching extra conditioning sessions, the injury rehabilitations and the big dreams mean in my life. They serve as preparation before the game and then as collateral during it, something else to fight and die for. Without these extra motivating factors I don't think I could honestly say I gave my all and strived to achieve my full potential.

> **"Nothing that I truly want ever seems to come easy. Maybe getting it wouldn't feel so great if it did"**

At home there is sometimes nothing more enjoyable than relaxing with my feet up in front of a great film after a fantastic meal. But with my life goals I don't like just being comfortable though, I don't like taking it easy or cruising along. I like to front up, to reach out and invite in something seemingly intimidating or worrying. It is not always easy, however. It often means putting one foot in front of the other and moving forward when inside I feel like freezing on the spot. Back before the final when it started to get pretty frightening, it meant taking it one step, one day at a time. It meant just enjoying each training session and continuing to strive for something amazing rather than holding on too tightly to a fear-based notion of possibly losing it.

I would like to grow by achieving experiences, not achieving material goods. I want things I can take with me wherever I go. It was not so much the World Cup winners' medal I desired in my back pocket but actually the intensity and unique opportunity to see rugby at the highest level. I was eager to discover what it might show me about myself. I also love the shared memories of such astonishing one-off experiences with a group of fantastic people on the field and a hell of a lot more in the stands and on sofas around the world.

> **Without these extra motivating factors I don't think I could honestly say I gave my all and strived to achieve my full potential**

Throughout the entire build up to the final and the match itself I remember my concentration breaking only twice. The last of the two occasions was during my personal warm-up when I was attempting goal kicks from near the touchline, five yards out from the try line. One of them struck the top of the near post and rebounded, almost perfectly along the same trajectory from which it had approached – straight back to me where I stood some twenty-five yards away with my kicking tee. As it fell into my hands I looked disbelievingly at Dave Alred – the England kicking coach – who was standing at the other side of the posts observing and catching. His timely smile put a grin on my own face and I found a few seconds for a chuckle. Then it was back to business. In fact it had been business all day.

Blackie: Evolution of a team

> 'How many years you have to keep on doing, until you know what to do and how to do!' Johann von Goethe

Winning the World Cup in 2003 was a wonderful achievement for all concerned. The architect of victory, Sir Clive Woodward, had vision, passion, and what seemed to be a relentless energy to drive the standards of his team.

That team wasn't thrown together overnight. It evolved over time. It went through the whole spectrum of emotional tests and came out stronger than before. At the start of that team's journey, they faltered at critical times, but still Clive's focus on them becoming the world's number one team didn't waver. He ensured the team learned lessons from their experiences, and moved on. His team grew together and the bonding of players and coaches was there for all to see. They believed in each other, they believed in the cause, and they eventually believed in the inevitability of winning the major tournament.

The dressing room was full of leaders and coaches. Many of the players coached each other on a daily basis. They supported, cajoled and demanded from one another a standard of teamwork that overwhelmed the opposition. The year before the World Cup, England were by some considerable margin the best team on the planet. Not only did *they* expect to beat whichever country they played, the *opposition* expected that as well. Invariably that expectation led to an English victory.

The preparation of the team was obviously excellent and the perception the players had of that preparation gave them enormous confidence. Once again Sir Clive and his team must take enormous credit for creating that environment. Yet, in a similar way to the Falcons episode in 1997, I feel the X-factor within the England group – the players, coaches and backroom staff – was their belief. They all believed that if they did X, Y and Z and put in the associated effort the inevitable result would be success.

So it was their choice to win. The opposition didn't really factor because if England did what they were capable of, as they had done regularly over a period of time, how well the other side performed was irrelevant: England's best would be better than any opponent's best. What was critical was that England knew they were the best. A team that had Martin Johnson, Jonny Wilkinson, Lawrence Dallaglio, Neil Back, Matt Dawson, Will Greenwood, Jason Leonard, Jason Robinson, Phil Vickery et al., all performing somewhere near their peak, would always be in with a shout.

The final stages of the competition were all evening kick-offs. A lot of players don't like them and for good reason. They can't stand the hanging around, they just want to get out there and get on with it. Me, well I fall somewhere in between. It does make for a long day, with nothing much to do but let your mind wander anxiously to what lies in store later on. However, when I know I have a big defining moment looming I am now able to make every second count. Every word on every page of the book I'm reading becomes doubly meaningful because I escape into it and I am so grateful for the chance to take deep breaths before the pressure of the big event. I allow myself to become so involved in the movies I watch it is almost as if I am starring in them.

When I search for the same intensity on a quiet summer's day off I never find it. I've always set ambitious goals, and therefore punctuated my life with events of immense perceived meaning, but now the moments around them seem to have accrued an incredible vibrancy too. But as the game grows ever nearer I cannot help but be sucked into the same impatient emotions of my team-mates.

The sensation of fear and insecurity is a horrible one. I cannot imagine what it must be like for those fighting in the armed forces before they do battle. We are, after all, only playing with a ball; we're not playing with life and possible death. A career in professional sport for me has, in a way, meant a continuous effort to deal with the worries and panic it creates inside me.

I've found a way to overcome this anxiety. But it requires a mental strength and commitment rather than the physical stuff which I find easier. However much I ignore or obsess about it, I just have to understand that kick-off will always arrive when it is time for it to do so, not a minute sooner, not a minute later. So the better way to deal with anxiety, in my opinion, is to allow it absolutely no time or space in my mind. I will embrace the nervousness because it will inspire my actions. The butterflies just let me know I care so much – not a bad thing! There is no point in letting them affect my preparation. It is better to focus all my thoughts and energy on a positive outcome and a great performance. If I allow mistakes and images of failure to exist in my mind, then I am offering them the opportunity to exist on the field.

I reckon I must have lost a good few weeks of my life through wanting to be a few hours ahead of myself. The sacrifices I've made have not been missing out on nights on the town, pizzas, fast food, or extreme sport holidays – as people often think – but of not living life to the full. This has been my choice – an unnecessary one at that. The question I was asking myself is, 'How do I deal with these feelings?' Trying to answer it has only invited more problems. The question I should have been asking was, 'What would it be like if I didn't have these feelings at all?'

> **In my mind I was already at the game, wishing away the whole afternoon**

On 22 November 2003, I hadn't even begun to understand this. As you can imagine I was struggling. I was cooped up in a room, pacing around. I wouldn't have been able to tell you the colour of the wallpaper or how the weather was outside. In my mind I was already at the game, wishing away the whole afternoon.

One thing which always helps salvage some kind of peace is speaking to my friends and family. For example, the night before each game Blackie sends me a fax to read over a few times. It is astounding how he can pull inspirational messages from all kinds of places, yet know that the interpretation I will make will include the exact words I need most at that time. Just when I'm thinking no one out there could possibly understand, those closest to me do just that. When I have really spent time getting to know someone, hanging out, talking and telling truths, a deep connection forms. It is a bond which goes deeper than words or distances. I have the link with my brother too. It comes from spending our childhoods in each other's pockets, sharing dreams, seeing things through each other's eyes. I have called upon these people far too much for the extra help I need and I am lucky to have such a brilliant group around me.

Blackie: Faxed inspiration

Hi Jonny,

I turn once more to the field notebook of General George S. Patton for this message to inspire your thought processes today.

'Success in War depends upon the Golden rule of War, Speed – Simplicity – Boldness.'

Be assertive, decisive and rapier-like in your execution of today's game-plan.

Your performance will ignite the flame of desire within your team to produce irresistibility . . . and victory.

God Bless,

Onwards and Upwards,

Blackie

***

Jonny,

Once again, you've prepared brilliantly . . . now for the game . . .

Today, in attack and defence go forward with purpose, guile and intent!

As a team, show massive ambition in attack and indefatigable spirit in defence.

This team, playing this way, led and inspired by yourself, barring a catastrophe of nature, can't be beaten.

Heart work will drive your Hard work.

Believe in this performance.

God Bless,

Onwards and Upwards,

Blackie

That day, however, like I said, was all business. Mike Tindall, the king of gizmos and gadgets, had taken charge of the pre-match journey soundtracks. He had mixed some belters. The CDs were burnt to fit the time scale perfectly. Eminem's 'Lose Yourself' was to fill our ears as we entered the stadium and stepped from the bus. The selection of songs was eclectic, to cater for practically all the squad's tastes. However, on the final journey the music system skipped a few times. The Leicester forwards may have been lifted to new emotional heights, but entering the arena to the tune of 'Rock the Casbah' was not quite as potent a motivating force as the power lyrics of America's biggest rapper's monster hit. That was the first of the two times I broke from my concentration.

'Yes, Daws, I'm here, mate, straight back.' *World Cup final, thirty-six seconds to go. Me calling for and praying for, one of Matt's best left-hand passes.*

The game was incredibly tense, like a boxing match between two prize fighters armed with the knock-out punch but afraid to wind it up in case the other struck in the meantime.

Australia did strike hard right at the beginning with a beautifully executed cross kick and catch exploiting their height advantage on the wing. We struck back when Jason Robinson, with lesser height, countered with a matching display of great finishing skill. We jabbed and jabbed with penalties and towards the end of the game we were still standing on steady feet. That is until a few expensive lapses in discipline sent us wobbling and helped level the scores at the end of eighty minutes. If that wasn't enough, at the end of extra time we were dealt a killer blow when the man with the whistle blew for a mysterious (at least to us) penalty. Then, with his country watching and hoping, it was the man with the strongest legs (and nerves) who popped over another three-pointer. Fair play to you Elton Flatley.

The Law of Attraction, which I spoke of earlier, involves making a fantasy play in your mind then turning it into reality by your intent and actions. When a squad of players align themselves and combine all their visualisations of what they desire, then the force multiplies. We tried to control all that we could to allow for the possibility of success. Our collective energy, pulled together, created an influence over what happened. If we'd sat back, let our heads drop, felt the power of our team spirit drain away, we would have lost. Combining your focus into one aim doesn't guarantee success, but it gives you a hell of a better chance of achieving it. And at the very last, we had enough self-determination to get the result we wanted. Throughout the years I think we had learned how not to waste too much of that energy along the way. There was still some left in the tank.

As a nine-year-old, when I set my goal of winning the World Cup, I also made myself a promise — that at some point I would do all I could to try to achieve that goal. I wanted to be the kicker and I wanted to play my part. Every little event over the years was important, what they taught me, how they strengthened my resolve, the feelings they offered me or even just the fun they afforded me. Every person whose path I had crossed, their input, however small, had redirected me in some way and now I found myself at this very point.

'This is the one. It's coming back for Jonny Wilkinson.' *World Cup final, thirty-five seconds to go.*

Matt Dawson made a fabulous break. Neil Back sent Martin Johnson piling into the Australian defence in order that we find a few more seconds to set ourselves and get Daws back on his feet to make the pass. He made it, a good one, right into my hands and I was left to do exactly what I had spent an unhealthy amount of time doing already in my life. All the hours of isolation, of dreaming, of crying, of screaming and of cheering, the practice sessions in car parks, on football pitches, in swimming pools, in hotel rooms and in my sleep added up to perhaps this one repetition. In a strange way that drop kick symbolised the bigger process of winning the cup. I had learned over time, with practice, with the influence of others, how to make something I wanted to happen, happen. This time of all times, it worked. Thank God!

* * *

Blackie: If you can't stand the heat

'Life is a sum of all your choices.' Albert Camus

A mistake here, a poor decision there ... personal performances make or break you. That's why the guys who can make
great decisions when the heat is on are worth more than their
weight in gold, in business and politics as well as sport. In team
sport, your destiny in so many cases lies in the hands of
someone else's contribution. So you need to surround yourself
with good managers, coaches and players who keep delivering
the right decisions and performances when needed.

'Use Catty, Daws!' *World Cup final, three seconds to go. Me getting
excited.*
'Catty, get rid of it!' *World Cup final, zero seconds to go. Me
screaming.*

Hit the pause button right there. This is the moment I want to
reside in for ever.

Trevor Woodman had secured the ball after the Australian
team's clever effort at a short restart. Daws readied himself to
pass to Mike Catt on the right with me on the left if needed. Catty
caught it knowing the game was won as soon as the ball went
dead. He put his cultured right foot on it and sent it spiralling into
the crowd. As he did I watched referee Andre Watson put the
whistle in his mouth. How I loved that split second before he went

ahead and blew it! Before the sharp shrill sound there was a beautiful mix of anticipation and security. It was the perfect recipe for bliss. I didn't want it to end.

'World Cup!' 'World Cup!' 'World Cup!'

I'm going to attribute Will Greenwood with these wise words but in reality they were probably coming out of my mouth. It was all I could shout as myself and Shaggy (Greenwood) performed an excruciatingly embarrassing dance of celebration.

The adulation, the noise and energy were too incredible to explain. To live in it, experiencing every day like that night as if it was new each time would be paradise on earth. But it just isn't possible. Is it?

Blackie: Legacy

'Treat people as if they are special and they will become special.' Brian Tracy

Sir Clive kept his head, kept his vision and stayed true to his belief that the big prize would be delivered. He didn't just push the standards within the team; he pushed the standards at head office. He made people in management feel uncomfortable with his demands in his unrelenting pursuit of excellence. With someone else leading that group of players, it could have gone wrong; it could have faltered. The fact that it didn't was down to the great foundations he'd put in place during the building of that team. He empowered the players to make decisions on the field of play and wholeheartedly supported their right to do so. By the time the World Cup was won Clive had grown the team to the extent that they could have turned up at the tournament without him and his coaching team and still won! That's the ultimate accolade in coaching. Clive and his management team left a legacy which could have, should have perhaps, lived on.

But the legacy wasn't handled as well as it could have been in the aftermath of that great victory. I think if England had consolidated the progress made and continued the journey with an open, developing mind, they would have been able to retain the number one spot. The challenge now is to regain it. When they do, I believe it will be down to two overriding factors that will finally finish the job: absolute belief and unwavering confidence. The other stuff, the training, the facilities and so forth, is a given. You have to get that right. It's like breathing.

The managerial challenge of doing what the England team did in 2003 must not be underestimated. The philosophy of putting together a group of individuals who are acknowledged leaders in their field, to coach other individuals, and to have all aspects of the preparation covered by experts screams of common sense. Yet this common sense appraisal doesn't begin to tell of the pitfalls involved in executing the strategy.

First of all, you've got to pick the right people. The choices will never please everyone all the time. Life isn't like that but Clive chose well enough to satisfy the people who mattered most: his players. He also brought together a backroom team that bought into the vision he was trying to bring to reality. It followed that they were all able to work together and complement each other's input. The whole structure became a group of people who had decided to get along and to dedicate their time and effort to fulfil a very worthy purpose. They wanted to become irresistible, and they did.

The problem with reaching the peak of the tallest mountain in your dreams is that the path can only wind down the other side further and further away from this idyllic moment. I had pictured this image – worshipped it even – for years, maybe as long as I could remember. As we walked around the field in our celebratory lap of honour I could feel my dream beginning to slip away. The brightness was already fading and with each second that passed so was my happiness. I knew that it would never be the same again. Had I had my moment at twenty-four years old?

> *The adulation, the noise and energy were too incredible to explain. To live in it, experiencing every day like that night as if it was brand new each time would be paradise on earth*

What a life I had had so far. I was so fortunate. I prided myself on making the most of it. I wanted to pay it back by showing my gratitude. It was definitely a worthy mission. And my life deserved some payback because, up to then, I think I had kind of abused it. I had surrounded myself with the fear of never achieving my ambitious goals and then with retrospective regret at the mistakes which I believed stained my best efforts.

Boy, was I missing the point. I was missing the bit between what I had done and what I might do. What I was doing right then and there was what was important. The present moment is the only place in which I believe the world can exist. The past is gone. It only provides memories and stepping stones. The future is just the mind's best guess as to what might happen, based on what you have learned from experiences. But what does it feel like in the here and now? For me it has always been fine when I'm out there competing. Then I don't feel anything because I'm too busy 'being' – in the thick of the game action, reacting and using my instincts. At these times it really doesn't matter who I am, where I've come from or where I'm heading. All the things which comprise my worries just seem to disappear. I have always lived in the now in those moments on the pitch. But back then, after the final whistle, I would sometimes sit in the changing room and try to find the same zone. I never did.

Two hours after we lifted the trophy above our heads we walked into the post-match party. We didn't need to queue which was nice but the 'private' affair had degenerated into something far from exclusive. I could feel myself being pulled from pillar to post when all I wanted to do was find the space I needed to get a handle on it all, just like after the semi-final. My fairy tale ending was turning out to be an altogether different story. I was not carefully treading a path down the mountainside and enjoying the view. No, I felt like I was tumbling out of control.

So how did I end up in that state of mind, on what should have been the happiest day of my life? What a waste. There were a number of reasons I let my life down even as I achieved my life goal. My ethos. My attitudes. My foolishness.

3

A No-fear Environment

> " *I didn't stop laughing until we arrived back at the hotel. I had, along with many others, managed to complete the rest of training in tears* "

Before I go on to explain how I think my own perspective on life at the time of the 2003 Rugby World Cup robbed me of my ability to enjoy the moment, in fact to do justice to what life was giving, I think it is worth pausing to reflect on one of the key reasons we won the trophy. Just when I needed it, one of the positive influences on me at the time – and indeed now – came from a man named Clive Woodward.

There were, of course, many reasons why England triumphed that autumn. But most of them, in my view, led inexorably back to Clive. Everything he did and thought in that run-up to the World

Cup was designed with one goal in mind. His attitude, his planning, his preparation and his foresight left a very big impression on me. The principles he employed then, I still use as a benchmark for attention to detail. Without that, I believe you lose your winning edge. In any facet of life. A lot of this book is about my journey to rediscover the flame of enjoyment in life – but never at the expense of wanting to succeed. Clive certainly showed me, and a lot of others, many of the attributes that are necessary to be victorious.

During my time with Clive I found him exceptional, especially when it came to reacting quickly to and preparing for the unexpected. But for me, that wasn't what made him stand apart from the rest. His trademark, in my eyes, was the way he managed to stay one step ahead of the game. At international level, when rugby gets really competitive, if circumstances are telling you that you must change then it is probably already too late to do so.

Tactically speaking, he possessed a brilliant mind, and to back this up, he never shied away from taking risks. He was happy to put his neck on the block and accept accountability for the team, provided we took responsibility too. He looked hard at where the game was moving to and then either raced ahead of the impending change or took rugby off in a totally different direction. Rather than do things the same as everyone else, he experimented to see if they could be done differently and then did them better.

Clive showed me how to break out of the box and view the action on the rugby field from different angles. This often meant overcoming enormous emotional urges in order to make calm, composed and clever decisions instead of rash or predictable ones.

He saw, I think, what the impact of professionalism was going to have on rugby union; he saw the way in which the sport was evolving and forced a quantum leap. Match play was becoming more physical, involving bigger contacts and the intensity was being sustained for much longer periods. Now fully employed by the game, players would have all the time they needed to boost and refine their skills. Everyone taking the field was exhibiting superior fitness and strength. Above all, teams were becoming enormously competitive. Victory and defeat were being decided by inches and seconds. Winning was now to be about the one per cent advantages you could muster across the team, and these were always hidden in the finer details.

Clive started accumulating these vital margins by organising the best of the best into an elite coaching team. The line-up covered every specific skill using world-class expertise in every area. Straight-talking Phil Larder was someone whose rugby guidance I trusted implicitly. He came from rugby league and

> **Clive showed me how to break out of the box and view the action on the rugby field from different angles**

had the job of making sure that even if we didn't score a point all year we might still draw many of our games with ruthless watertight defence. Dave Alred delivered practically perfect kicking and kicking tactics with experience drawn from rugby union, rugby league, Australian rules football, soccer and a spell in the American Football League. He could well boast of being the best in the world with enough qualifications to use up most of the alphabet after his name. And he was the psychology man too. Andy Robinson, famed for his ruthless animal-like approach to his own England

and Bath rugby career, would fire up the forwards while at the same time keeping them smart and switched on. Brian Ashton brought his lateral thinking and natural flair to organising the backs into a formidable attacking outfit capable of scoring from anywhere. Dave 'Otis' Reddin was responsible for physically challenging the players, drawing out the very best of them, giving them the strength and potential to battle out of their comfort zones from the first to the final whistle. He would spend a lot of time with the boys and, therefore, probably required a great sense of humour as well as thick skin. He had both, and his experience of elite sport at all levels helped massively.

Phil Keith-Roach was a scrummaging genius. Thankfully, on his specialist subject, I had very little to do with him. The forwards simply swore by him, and on a social level he was an incredibly nice guy, flawless in fact.

Simon Hardy was the man to strengthen up the lineout throwers, and to add some important guidance on all lineout situations. The precision which he brought to this facet of the game would make a big difference.

Also on board was Adam Carey, nutritional specialist and now TV star. He revolutionised the way we ate and thought about our food. I never realised until I met Adam just how important it all was. Team energy levels went through the roof, physiques changed and reshaped and smiles started to fill the rooms and the pitches.

A later addition came in the form of Sheryl Calder – vision expert whose talent was in broadening our field of peripheral sight and decision-making. Every day I found I was taking more information in with each glance, seeing opportunity where there used to be brick wall defences. And still I was able to keep my eyes on the ball and the game at the same time.

Blackie: Good vibrations

'Align yourself with ambitious, like-minded people...
it's the best way.' A delegate at the Leaders
in London Conference, 2007

If you allow yourself to be authentic and live the way you really want to, doing the things you enjoy doing, and, as is often the case, doing them well (because we tend to want to do what we're good at) you'll almost certainly find yourself working and living with like-minded people. You'll be naturally drawn to these people, and them to you. Our thinking dictates our actions, and through our actions other people view us. So it is our thoughts that start the process. Now, imagine that those thoughts actually produce vibrations which resonate with other like-minded people. They are drawn to you, and you to them.

Think of your own lives. How many times have you inexplicably had a chance meeting with someone who went on to play a huge role or have a huge effect in your future – if you had not gone to that meeting/party/conference/shop/social gathering on that particular day, the course of your life may have been steered in a completely different direction. Was it a chance meeting? Is it simply a coincidence you were both there on that day? I don't believe so. There is something which attracts people towards each other for mutual gain. So just think what can happen if you can get a group of people operating on the same wavelength with a shared goal. They'll become almost unbeatable.

There are some people who make you smile when you see them. They always seem to be in a happy, upbeat mood which is very contagious and persuasive. When we leave their company we feel better for having spent time with them. It's great when a bunch of people with those characteristics are drawn together because their collaboration can provide a very strong base for whatever they are doing. A weak base for a team would be one with a group of complainers and moaners, because they'll start to attract others who are more like them. And nobody who desires success is going to want to hang around with a bunch of wet blankets! So, wherever you go, no matter what the weather, always try to bring your own sunshine. It'll make people, your team-mates, feel better than they did before meeting up with you.

The 2003 England team had that chemistry, that bonding of intent. Here was a group of winners drawn together by a common purpose. Was it a coincidence that each player in the team just so happened to be in the right place at the right time? Or was each attracted to positive vibrations/energy? At the time they were together, they were undoubtedly irresistible. The blend of talent, personality and ambition was the most potent of forces, not just in a one-off game, but over a relatively prolonged period of time.

Their intellectual leader, Sir Clive Woodward, by his own admission grew from that event and took charge of the 2005 Lions tour to New Zealand as a more experienced and wiser manager. I've no doubt his intentions were to lead a triumphant Lions team who were prepared as well as they could possibly have been. Unfortunately, the series was lost ... every Test lost in fact and the team's expectations were shattered. The main reason for this result, I think, lay in the chemistry of the entire squad. All good people I'm sure, who practised hard and regularly. But let's face it – most teams do that. The key, I suspect, was that the squad's thoughts and feelings were not on the same wavelength and the resultant performances reflected that. Are there any lessons to be learned from this? Only in realising that reliable processes and good players simply aren't enough. Of course they help, but if the chemistry of the characters within that group doesn't gel it can't, not won't, perform.

Individual and personal development had never been so good. This was the beginning of the optimal performance environment which England rugby had been crying out for. A great team had to be world class both on and off the field, and a lot of this came down to the players themselves. Early on, Clive and his team sat down in a locked room and didn't re-emerge until there was a full self-explanatory behavioural team code in place. This rule book would ensure collective strength and cohesion and as few distractions as possible. It was all about being the best any player could be for his team. Mobile phones were banned, except in your own rooms, respectable dress for meal times, and impeccable dress for training, was required. One of my favourite suggestions was to do with selection. If another player was named to start in your position for the match, it was your responsibility to congratulate him immediately. No time or space for sulking or bitterness, just unconditional support and humility.

The law that was most revered by the players and management alike involved timings. You had to arrive at any engagement, especially meetings and training sessions, at least ten minutes before it was officially due to begin.

Some guys broke this rule, but rarely through lack of self-discipline. It was usually because they had been misinformed.

> *The sight of the biggest guy in the squad appearing around the door in top-to-toe biker leather achieved the seemingly impossible*

There were few worse feelings during that time for me than the realisation I was going to break the time rule. I ran so hard on a couple of occasions that I almost threw up on the meeting-room door. England prop Julian White provided perhaps the most memorable meeting infringement. He had encountered some heavy traffic on his motorbike in central London, the meeting in Bagshot was already twenty minutes old, the lone spare seat had by this time almost been forgotten. Then there was a light knock. The players looked at each other, and winced. There may have even been an 'Oooh' sound from one brave corner of the room.

The sight of the biggest guy in the squad appearing around the door in top-to-toe biker leather achieved the seemingly impossible. The bollocking was avoided; the sheer sight of a nineteen-stone man squeaking his way to his seat in a one-piece leather suit with helmet in hand took everyone's mind to a totally different place. I don't remember ever seeing anyone that uncomfortable in a meeting. Those rooms were too hot at the best of times, and in that gear it must have been unbearable. Julian did really well to get through that morning. The fact he was able to carry it off says a huge amount about him.

The overall effect of following this team 'ethos' was to create a reciprocal relationship in which the daily behaviour (performance) of the individual embodied perfectly the approach of the whole team and gave it its overall strength, and vice versa. The more the players put in, the more together we became as a group and the better we played. The more successful we were in our matches, the more each individual improved and the more committed and dedicated we could become. It was a positive upward spiral, a virtuously successful cycle.

I remember watching Clive in the meeting-room environment and thinking that I could almost see the ideas buzzing around in his mind. He was always challenging the conventional beliefs of the time and regularly offered me his own considerations.

'How many drop goals could we score in a game?'

'What if we took a penalty from such a narrow angle that if we missed we could catch the ball in the in-goal area, on the far side of the field and score a try?'

'Why don't we put Will Greenwood in the scrum and Lawrence Dallaglio at fly-half so he can run straight over their weakest defender?'

'Let's leave Jason Robinson all on his own in two-thirds of the field and see how they mark him (if they put any less than five we were still going to give the ball to him!).'

We had calls for everything. There were names for moves, for taking a breather, for trapping opposition players, for all the kicks including a reverse, no-look hook to the blindside wing. It was a 'no-fear' environment for everyone. There was a pressure to be accountable for all your actions, but it was an energy on which we thrived. It was mightily empowering to be told to go out there and try things, to be innovative. It was a great feeling to know that someone had confidence in you. We also needed to practise it too though, and sessions were often tough.

One of my favourite plays at that time was to shorten the lineout to only four men while the other three positioned themselves on the (very far) opposite touchline. Those three were invariably the back rowers, perhaps Lawrence Dallaglio, Neil Back, Richard Hill, Lewis Moody, Joe Worsley – guys like that, fast but tall. The formation provided us with all kinds of options depending upon how the defensive team formed up. If they kept their back row close to the back of the lineout and pushed their backs out wider to mark our big boys, we had the idea to smash a cross kick over their winger's head for our bigger, stronger forwards to catch. This move was reserved for their end of the field, the kick would ideally land over the try area, so it could be downed straight away for the try and it was my job to put it there.

During a team practice run, a day or two before we played South Africa in the second Test in Bloemfontein in 2000, we set the move up. We were really focusing on playing the game fast to cut down opposition thinking time, however on this occasion that speed caused a problem. Dorian West or Phil Greening, I can't now remember who it was throwing the ball into the lineout, had taken the lineout way too far back from the try line. So now only a gargantuan bomb (high kick) from me would suffice. It was meant to be thirty metres at the most.

Clive had always tried to encourage me just to drop the ball and stop training if I, the decision maker, wasn't happy. I was too young and reserved at this stage to make such a call and, with my desire to impress and basic stubbornness, thought I could make it, especially with a high altitude on my side. I couldn't resist such a challenge.

The ball came to me from Kyran Bracken and I just emptied all I had into this kick. It needed to be in the air for a good five seconds in order that the back row be able to chase from an onside position and still arrive in time to leap and challenge. It was up there for five and a half. I loved the look of it but not all the back row boys shared the feeling. Knowing that the move was perhaps a little unrealistic from that distance they held back, not wishing to pull any muscles at this late stage in the week. All of them, that was, except my good pal Richard Hill. Hilly must have relished the challenge, as I had. Either that or he had seen the look on my face and wanted to help me out.

> **The ball flew untouched through both his hands and landed sweetly on Hilly's forehead with a sound I can still hear today**

Hilly probably maxed out his personal rev-counter as he crossed the twenty-two-metre line. He ran so fast that he even arrived a little too soon. Totally alone and with the half a second he'd saved he took three stutter steps and then leapt gloriously from one foot, hands ready above his head, opposite knee raised for protection just as Dave Alred had shown us. It was immaculate technique. The pitch fell silent as twenty-odd players stood admiring the one-man show. The weather was beautiful that afternoon, there was not a breath of wind, but the sun was bright and high in the sky, directly behind the ball as it descended.

Dave Alred had also taught us to look straight through our hands when catching high balls above the head. It was an Australian rules technique and it works brilliantly. Richard Hill squinted hard, following this tip to the letter, but at the last second I think the intense UV rays just became too much for him. He moved his head slightly and closed his eyes. The ball flew untouched through both his hands and landed sweetly on Hilly's forehead with a sound I can still hear today. The connection was so pure that the ball travelled back a good fifteen feet almost exactly along the same trajectory from where it had come. It was very funny, Hilly's instantaneous reaction to start rubbing his forehead (Laurel and Hardy style) whilst still trying to regain his sight only serving to make it more so. Ben Cohen – in typical Ben Cohen style – ran in, jumped high, knee raised, caught the rebound and dotted the ball down whilst screaming 'yes' and setting off on a celebratory run.

I wanted to laugh so badly. It was perhaps the funniest thing I'd ever seen, but I didn't dare appear unprofessional. I turned to try and find Clive (Mr Serious – The Boss) and I saw him, bent over double, one hand on the floor to stop himself from falling, in fits of hysterical laughter. The whole field erupted. I almost wept as Hilly jogged back still shaking and massaging his head. I didn't stop laughing until we arrived back at the hotel. I had, along with many others, managed to complete the rest of training in tears. And I'm glad to report that it didn't affect our performance. We won the following Test, the first time we had won in South Africa, I think, for a long time.

* * *

Blackie: Don't play favourites

'Treat everyone with common decency, behave with integrity... earn their trust.' Tom Peters

If you want your players or staff to win for you then you've got to want to win for them. In my opinion, we could all do with a crash course of understanding regarding that thought, because in just about every team I've ever been involved with this just hasn't been the case. If you lack a sense of commitment for, say, twenty per cent of your team, in turn they will have a lack of commitment to win for you. Disastrous.

Nobody likes to think they are inconsequential or that they aren't an integral part of the success of a team. Players in just about all clubs feel that way and I don't think coaches and managers do enough to reassure them that they are valued, wanted and needed. Some get treated not just differently (that's OK; that's right and proper because we are all different and have different needs) but are actually treated with a definite bias which certainly isn't healthy. Don't allow for certain behaviours to be punished in one player's performances but ignored or laughed at when another player does the same thing.

This happens at all levels. People play favourites and not just because the chosen individuals are committed, hard-working professionals who win everyone over with their engaging personalities and determination to deliver. It would still be wrong to afford these favoured individuals extra leeway that would not be granted to another employee, even though the motivation to do so would be understandable. The problem is that some people are treated differently because of their perceived power, whether they have that power or not. If managers and coaches can really understand that point, we would perhaps see a resultant change upwards in their results which would lead to fewer sackings and less management upheaval. Please take this blunt and passionate message on board. It could make or save your career.

In a nutshell, do what you resolve to do and treat all your staff with common courtesy and decency. If you do, they'll respond better and with more genuine energy and passion than if you don't. The effect will be like signing another couple of very good players. You don't need to do this of course . . . especially if winning isn't really important to you. On the other hand if winning is important then start practising this philosophy every day. Be accountable. Make sure your players have everything they need in order to perform well, both for themselves and for you. Go out of your way to show your interest in them as people as well as managers, coaches and players. It's hard work at first but if you persist and make it a habit then it will reap great rewards.

Clive was a visionary. But there was an area where I questioned his decisions and his imagination. This area involved dress sense. It had nothing to do with what Clive wore himself, his attire was actually very smart, but it did have something to do with what he pictured the team wearing.

By the time the 1999 Rugby World Cup had rolled into town

England had secured Hackett as the formal clothing sponsor. Hackett are actually a long-time personal sponsor of mine. They are a quintessentially British fashion company of respect and understated class and they cater for almost all walks of formal

> **" *Do not be afraid of change, embrace it and sometimes lead it. Take responsibility for what you do and make sure it helps the team* "**

and more casual life. Clive had free reign to explore the full spectrum. The brown chinos and green tweed jacket (with red check), blue shirt and red tie wouldn't have been my first choice for informal wear, but it worked nicely, smart and different, not arrogant in any way.

The other look he chose involved thick, deep, purple/maroon cords with a cinched- ankle finish and I never really saw eye to eye with him on that one. I went home one day and decided to layer these extravagant numbers with a pair of tangerine-coloured high-cut boots (that Clive chose from a separate sponsor for the previous tour) and I created maybe the single most striking ensemble in the fashion world. I managed to miss the photo shoot with the velvet cords but the boys actually looked great.

Clive was, and still is, fabulous for me, always taking time out to ensure I had everything I needed and felt happy and secure. We chatted on many occasions about balance in life and enjoying what you do. I wish now I'd listened more to what he was saying then. Perhaps that's not quite right. I did listen, I just wasn't ready to absorb. I believe he really enjoyed his experiences, and he taught me a massive amount from what he had learned from them. He never did anything that he wasn't a hundred per cent committed to. When you approach things like that, without fear, they normally work out – even somewhat lurid-coloured cords – but when they don't you almost always find yourself with a better idea of what might do instead. That's how Clive made his progress and made the 2003 Rugby World Cup happen. Do not be afraid of change, embrace it and sometimes lead it. Take responsibility for what you do and make sure it helps the team. As Clive said in many ways to me, life is too short to hold back yourself or others, so give it a damn good go.

No Pain, No Gain

" I thought I had 'success' nailed. I thought I knew how to achieve it and I thought I knew how I could throw it away "

'No pain, no gain.' Welcome to my personal ethos: it has single-handedly shaped my view of the way the world works. I have used it to form the core of my motivations. I pushed myself hard and I always believed it would bring results. I still do in many ways – when you put a limit on the effort you are willing to invest, you immediately put one on the reward you're hoping to receive.

Nothing ever comes for free; if you want it you have to earn it.

If I craved the better things in life then I had to pay the going rate. I figured those who worked long and hard enough would have the right to own their success. It was like saving up your money for a new pair of boots or a holiday in the sun. Over the years I have tried to gather as much credit in my 'dream bank account' as

I can by practising and training. The more I banked, the greater my ability to fund my goals. That at least was the idea.

I have kicked a lot of balls in my life, perhaps a million. The average number of goal kicks I take per game is maybe four or five, depending upon team disciplinary tactics. The number of punts adds up to just a few more, something like seven to ten. A single drop goal and roughly four restarts would be about right too. In total I might kick the ball at most twenty times.

> **I have been totally obsessive when it comes to getting things right, never stopping until I was happy**

Each week leading up to the big day, however, I hit about two hundred and fifty to three hundred practice place kicks alone. I average two hundred to two hundred and fifty punts using my left foot, and exactly the same number using my right. A daily total of twenty drop goals with each foot and fifteen to twenty restarts, six to seven times a week would pretty much constitute a solid preparational build up. That makes a total of about a thousand kicks to prepare for just twenty. That's near enough fifty rehearsals for each single defining event. To me that has been a totally acceptable ratio.

Apart from the final session on the morning of the match, I would never spend less than one hour and thirty minutes, and sometimes up to three hours, kicking and fetching my rugby balls. A full game is defined as having two equal halves of forty minutes, even with injury time added on the whole event very rarely exceeds ninety minutes. I spent more time kicking daily than I did playing on the weekend. Not so long ago, during the 2008 Six

Nations I was measured as physically covering well in excess of five and a half kilometres in one of my shortest sessions. I did all of this in the name of adding to my personal 'I deserve to be successful' fund.

My longest session on record ran for a hefty five hours and then another hour and a half later that same evening. I have been totally obsessive when it comes to getting things right, never stopping until I was happy.

At the end of each kicking practice I would need proof that I was in good enough form to play a big game right there and then. That meant a kick challenge from anywhere on the field: six in all. If I missed one then I started the set again, if I missed another one I was capable, in my most irrational and angry moods, of starting the whole session from the beginning. If I thought I struck the ball poorly but it still went over, then I'd also head back to the start. The key was not just putting them all over, but also in knowing I actually deserved to succeed with them all. I actually believed that getting lucky was worse than missing. I never knew where I stood with luck, especially the good stuff; it seemed to take away from the level of my control. I aimed for the middle of the middle, nothing else was good enough.

When good fortune did fall at my feet unexpectedly, like a lucky drop goal, it was like I had taken out a loan (I would have to hit another ten 'perfect' kicks as my way of paying it back).

In my eyes, if you weren't prepared to, or couldn't afford to cover the cost of this payment, then you simply had to buy your entry ticket into the game of chance. The rules stated bad luck evened out the good. It was a playground of swings and roundabouts in which catching a lucky break or two was like playing with fire.

I attributed all of my positive outcomes to the hours upon hours of practice. I tried to give the weekend's game an air of inevitability with the quality and quantity of my preparations. If the experience didn't satisfy my expectations then I saw the result as one of gross injustice (in other words very bad luck). I didn't mind this so much because in this way I knew my compensation was coming in the form of an equal share of good luck.

'You can't always win but you can always deserve to.'

I thought that, in time, everything had to balance out. When everything did fall into place, I knew it was only down to the fact that I had truly earned it. These awesome moments strengthened my faith in what I considered to be the way that life worked.

> " *I attributed all of my positive outcomes to the hours upon hours of practice* "

This outlook did, however, mean foregoing and sacrificing certain pleasures like relaxation and just enjoying one's self. I was convinced it was a reasonable deal though. I would trade all the immediate joy around me at that time for what would undoubtedly be an even greater, more worthwhile and lasting experience further down the line. I did not intend to go laughing, joking, smiling and therefore wasting all my dream savings away. I took this as a severe test of discipline and in doing so I believed it made me stronger and more deserving than my fun-loving competitors.

* * *

Blackie: No train, no gain

> 'Be effective: do what works ... and keep doing it.'
> Stephen Covey

I understand talent as being those things that you seem to be able to excel at with no great discernible effort. I see hard work as the tool you'll employ to develop that talent to the optimum. I think that talent shows its hand early, then hard work must be recruited in order to effectively hone your skills to allow you to make a valuable and significant contribution to your life's journey.

From a coach's standpoint talent is reason. It's the reason you're drawn towards working with a player or a team. Hard work, on the other hand, is habit, and effective good habits get the job done. I've always said that no matter how important reason and understanding undoubtedly are, they're not nearly as powerful as habit. 'No train, no gain!' I know, I know, it's 'No pain, no gain' or it's 'Practice makes permanent not perfect.' But I must tell you, cultivating the habit of simply *trying* on a regular basis is pretty good advice. Assuming that your continual efforts involve trying in the *right* areas, learning from the outcome, modifying your preparation and upgrading your performance, then that practice will ensure you make progress. Give it a go!

For whatever reason, the talents you are blessed with sometimes aren't given a chance to air themselves and as such you must always keep searching for them throughout life. We all have a special gift which makes us unique. Maybe you have already found something that you obviously excel at. If you have, then great! Congratulations. However, many people don't clearly recognise what makes them distinctive. In this case, my advice would be to keep your radar open for unlikely opportunities that may present themselves. It can happen anywhere at any time, so be ready and keep your mind fresh and ready to take on challenges in a successful and positive manner.

Talent needs to be discovered. It needs to be allowed to expose itself. It may be that your talent has lain dormant within you for many years, without the necessary stimulus to bring it into the open. This is more common than you think and I see it all the time in individuals I have worked with. They have kept their minds so restricted that they have missed great opportunities, preferring to stay within their comfort zone. You need to ensure that you seize those key moments when they arise. They can be testing but they also let us know exactly who it is we are; what strengths we possess and what fears we can overcome. Without taking risks (albeit small risks ... I don't recommend you take uncertain large leaps of faith!) you fail to stimulate your hidden talents and thus restrain yourself to a life of mediocrity.

To bring into play the valuable strengths of hard work, camaraderie and sharing in our daily lives, we need to have something to contribute. Something to share with our colleagues and our team-mates to stimulate them into contributing back. That something we share is *talent*. How often we share that will be determined by our work ethic and discipline. But you can only share what has been discovered.

I'm of the viewpoint that talent is God-given and our skill

lies in putting that God-given talent to its best use. In this way we are an integral part of our own success. It is an interactive journey and we must make sure that we work hard to allow our talent to fulfil its potential. In general, the more we practice, the better we'll become ... or at least, the more confident we'll become. Slightly different, I know, but more accurate. Utilising our talent will become second nature to us. It's that habit thing rearing its head again.

The confidence to repeatedly execute a particular behaviour will be reinforced, or eroded, by the success or otherwise of actually doing. In Jonny's case, he had the gift of having both talent and skill. His natural talent was exceptional as was his propensity to practise. He was intrinsically rewarded for the habit *and* the success of his individual actions. When I first met Jonny, he would probably successfully kick, on average, say seventeen or eighteen out of every twenty practice kicks. Now, twelve years later, he still successfully kicks, on average, seventeen or eighteen out of every twenty practice kicks. Has he improved? He's probably more confident and more disciplined now and when the chips are down, he's probably the man you'd want to be kicking to save your life. A bit dramatic I know, but you know what I mean. But statistically, he was pretty good then and he's pretty good now. No change there then. Not surprising when you consider he's the world points record holder and as good a kicker as has ever played the game. Statistics fail to show the rounded improvement he has made as his playing career has matured. Stastistical feedback plays an important part, there's no doubt, but ahead of that we should value our intuitive take on any situation.

Jonny applied himself to the task at hand, improved in execution and confidence and, as a result, has been able to deliver a very high standard of play and behaviour over ... well, a lifetime. His discipline is his greatest attribute, and he's got a few!

Jonny's efforts have had an element of 'paying-the-price' about them. I think evolution has taken that payment and invested the funds in allowing him to give of his best, to afford him the patience to practise and to finally become happy with the person he is. Meanwhile the intention behind each effort each day remains strong. He is happy but not content I'd say ... and that's as it should be.

I used to coach Neil Jenkins, the former record holder, and he wasn't bad either! Strangely enough, he used to practise too, although maybe not quite as much as Jonny. Nevertheless he was incredibly disciplined in his preparation and approach to playing the game. Rob Andrew was the same. Matt Burke worked on his technique and 'feel' to become another prolific kicker. I don't actually know of any kickers who were so talented that they did not need to practise. There have been kickers who have been so gifted that they need only practise occasionally. But guess what ... they were only excellent and at their true potential occasionally, and were often erratic and unpredictable.

A lot of individuals rely on what we term the 'luck factor'. It is never, ever, wise to let your achievements rest on the shoulders of luck. There is no easy and quick cheat's guide to attaining great success. We must all, without fail, invest copious amounts of time and effort into achieving what it is that we deeply desire. The irony is summed up by golfing legend Gary Player who said: 'It's funny that the harder I practise, the luckier I seem to get.'

The secret, of course, is to avoid the luck factor and instead work on ensuring that you enjoy your practice. If you enjoy practising a lot, then practise a lot! It makes sense if it makes you happy, as it will only feed into your confidence for you to draw on during your performances. But there are pitfalls to be aware of, as I've discussed often with Jonny. Not least in the risk of injury through over-practising. I'll leave Jonny to discuss how he feels about this aspect elsewhere in the book. But if you are victim to various injuries and feel yourself getting stale, then consider shortening your practice sessions. If you don't, you will only find yourself becoming frustrated and stressed which, in turn, will drain enjoyment. And the less you enjoy your practice, the less effective it will be. Recall that we naturally lean to what we enjoy and what we enjoy tends to be what we're intrinsically good at. With this in mind, you must not drown your thirst for the game through flooding yourself with negative emotions and feelings as you miss that hundredth kick, or feel disappointed at your tiredness and lethargy during your sessions.

Despite the nerves and anxiety that underpinned that stage in my career when practising was so dominant, it certainly was an interesting period of my life. The self-exerted pressures and extreme expectations which came from letting so much ride on practice and games were exhausting, but again I latched on to the pain and probably encouraged it. I knew deep down it would all be fine if I stuck to the rules.

It worked in many ways but it was a fairly destructive method and the success made it an addictive one. It seemed to touch on my obsessive streak, taking it to a new level, and before long it was getting well out of hand. The final whistles had barely sounded and I had already begun sacrificing for the next weekend, afraid that if I stopped to celebrate and embrace it I would have severe consequences to face.

I thought I was a winner, and statistically at times I could back that statement up. After all I was achieving my goals but now, today, I wonder if I was achieving anything at all. I was playing a version of life in which I barely featured. I totally negated any contribution of my own. I was the organiser of my experiences, but not the experiencer. I left no room for any personal X-factors in the formula by which I ran my life's journey: my theory that what you put in is what you get out. What I'd forgotten all about was growth, enjoyment, natural ability, life. Me.

> **" It worked in many ways but it was a fairly destructive method and the success made it an addictive one "**

I couldn't find a way to enjoy what I was achieving because I didn't perceive myself – my natural talent and instincts – to be playing any real part in it, therefore I didn't warrant the success. I was living the old adage – and only this: 'How do I get to Carnegie Hall? Practice, practice, practice.' On top of this I was scared to upset the equation. I was earning a good living but not living a good life. I was frightened to cash in my chips in case it came back to hurt me later on, where my 'fabulous' future lay.

Talent and natural ability represent our instinctive and creative sides. They are an expression of our true selves and the bits which make us brilliant. We all have slightly different 'special talents' but they are all equally worthy and deserving. By denying mine I was denying myself the experience of real life.

I no longer want to be afraid to celebrate good performances or enjoy talking about the things I've been involved in. It is not an arrogant desire, more an open expression of gratitude for my gifts and for letting me find a place of value where I can use them. When I recognise the existence of my talents then I get a better idea of how to add to them. When I become aware of my personal contributions then maybe I can allow myself to have that fabulous future. The one I've been saving for all these years. But maybe I can actually have it today. Up until now it has been lodged right there in the future, just out of arm's reach. I always felt that if I could survive the next big challenge, it would be there waiting for me, but it's been waiting a hell of a long time. Now perhaps I think I might start enjoying it.

Blackie: Where do you want to go?

> 'If you don't know where you are going you will wind up somewhere else.' Yogi Berra

Our expectations of life are set early in this journey ... in childhood. As we mature into youth we intrinsically employ fear to curtail our innocent exuberance as a precautionary safety mechanism. Experience determines to what extent the brakes are applied to our natural behaviours. We get recognition and reward for certain actions and the reverse for others. What seems to bring us pleasure is repeated and hopefully reinforced, whereas the consequences of other behaviours gives us our understanding of what pain is. Those actions are ceremoniously dumped!

The answer seems easier the younger you are. The no-brainer response is somehow less clear at times during adulthood, although I fail to understand why. As a child we are consistently conditioned by daily exposure to those experiences of pain and pleasure; and from there, what we come to understand as right and wrong. Invariably we are rewarded for winning. We are treated in a more positive manner if we do well at something. We feel valuable in those areas for which we receive praise and recognition, and very insecure in areas where our performance seems to incur displeasure and disregard. Personal evolution should suggest we gravitate towards things that we are good at, disregarding those things we don't easily complete to a satisfactory degree ... or at least to a level the most influential people in our lives come to expect from us.

This initial grounding underwrites our life philosophy, and it can endure many shifts throughout our lives, although I think the basic values we hold remain within the early framework that we acquire during childhood.

Life seems to give us a wide exposure to what's on offer at an early age, then steers us towards our specific purpose. This enables our strengths to flourish and relegates our weaknesses, on the whole, to a sideline role as we pursue our chosen pathway. That's just the way things work.

I suggested to Jonny, and the same applies to everyone, that he give little attention to fears and revert to the simplicity of childhood learning. If it feels right to go along a certain path then do it. That safety net of intrinsic intuition may save your life. But don't hide behind it either! There's a fine line between feeling it is wrong to take a certain path and simply being too frightened to rationally consider it. Try to sideline fears. If you commit increasing energy to them, you'll find they become drawn towards you and their effect may even be amplified.

It is as Jim Rohn, the US business philosopher, entrepreneur and author said: 'From testimonials and personal experience we have enough information to conclude that it is possible to design and live an extraordinary life.' To do this, we all need to find out what it is that we are good at and then devote the majority of our lives into putting our best energy into achieving that potential. We must ensure that we know exactly where we are going and then develop a burning desire within ourselves to get there. If you do this, then you'll have a greater chance of achieving that happiness and fulfilment that we all crave.

I wore through both sides of my groin – the right side twice – kicking balls. I wrecked my back and tore muscles up and down my legs. I still kick every day but not for as long now. I didn't fully understand that it is not just about how much time and effort you devote in practice, but also how, and to what, you devote it. I still

" I wore through both sides of my groin – the right side twice – kicking balls. I wrecked my back and tore muscles up and down my legs "

challenge myself with my six vital kicks from all parts of the field but I realise that I don't get two chances in a match so I try even harder to make the most of the first go. If I miss I learn from it and ensure that the uncomfortable feeling keeps inspiring me to improve. This way I leave a little extra gas in the tank for the little 'me' inside to thrive on, the 'me' that is my instinct and my ability. Because that's what I'm supposed to do, feed him – with information and energy – and let him do his stuff like he's been doing all my career.

What I was doing, in essence, was just surviving rather than thriving. I thought I had 'success' nailed. I thought I knew how to achieve it and I thought I knew how I could throw it away. My values and my understandings had convinced me that the only way I would blow it would be by changing my written-in-stone-inflexible-tunnel-vision-practice-practice-practice way of life. This was not healthy. And not a route to real success or happiness. It was bound to fail me at some stage – and it did, of course. So I became rigid with the fear of altering my routine, and the fear of letting myself and my team-mates down.

5

Mountain Climbing

> *"I'd had two opportunities to stamp my mark and define my purpose in life – in my eyes anyway. I'd put myself through the pain and the pressure and I needed something back"*

Newcastle kicked off the 2005 season against Sale at Edgeley Park and I was on the reserves bench. I wasn't moaning though, after all I had just spent eight days of the nine-day pre-season tour to Japan in hospital and, therefore, had played very little rugby. I'd developed a solid case of appendicitis on the first night we arrived. I remember it well because it started to kick in shortly after my evening practice session when a Japanese gentleman asked me if I would sign his dog!

I was sharing a room with my brother, Mark (Sparks to

everyone), and at one point during the night there was a rumbling that shook the entire room. It turned out to be just your basic earthquake, not my gut. My stomach started up a little later on and it was a lot, lot worse on my personal Richter scale. Seven days of antibiotics through a drip and I was just healthy enough to fly home. So to be sat on the sidelines with a chance to play was an absolute blessing after the week I'd had.

I struggle with benching, although it does make the pre-game stuff a little less stressful. It is the not knowing when you might come on which drives me crazy. It's as if someone has trapped me in that one-minute-to-go-before-kick-off scenario and my nerves are locked in at a level just below where I start to feel I can't bear it any longer. Our coach, Rob Andrew, had hinted that he would put me on at half time, so for now I was just watching out for injuries and keeping my body warm.

We were down by a few points at the interval and I ran out after the break feeling like the new kid in ice-white shorts and a sparklingly clean shirt. I settled in quickly when we scored early on. My conversion was successful, and after two penalty conversions from Sale, we managed to regain the lead with my kick for three points. Now both the team and I were in the game. However, I soon found out that lows do follow highs sometimes as I misplaced my next pass, which proved to be a big downer.

Sale snapped up the loose ball and, in what seemed like only a flash, I was joining my team under the posts five points worse off. My heart rising into my throat, I felt terrible. Plenty of time, I told myself, there is plenty of time to sort this out. Stay calm, play each second on its merits.

After a huge team effort we crept over in the left corner. It took two minutes of solid action and several phases of play. It was a great score which brought us to within one point, and when the referee then informed me that time was officially up, I was presented with the chance I had asked for, to set the record straight. I had a conversion to win us the game, or lose it.

I live for these moments, they are so rare in life. I love the challenge, the possibility of pulling off the incomprehensible, but at the same time there is much pressure. It is the potential regret, the disappointment, the possibility of waste and desperation which lies in missing your one and only shot that creates the almost unbearable tension. It is the same feeling I have in the dressing room before a big game. I experience a unique buzz and energy, an anticipation, a pride and an open field of dreams but there is also an opening for humiliation and emotional pain. A type of sickness turns over in my stomach which is begging me to stop putting myself in these positions where there is no easy middle road, just tons to gain and it all to lose. There is a desire to hold on to all that I am but I know that this is what I must trade for what more I can be.

Place kicks are never easy from the corner but in essence it is the same kick from any-where, so I didn't let it bother me. I'd made two from two so far but I wanted this one, really, really badly. My head was pounding, my now not-so-clean shirt was resonating with every audible heartbeat. But still, this wasn't unusual for me. I'd done this a thousand times in matches and practice. All I wanted was one more.

> **" I love the challenge, the possibility of pulling off the incomprehensible, but at the same time there is much pressure "**

Everything went as usual, I was calm and composed in my

preparation and run-up. But then I felt it. The point of contact between foot and ball was perhaps a millimetre or two to the inside of my leg swing. By the time the ball was halfway to the posts this millimetre had become six feet to the right of the far upright. I knew it would come back to about three feet on the wind but that would be it. Before the crowd had even seen the ball in the air, my heart was already broken. My mind raced, and when the ball landed I was too busy staring at the floor to notice, wishing everyone would leave me there to work it out. I had let my team down, I had let myself down, I had missed my chance, this was going to haunt me for a long time.

A year later, almost to the day, and this time round I was fit and in the starting team for the first game of 2006. Pre-season had been spent working on my ability to enjoy the game as much as the game itself. I wanted to have more faith in myself, to embrace and savour the occasion. Northampton away was the first test of that idea. In the build up to the match the pressure of the game was already convincing me to forget fun and drop back into the old habits. I decided I would work out how actually to enjoy life once I got through this challenge . . . the usual story then.

It was a fabulously sunny afternoon and the game provided an exciting spectacle to go with it. The lead changed several times; we all fought to help in any way we could, running and tackling for our lives. I even scored a try. After seventy-seven minutes of knocks and scrapes I ended up in pretty much the same place as I had been fifty-two weeks before. This time it was a penalty from wide out on the right-hand side. All in all it was a forty-yard shot. We were down by two with three points on offer and one final chance, perhaps, to right the wrong I perceived from last year. Good things come to those who wait? I had carried the memory of my miss with me a long while now. I wanted to pay my team-mates back. Maybe this was life's way of letting me even up the scores, of showing me that I could and should enjoy this rugby business, of helping me to see that it all works out in the end. Then again maybe it wasn't.

I didn't get hold of this one at all. I hated it. I didn't even want to look at it after it had touched my boot. I did though – just to see if it might miraculously turn a corner in the air – but that sort of behaviour was for the

> **"*I had carried the memory of my miss with me a long while now. I wanted to pay my team-mates back*"**

weak. I knew I'd messed this one up. I wanted a rewind button or, at second best, an eject button. Then I could spring myself out of the stadium or I could catapult my mind clean from my body, because this one was going to hurt twice as badly for twice as long. Once is forgivable – maybe – but twice – not a chance. So much for enjoying myself. I'd had two opportunities to stamp my mark and define my purpose in life – in my eyes anyway. I'd put myself through the pain and the pressure and I needed something back. I couldn't handle missing opportunities. I'd done everything I thought I needed to do. It wasn't worth the price I was paying.

Blackie: Stop beating yourself up

'If a man does his best, what else is there?'
General Patton

High energy comes from pursuing a course of action you think is the right thing and which will deliver a worthwhile reward for your actions. And, as has been said before, what gets rewarded gets done. The greater the interest you have in the project, the greater your energy will be. If you are doing something you love, something you're good at it, and you're doing it with people you like, then a lack of energy should never be an issue. You'll be buzzing all the time!

Of course you need to look after yourself in order to be able to use that energy effectively. If you don't, it will just dissipate, never taking you anywhere near to where you want to be. So you have to make sure you eat a predominantly healthy diet, drink plenty of water, take regular exercise that includes aerobic, strength and flexibility, sleep well and hang around with positive, ambitious, well-meaning people. Then you can't go wrong! Not much to ask is it? Still, that's the reality in a nutshell. If you have the discipline to put these considerations in place, you've got a chance, a very good chance actually.

If you are lethargic and not very enthusiastic the chances of success are pretty remote, especially in professional sport. Being energetic is associated with being ambitious, enthusiastic, optimistic and with doing something you actually enjoy doing. Being pro-active and seizing the moment are admirable qualities that we all try to achieve. Being in this state is contagious and lifts everyone around you; pretty important if you are a team player.

Be aware though that lethargy is also highly infectious, maybe even more so than enthusiasm, and it can dampen the most positive of spirits. Enthusiasm and lethargy manifest themselves in everything you do, in the way you talk, listen and carry yourself. So I'd suggest you actually think in a positive manner. If you begin there, the rest – how you look, how others see you – tends to follow. This is especially important when you are around other individuals. So how do you think positively? See yourself as being successful at whatever you do, in an environment you thrive in, alongside people you want to be with. Do it often enough and it'll cement the habitual behaviour that gives you the best chance to succeed in whatever you do.

Creating a mental image of success is a hugely beneficial method of developing positive energy. But is it enough? Stress can creep in and chip away at the image. I will look at ways in which that can be turned around in a later chapter. But what about all those other 'negative' thoughts we know all too well? The niggles, the annoyances, the sometimes irrational throwing of our toys out of the pram. The writer Byron Katie has influenced my thinking in recent years. She has helped me to understand and deal with all those pain-in-the-ass things that life throws at me, and at the same time has helped make sure I never relinquish my ambition.

The premise to her work is that you should ask yourself the question: 'How would you feel if you were not having those negative thoughts?' – frustration, anger, disappointment, and so on. The answer is generally 'OK'. Katie then asks: 'Is having a feeling of being OK better than feeling angry, frustrated and in many cases, not valued?' Most people would answer in the affirmative. She then goes on to suggest that all we need to do is to release negative thoughts and re-establish control of our lives. Generally, the frustration we feel is the result of something at home or work not going to plan. In other words, there are other people and things in the equation over which we have no influence. We can only control and influence what we do and thus are only responsible for our actions, which in turn give us control over what we think. Once we appreciate this, we stop beating ourselves up, wasting energy and time and begin to get on with enjoying our lives.

I think this understanding has helped Jonny but it is not a cure-all. I'm not suggesting that there aren't moments when the frustrations of life still prove a challenge. But I know Jonny would agree that today their impact is nowhere near as potent an adversary, and indeed frustrations appear in his life not nearly as often as they would have if we had been writing this book a few years back. This change in habitual thinking will undoubtedly help Jonny towards fulfilling his playing potential.

It is a fine line which has divided hope and fear for me. Like the excitement of scaling a rock face higher and higher while all the time knowing that I have further to fall. To a degree, I had let my life become a climb of sorts, holding my fear of heights at bay by focusing on just how high I could reach, inevitably becoming more and more troubled by the size of the drop growing bigger, and the fall potentially more painful each time I looked down.

Every event had become a shift upwards or a tumble down. I had given myself no flat ledge from which I could relax and enjoy the view. What started off this fear was actually worrying about death when I was a lot younger. I couldn't work out how I was going to avoid that most fatal of falls. This was a game I couldn't win. The closer I got to family and friends the more I had to lose. With rules like these what was the point of playing at all?

I worked effectively with fear under my skin, it drove my naturally obsessive side to fight and compete in every way. I was incredibly persistent. I began to see each challenge as vitally important. Success meant climbing higher. In my mind, he who reached the furthest point would be saved somehow from life's greatest certainty – the end. So, I set my sights on the peak.

I felt like the events of my life were tests put in front of me by the powers that be. My role was to overcome them while making the most of the gifts I had been given. I had to do the right thing every time of asking.

> **" *Every event had become a shift upwards or a tumble down. I had given myself no flat ledge from which I could relax and enjoy the view* "**

I needed extensive preparation and harsh analysis. To smile and bask in the glory of this existence was wasted time. It meant standing still whilst others moved past me. I had my formula – win at all costs, do your best, worry like crazy, sulk like mad and forget the celebrations. Brilliant!

My life was spent tiptoeing between fear and greatness. A favourable result lifted me up and allowed me to turn my attention to the next foothold. When it didn't go my way, I crumbled and dwelt in the pain and misery of what should have been. The apparent need to analyse every failed step opened up the wounds over and over again.

Did I spend my time well in those years?

What if someone asked me that at the end of my rugby career, how would I reply? Maybe I could show them some video footage, a few trophies, some statistical records. A phrase that comes to mind is 'missing the deeper meaning'.

I got to thinking about what makes time well spent and I thought about the first time I played the game.

When I took hold of a ball in my first rugby session, yes I was nervous, but it was a glorious feeling of anticipation. I stood at the base of this mountain and my knees shook. I had everything ahead of me; so much to explore and learn. The action was bright and engaging, the rules of the game and the play itself all engrossing. The competition existed without huge consequence and the learning experience was such fun.

That was way back then, and if I am honest with myself, that feeling of hope and excitement was soon overshadowed by the fear of failure. The good stuff didn't disappear, but it was struggling to get out. Maybe I climbed too quickly and started looking down way more than I was looking up. I misunderstood what ambition is all about. What striving for 'perfection' actually means. I feel differently now. Much better. I've been on a journey. I'm still on it. I realise that actually experiencing all that life has to offer will not compromise my passion for performing and winning, but will in fact undoubtedly strengthen it.

So, if tomorrow was my last game I would want to take it all in. I would want my attitude and my performance to portray the gratitude I feel inside for the opportunities I have been given. I don't want to pussyfoot around trying not to make mistakes. I would charge headlong into big tackles and take people on with the ball in hand. I would hope to express my willingness to do something special for my team even if it took all eighty minutes. On my face would be a grin that says, 'Isn't this amazing!' no matter how tense or tight the situation.

Blackie: 'The quick fix doesn't work . . .

Successful people know that. It doesn't stop them looking for instant gratification but they keep that searching in perspective.' Steve Black

When we talk about working in a team, we undoubtedly invoke the issue of the integrity of the individuals within that team. You will hear the term integrity a lot when people talk about a team's collective playing performance and may ask: 'But what does that actually mean?' It means showing your team-mates and the world who you really are in your daily interactions with them either on the training ground, in games or in some social setting. It means consistently doing the right, honest thing. As an aside, doing that greatly reduces your stress as you ensure that you have nothing to hide as you live your life with the very best of intentions for yourself and your team.

As human beings we tend to look for ways to negotiate the rules, to bring our future desires to the here and now. We have a natural longing to try to change the rules to get an immediate, or at least the immediate promise of, a benefit from doing so. This rarely works. It compromises our ongoing integrity and we will likely experience diminishing rewards.

The lesson to take from integrity in relation to teamwork is that we should always be honest with our team-mates. We should tell it as it is but I must quickly point out that if being honest will hurt their pride in any way then we should ensure we do it with sensitivity. We should never mislead people, and should always ensure that our actions will lead to a better outcome for the team and the individuals of which it is comprised.

Life is, I think, about experiencing and embracing. It is not, at least for me any more, about looking back or looking down, about titles, status and numbers. I desperately want to win but it is not the only thing that will sustain me. I want to win so badly because in so doing, it makes life in general even more exciting. It makes living more thrilling and fun. That is a massive motivator. One of the strongest. But it is different from how I felt previously. This climb comes with a safety rope. Once I experience something, success or failure, I see it and embrace it for what it really is. Only then does it become not just something I own briefly but an essential ingredient in a better me which can never be taken away. That is the safety net stopping the fall, these stored experiences actually tend to help with the next ones, forever steering me towards that brilliant existence.

> *" Life is, I think, about experiencing and embracing. It is not, at least for me any more, about looking back or looking down, about titles, status and numbers "*

We'll all get to face the end at some point, and I'm going to deal with that, but not now. I reckon I'll wait a bit. If I sit here worrying about it then I'll miss the very reasons for which I started the journey in the first place.

If someone asks me now, 'Did you use your time wisely?' I am not going to hand over a piece of paper with my CV and other achievements on it, with an explanation of why I might be better than anyone else. I am simply going to stand up, talk and smile a smile which lets people know I am fulfilled. I tried, I never gave up, I never hid and, win or lose, succeed or fail, I loved every second of it.

Some of those amazing seconds of my career stand out in my memory more than others, of course. Like one second of the sixty in the seventy-eighth minute of a game played in Twickenham on 4 April 1998. That second changed me. At the time I thought wholeheartedly for the better. But even if there were a few less than positive side effects, the opportunities that came my way from that second onwards have shaped my life forever.

Beginnings

> " *I jumped on the spot, shook out my legs, clenched my fists. My mind was over-heating so badly that I felt my face burning up. I was desperate to get on. Then it happened* "

As I remember it, there were seventy-four or so minutes already on the clock. I was on my third length of the goal area, keeping warm just in case. That's when I got an urgent call to get myself back to the reserves bench. Rich, our team masseur and match-day handyman, had sprinted over to tell me that Mike Catt was struggling with his hamstring.

'Clive wants you on!' he blurted out.

My heart skipped a few beats and I caught my breath. I suddenly became aware of almost every one of the 85,000 spectators filling Twickenham Stadium and the sheer noise they were making. I started peeling off my tracksuit as I hurried over. Dave Reddin, the team's physical conditioner and match-day substitute coordinator, came and knelt down beside me, putting a hand on my shoulder.

'You're on the wing, mate.'

'What! I've never played there in my life.'

'He wants you to, you'll be fine, really enjoy it.'

We'd used up a few replacements already and I knew it was the right call, I just wished it wasn't.

I stood on the sideline, now stripped down to my kit, fidgeting. I jumped on the spot, shook out my legs, clenched my fists. My mind was overheating so badly that I felt my face burning up. I was desperate to get on. Then it happened.

I somehow managed to make out the loudspeaker announcement over the noise as I ran on. The message alerted everyone to the fact that it was my debut, I was only eighteen years old and I was coming on to play wing. In other words, it told the Irish team that I was totally inexperienced, young, nervous and completely out of position. So no prizes for guessing where the next ball was going. Thankfully I caught the high kick and now I was in the game, my first game for my country. It was a dream come true.

What a brilliant moment, it was as though I'd found a new level to living, like I was on top of the world. My phone was beeping a hole in my pocket afterwards with all the text messages of congratulations and support. I was so proud. I was now an international rugby player, in fact the youngest to play for England for seventy-one years.

After the game we walked through the corporate tents outside the ground in our sharp suits and were met with applause. I was being pulled around by autograph hunters and people I didn't know wanting to shake my hand. Everywhere I went I felt like I was being watched and talked about. I reminded myself I didn't really want any of this. All I wanted to do was pay back those who had helped me but it was very infectious. Subconsciously I was beginning to feel a little bit important.

I had attached a huge amount of worth and value on to who I was because of the events of one afternoon and a brief pitch appearance. I had new status; although I tried not to involve myself in all this fuss, deep down I couldn't help it. It was the front of the queue syndrome and maybe I actually believed I warranted the special treatment. I am loathe to admit it but I guess I formed a new understanding in my values which told me I was suddenly more significant than others. I prided myself on being the ultimate team man but away from the rugby field I was definitely taking way more than I was giving.

> *What a brilliant moment, it was as though I'd found a new level to living, like I was on top of the world*

People around me started to treat me differently, maybe because I was acting differently or maybe because their perception of me had changed much like my own had. Either way it made it very tough to recognise what was happening. A more pronounced public profile brings more opportunity and reward in today's world. When I started achieving what I wanted I started getting more sponsorship offers. Sadly those who aren't in need are normally the ones who get given things for free.

I look back at this interesting time and what I see is the start of a vicious cycle. I began to see myself as something bigger than my

> *I prided myself on being the ultimate team man but away from the rugby field I was definitely taking way more than I was giving*

own boots and everything I was experiencing therefore served to strengthen my identification with this view. I feel capable of looking at it differently now.

Blackie: Checklist – New recruit

'It's great here! Come and join us, we can and will be good for each other.' A highly effective welcome

ONE
Before bringing on board the potential new recruit, you need to assess their general behaviour and character, in as much depth as possible and over a period time. If you are not able to do that personally, you must obtain the information from as worthy a set of external sources as possible. Previous teams, employers, and so on.

TWO
You should assess whether this is someone who can, and will, contribute to making your team more valuable. They should possess the potential to grow in the job as an individual and as a team member.

THREE

You should tell them exactly what you expect from them – behaviour, standards and ballpark results. Tell them what you will stand for and what you won't stand for. Explain they will be supported fully if they buy into the team's philosophy and culture.

FOUR

Your new recruit should want to join you and should know why.

FIVE

Look beyond references but pay some attention when a person who commands respect puts their reputation on the line to endorse the new recruit's effectiveness.

SIX

Look for pride and passion in their profession. Add good personal standards and you've got a winner.

SEVEN

Ask yourself: 'Will they fit in and flourish in our environment?' If no, then don't touch them with a barge pole. In just about all cases, people don't really change from bad to good. They can change from good to better, but invariably the 'bad' need to find another environment in which to flourish.

EIGHT

Ensure the new recruit's introduction to the team is carried out by someone who both loves what they do and where the team is going. They'll paint a genuinely positive picture and give the new relationship the momentum it needs.

NINE
Ensure the new recruit can see that his team-mates are professionally optimistic and their ambitions are being fulfilled. Make it clear that being socially comfortable and content isn't what breeds success.

TEN
Agree a development plan, with both behavioural and physical goals. Write them down and monitor progress regularly.

I made a pact with myself, as a young boy, that I would try to be the best person and best rugby player I could ever be. I even wrote down, 'I want to be the best player in the world,' in a little book of goals when I started out on my professional career. Somehow along the way the vision became distorted and I became more focused on just being better than others.

In sport, as in life, despite what results may indicate, there can be no better, best, worse or worst in my opinion. We can only try to contribute wholeheartedly. We all face different circumstances and we all play under slightly different rules because we play for different teams – be it within a family, in a workplace or indeed, another sports team. We possess unique motivations which drive us in different ways, to achieve different things. But they are all achievements, and each matters to the individual. After all there is no set path. Life experiences vary and what constitutes success is open to our own interpretation.

We are all equal, equally great. We do seem inclined to place huge importance on certain areas of life: though – sport is perhaps one of those. Being involved in it certainly does not make you more important by association. In fact, nothing could be further from the truth in my eyes.

I have tried to digest something I read not so long ago, and I feel it fits here. It has come from my understanding of a Buddhist principle called 'emptiness'.

Everything on earth, every person and every single object completely depends upon something else in order to exist. At a basic level the world cannot exist as it does without the human mind to perceive it and display it. The human body relies upon its parts, its cells, its atoms and energy for its appearance and function. By definition all teams will rely upon their members and their every move for the team's overall performance. These individuals are themselves the collective result of their own experiences, families and other guiding moments. This is the message which helps me keep my feet firmly on the ground. If you take any of these parts away, no matter how seemingly small, the final outcome will not be the same, in fact displacing the wrong brick can bring the whole building crumbling to the ground.

> " *I made a pact with myself, as a young boy, that I would try to be the best person and rugby player I could ever be. Somehow along the way the vision became distorted and I became more focused on just being better than others* "

The drop goal at the end of the 2003 Rugby World Cup may not have occurred in the manner it did without every one of my million or so practice kicks which preceded it. It certainly wouldn't have happened without Matt Dawson's pass or his break a little earlier. Or Lewis Moody's lineout take, or Mike Catt's charge. I could go on right back to the day I was born, in fact the day William Webb Ellis was born! You get the point.

We are all interacting as parts of each other's journeys, dreams and failures. Life is the ultimate team game which never sleeps or breaks for half time. I am not even the most important part of my own life, let alone the lives of others. I like to try and make the most of every second because you never know what role it may play in your future or the future of others. Being a contributor to the team effort, that is the most fantastic feeling. And that is something you just have to learn sometimes.

Blackie: Allow yourself to be successful

'Remove those obstacles . . . give yourself a clear run.'
Bob Proctor

Just how important are goals? In one sense, I would say, unhesitatingly, massive. In another, not at all.

Depending on the type of personality you are, the setting of conventional goals, i.e. going from A to B in a given time, can not only be hugely motivational but can keep you on track in your career and in life. Doing five of something today then setting a goal of ten in three months' time gives you something to aim for. If that goal is worthwhile, and will stretch you while still being attainable, and by reaching that level you'll get recognised and rewarded as becoming a more valuable person, then great! Especially if the pressure and stress associated with meeting the goal is not prohibitive and is actually one of the stimuli which make the journey rewarding.

On the other hand, striving for a goal that you probably realise is not attainable and for which your very best efforts won't be recognised or rewarded, won't be a life-enhancing experience for you. In fact, the stresses associated will make you unhappy at best and physically and psychologically ill at worst.

But there is one goal everyone should aim for: to be your very best on any given day, doing whatever you've chosen to focus your attentions on. We are all capable of achieving that goal. And the reward of being successful can be very powerful and liberating. If we strive to be our very best each day, not only in our physical training sessions and so forth but also in our compassion to help others and in our desire to make the world around us a better place, then we can't help but leave a positive impact in our wake. Surely that is everyone's goal.

So allow yourself to be successful. Allow yourself to give it all you've got. And do it in as relaxed a manner as you possibly can. You don't need to experience angst and stress. When we work on improving the absolute speed of a player or athlete, we need to cultivate 'relaxation' and increase flexibility to allow the athlete to move powerfully into optimum mode; knee lift, stride length and arm/shoulder movement allied to a relaxation in the neck and especially facial musculature all contribute to attaining top speed. If we extrapolate that principle to 'mental muscles', tightened and stressed due to conventional and, at times ill-conceived, goal-setting, then relaxing the 'have to achieve' thought process and changing it to 'allowing yourself to achieve' will bring success to you more effectively.

Before I started playing rugby, I used to watch my brother play. I used to throw a ball around with my dad on the sidelines. I was so charged by the feelings of anticipation, I simply could wait no longer. Admittedly I was only three years old and most kids that age are indeed ridiculously excitable about something or other. I have a favourite photo at home of this moment with my dad, and it always reminds me of my early love for the game and everything it stood for.

The following September, in 1983, I finally joined my brother in the Under-8s mini set-up at Farnham RUFC. Almost immediately I began receiving my first lessons in teamwork and these, I firmly believe, still apply today. They are not messages that can be easily conveyed through explanations and definitions, it is better if you experience them. Maybe my dad knew that because, as a team coach, what he did was let us get out there and get stuck in. But there were a few key principles he was definitely keen to instil in both of us back then. The games I have competed in and the teams I have played with have only made these points more powerful and relevant.

* * *

No. 1: No-one likes a show off

I learned slowly, bit by bit, that nothing has a more detrimental effect on collective togetherness and team spirit than an individual concerned first with seeking glory for himself, and looking good before doing good.

I have always been fascinated by sports performers' reactions after scoring. I have been intrigued by seeing a soccer player celebrating a goal-line tap-in pushing away his team-mates, who have essentially just set it up for him, in order to follow his rigorously choreographed, individual dance routine using a corner flag or possibly a theatrical device stored down his sock.

Mind you, 'dance' routines are not confined to the soccer pitch. In rugby I've see my fair share of signature moves. To name a few:

THE SPRINKLER – player drops to one knee and rotates body whilst using one arm to simulate pumping water from out of the other one.

THE LAWN MOWER – player places ball horizontally on the pitch then rolls it away with the foot. The scorer then walks behind the ball pretending he is pushing it along like a regular Flymo.

THE CIGAR – player flicks ball into hand using his feet. He then spins ball on finger for dramatic effect before placing it in the corner of the mouth, pretending to light it. It is then removed and the scorer simulates exhaling the smoke ring.

I do admire the imagination required for these ideas but – call me old-fashioned – I keep asking, 'What about the other fourteen guys who have worked hard to help that one lucky man over the line?' Perhaps this one represents an answer of sorts:

THE GRENADE – team-mates stand in a huddle whilst the scorer lobs the ball into the middle of them then covers his ears and crouches down. Supporting players are launched into the air and onto the ground by the explosion.

There are certain celebrations that I have enjoyed seeing though. I love watching Jason Robinson cross the line, he embodies a great sporting ethos. In both the 2001 Lions tour and the 2003 Rugby World Cup he scored big tries. His actions afterwards spoke of pure emotion, a kind of outpour that says 'we have scored and I'm fired up'. It lifts the team no end, and makes me feel like I have been a part of contributing to that power which propels him to be his most destructive and ruthless best. I know there is nothing premeditated about the shake of his fist or the way he punches the ball into the air, that kind of passion.

> " *Nothing has a more detrimental effect on collective togetherness and team spirit than an individual concerned first with seeking glory for himself, and looking good before doing good* "

In the third game of the same 2001 Lions series, which the Australian team won, they scored a classic try symbolic of their tactical mastery. In just three phases of play, starting with a lineout, they pulled our defenders out, jammed us back in, then flew down the short side with a slight overlap and finished it off in the corner. I saw it coming but too late. I was urgently tracking across, the last defender to attempt a tackle. It felt as I imagine it would be like trapped under a tornado, as the other fourteen members of their team emerged from nowhere. They picked up the try scorer, screamed and high-fived. It had quite an effect, it was all about the team, all together, feeding each other's spirits. There was nothing arrogant about it, there was nothing in the act that I felt I could use as a motivational tool to feed my own desire to fight back later in the game. All it did was let me know that they were running hot and about to get hotter. This was not a comfortable feeling when I considered how well they were already playing.

In my view, every member of a team is hugely important, we are all equal and therefore equally worthy of sharing the praise, the responsibility, the blame and the memories. For me this is a huge part of being a team man. It is the attitude which says, 'I will do whatever I can to help you guys to be at your best.' If every member of the team is pushing others to excel while also being propelled forward by the rest of the team, this will bring the best part of everyone to the fore.

No. 2: The best way to achieve one's goals is to help as many others to achieve their own goals

The easiest way to illustrate this concept using rugby is undoubtedly when you consider what is really happening during a spell in defence. It doesn't matter which system of defence the team employs, the fundamental principle is that everyone works together. It means you must take notice of the player in the defensive line on your inside and on your outside, who they are, their strengths and weaknesses and exactly what they will require from you to help them play their own part brilliantly. You must be technically sound and have worked on your tackling during practice. You must be able to react quickly to the unexpected and learn to be aware of your team-mates' body language so that you can read their more instinctive moves. Finally, the ultimate component behind good defending is an enormous work rate, the desire to get up from the floor and to get back into a useful position. Good defenders are those who want to make hit after hit with no concern for recognition or their own physical state. It is about the team.

There is something in rugby called the 'tackle count'. It basically highlights the number of tackles an individual attempts in a game. It then breaks those tackles down into missed tackles and tackles made. The successfully completed tackles are then judged on their outcome, whether it be deemed as dominant (knocking them back/dislodging the ball), OK (attacker is put straight to the floor), or submissive (attacker makes valuable yards forward towards the try line). Ideally we all aim for a one hundred per cent completion rate with as great percentage of dominant hits as possible.

On the whole I disagree with tackle counts. Teamwork is an attitude, a state of mind, and is very difficult to measure in stats. Aspiring to do more to help the team should not be discouraged by fear of mistakes and being labelled 'not good enough' or looked down upon. I have played with players who will knock an attacker to the floor, thereby taking himself out of the game, when he knows that it will not stop the ball being passed on or the attack from continuing. It will have been a 'dominant' tackle. But to what effect? Although it may sound strange, defending against five attackers with only three defenders is sometimes quite simple, whereas defending against four with two is not. Trying to stop three guys on your own is damn near impossible. The statistics may show the big hit as a successful bit of defending but, in essence, the act hangs other players, and therefore the team, a little bit out to dry.

One of the best team players I have ever had the joy of playing alongside is recently retired: England and Saracens back rower,

Richard Hill. He defends superbly, always managing to stay alive and active in the game to help others but at the same time the first to strike when the time is right. He has put his body in places I would struggle to peer into, let alone dive into. He would fight right up to the final whistle but never for himself – just for the boys around him. It was astonishing to watch him at times, jets of blood gushing from his forehead, bits of face hanging off and fingers pointing the wrong way and yet his only consideration: 'What more can I be doing to help?' And people wonder why England were successful during that era . . .

No. 3: The team is only as strong as the weakest player

In a successful team people look after one another. Players listen as much as they talk and in doing so they gather as much information about one another as possible. The better you know someone, the easier it is to help them along their own path to their potential. If you know the guy next to you doesn't have a particularly strong turn of pace but is a giant in other areas, then you make sure he isn't put in a position where his lack of speed will be a problem. In turn, he'll help you out in the areas where you are weakest. But you only truly know that about someone when you know they have been totally honest in giving their all every time they take to the field – on match days and training days.

> " Training-game players are ten-a-penny "
>
> Bobby Saxton

Whenever a player trains, or plays, he represents the team in

119

every way. He embodies what the team and its members are about. If during the week I choose to operate at sixty per cent energy and concentration then I make a statement that it is OK to do so in the team at the weekend. It shows a lack of respect for my friends and becomes an illustration of how we all see the game. This is a large part of sharing responsibility, a conscious decision every day to arrive ready to be better than yesterday.

Blackie: Checklist – Managing a team

'Be a strong, supportive, knowledgeable and reassuring catalyst.' Anon

ONE
When talking to a team member about their performance and effectiveness, be constructive, fair and consistent with your comments. Give tips for consideration and objective examples concerning acceptable behaviours and practices. Don't get personal or be negative. Communicate what you want to see, not what you don't.

TWO
You must recognise effort and good performance and you must reward meaningfully and as individually as possible. What gets rewarded becomes habit and good habits get the job done.

THREE

Care for all your players no matter who they are, what perceived seniority they have and what they do. Their self-worth and confidence will increase and so will your reputation.

FOUR

Each team member has an optimal environment that will support a consistently good performance. Whatever it is, find it. Keep searching until you do.

FIVE

Always be honest in a caring and compassionate way, but honest nonetheless. Reward those who deserve to be rewarded and discipline those who deserve to be disciplined, no matter who they are. Period. If you do this the players will trust you.

SIX

Ensure your players see you in control of the situations and challenges your job demands of you.

SEVEN

When the team faces a dilemma, show the ability to simplify how you look at it and what you'll do to resolve it. 'Let's narrow this down and focus on doing this...'

EIGHT

Tell your players what's going to happen over and over again, more clearly each time. Believe in yourself that it will happen. Picture that it has already occurred and behave accordingly. Give all your attention to the victory, never mention the possibility of defeat.

NINE

Bypass the golden rule of doing unto others as you would have them do unto you. This doesn't make much sense really, as we're all different. Replace it with what I term my Platinum rule: 'Treat others the way *they* would like to be treated.' As long as you've recruited the right individuals, with ballpark talent and character, this will be your X-factor.

TEN

Know when someone just isn't good enough. I'm not saying you don't continue to try and support that person in every way possible. You should keep offering all your skill development, strategic and tactical coaching abilities. But you must aware that the results will be less effective. Don't disappoint yourself — it will show to the other team members and will reduce overall effectiveness. Know when your efforts are worthwhile and act accordingly. If there is nothing to be extracted from the coach-player, manager-employee relationship, then the mutual benefit has gone. It is no longer healthy to continue to try to create something out of nothing. At such times, you have to be brave and admit it's time to let the individual move on, for both your sakes.

Everything you do as an individual, and everything you think, is important in a team environment. Being positive is vital. Even the slightest touch of negativity (a motivation, fear or attitude) will act as an enemy

> **Each player can only ever be doing whatever he or she can to help the team succeed**

and will confuse overall confidence. Most importantly, each and every player must endeavour to step up and put themselves on the line when the pressure is on. Not to do so is to decide not to. It is a conscious decision to hide – undoubtedly the most negative of actions on a team sports field. To fear for one's own failure and to give this fear priority over the opportunity to stand up and at least try to improve a difficult situation is the ultimate game breaker in my view.

Richard Hill did not know what an easy option was, he couldn't hide even if he wanted to. He would do the extra work so that others wouldn't have to; he would not drop to a knee or join a ruck that had already finished just so he could avoid having to face uncomfortable circumstances. He never fell silent in the middle of play so that someone else would have to face the opposition's strongest or fastest runner. He took blame, he took praise and he treated them both the same, it was all in a day's work for a true team player.

I wonder what I was thinking now when I made that original goal about being the best in the world. I'm pretty sure I meant well but I understand things differently now.

Each player can only ever be doing whatever he or she can to help the team succeed. The very concept of being interested in how you fare against others is to buy into what the statistics say.

And when you play for numbers, you play first for yourself.

I want to be the best I can be; that has to be good enough. The best I can be in whatever my team needs me to be. Even when things are going very, very badly.

The Road Back from Hell

> " *When I realised that I had done pretty much everything I could possibly do before and throughout every second of the match, I found a touch of peace for the first time* "

There are few more horrific feelings in any sport than the experience of being humiliated. I can't even stand to watch it happen to somebody else.

I began secondary school about a year and a half sooner than what is considered normal. It meant that I played my rugby with a bunch of lads a fair bit older and bigger than myself.

I remember the first game of my first season. We were playing away down at a school in the south. I was ten years old in an Under-13 team and not completely up to scratch with the game's more advanced rulings. We had just conceded a second try very early on and the situation was already looking bleak. Underneath the posts, we waited for the conversion kick attempt which struck one of the uprights and bounced towards me. No one had told me that, after a conversion, play is dead until the halfway restart. Feeling like my team needed a boost I picked up the ball and set off on a heroic but completely illegal run. I can picture the scene now. I was about three feet high with blond hair straight from the candy-floss machine and my little legs just a blur as I tore up the field, completely on my own. I must have thought I'd caught everyone napping. Everyone that is but their confused kicker who, probably twice my size, promptly turned around and decked me.

I was knocked unconscious by the tackle. When I came to, I remember hearing some sniggering from what I perceived to be both teams and I think also the referee. My brother, playing in the second row and captaining the side, took it upon himself to carry me from the field in an act very similar to cradling a huge baby. He laid me down on the sidelines where I had plenty of time and space to mull the whole thing over.

> **The ball wobbled, and gently toppled over. It marked possibly the most anticlimactic and embarrassing moment of my life**

A year or so later and this time at least I was on the winning side. We were several scores ahead and I was enjoying myself. There was even a small crowd forming, certainly more than the usual mix of teachers and parents. We had scored out wide on the right and I was in the process of digging a hole in the overgrown turf for my place-kick attempt.

The coach had pumped the ball absolutely rock solid, as was his way. It was so hard I could feel my teeth clatter as my foot struck it. I had had to fight that little pellet for every inch of height and length my whole school career. With a tough kick like this one ahead of me, my confidence and optimism wavered slightly.

I decided I'd give it everything anyway. I could slot this one and give the spectators standing a few yards behind me something to cheer and admire. Energy surged up my spine. The excitement in the air was palpable. To me at least. I tensed my body in anticipation of incredible success, swung my left foot very hard . . . 'thump', straight into the ground behind the ball. In those tiny moments before the inevitable happened, I was reminded of a chopped tree just at the call of 'Timber!'. The ball wobbled, and gently toppled over. It marked possibly the most anticlimactic and embarrassing moment of my life. As I sheepishly jogged back towards my team trying to hide the obvious limp, I felt a wave of nausea and self-loathing rush over me. I don't really remember anything else of the game after that. What I do recall, however, is driving my parents absolutely mad for the next few weeks, months even, by tearfully pulling apart the event in obscene detail every night without fail. I was obsessed with what each person on the field and the sidelines might have thought about me. I felt like I was never going to be able to get over the shame.

When it comes to my sport I have never really been able to laugh at myself enough. My strict views on professionalism and competition have caused me to become ridiculously serious at times. In my sporting values, success was all about sacrifice, hard work and being ultra self-critical. I saw no benefit in, or room for, relaxation – mental or physical. To me, that was the reserve of the weak and unambitious. When all combined, these beliefs created a fairly stubborn and self-perpetuating mindset. Every second counted, each performance made a difference to who I was and my identity. If I did well then I felt strong and worthy; if I made a lot of errors then I too was full of faults as a person. I could no longer distinguish between me and my job, between me and what I did, between me and the rugby-playing me.

My pride is mostly my own perception of what I feel I am worth and it works in relation to other people. Often I reckon it behaves like glue, sticking me to my values and ensuring that I never stop fighting for what I believe in and what I see as the right way to live. With compassionate and ambitious values, pride is a very valuable asset and a great personal trait. With self-centred values, pride isn't a worthy attribute. In my opinion, pride combined with selfishness simply brings humiliation and smacks more of stubbornness and insensitivity.

I cannot recall meeting anyone who deeply relishes coming second. When you've poured your heart into a challenge it is the last thing you desire

I wonder what my brother, Sparks, must have thought over the years as my kicking aide. So many times have I taken kicking practice past the point of preparing for a game and past the boundaries of enjoyment to a level only serving to fulfil my own ego. It was to make me feel better about myself whilst he stood there bored and cold behind the post, pondering whatever happened to his evening's plans.

* * *

Blackie: Behave like you are the best

'Behave like you are the best . . . and you'll have the best chance of being the best you can be.' Tony Robbins

How many times do you hear someone complain about the fact they never get the recognition they deserve for the amount of time and effort they put into whatever they do? I see great players who shy away from telling their coaches just how good they are for fear of seeming above their station. My good pal Jamie Noon at Newcastle would probably have been an England regular long before he achieved that status if he had been more openly positive about his abilities and what he would bring to the international set-up. Fortunately, Jamie has secured a rightly deserved senior status within the current England squad. Jamie, I feel, was held back not in the performance department, because he's been a great player for years, but in his propensity to talk up his personally perceived weaknesses. When he ditched that habit, and a habit was all it was, strangely enough the aspects of his play that had been evident for many years but had remained hidden, seemed to become increasingly attractive to those making the key decisions.

I remember Rocky Marciano, the great Italian-American heavyweight boxing champion, telling a bunch of young fighters that if they didn't have courage naturally they should pretend they did up until, and sometimes during, the fight because nobody would be able to tell the difference. So the message is, don't be arrogant, but sometimes you have to behave like you are the best. Tell us what you are good at and what you like doing, not what you don't excel at or what you don't like doing or what you perceive to be your weaknesses. That won't get you to the destination of your dreams unless your dreams are full of very low self-esteem.

Many times players and coaches are offered contracts because some amateur psychologist among the senior management has heard their love of that particular environment, that team, that club, that area, those players, and so forth, without any discernible results coming from their professional efforts. At the same time, other, more effective and worthy contenders are dropped and get lost along the way because of their answer to the everyday question, 'How are you doing?' The players you've never heard of answer, 'Not too bad ... OK ... could be better ... you've got to get on with it I guess ... etc.' Unless you truly mean it, cut it out – for your and everyone else's best interests. If you are really enjoying what you are doing and where you are, and this is just an habitual response, then don't keep your enjoyment a secret. People want to hear and want to be energised by positive feedback and optimism.

Believing in my own self-importance as I did, the 1998 'Tour of Hell', as it was dubbed, was always going to hurt me. The humiliation wasn't confined to the pitch either.

In life everyone loses at some point. It is the same in sport. There may be a few boxers who aren't very familiar with the feeling but on the whole it is the unwritten rule.

I cannot recall meeting anyone who deeply relishes coming second. When you've poured your heart into a challenge it is the last thing you desire. I believe how we react at these times, the interpretations we place on events, are the most influential steps in deciding whether we go on to achieve what we really desire.

I had just made my England debut, won the league title with Newcastle and we'd beaten the Rest of World team at Twickenham. As my first season was drawing to a close I was feeling pretty good about myself and this rugby lark. I believed that I had a good formula for getting what I craved from the world. However, I was about to receive something I certainly didn't want but which I guess, looking back, I really needed.

There was a considerably different look to the 1998 England squad named for the tour to the Southern Hemisphere compared with the one which had finished the regular season. Almost twenty first-line players had been rendered unavailable. It didn't matter to me though; I foresaw a bit of an upset Down Under. Clive Woodward had already told me that I would be his starting fly-half and, right then, anything was possible.

Not long after we had touched down, the Australian press began billing me as the 'wonder boy' who would ruin their country's plans. We were young and inexperienced but in all fairness we pulled together well. Our training ran smoothly and the final team rehearsal on the Thursday night was our best to

> **Midway through the second half the scoreboard had hit fifty, and the press-up gang began to hit the wall. One by one they shook and trembled then collapsed to the ground**

date. We were confident, enthusiastic and peaking at the right time.

I remember running out on to the field in Brisbane shortly before kick-off and almost being hit in the face by a stray firework from the raucous pre-match entertainment. It was to be a symbol for what was about to come.

It was 0–0 after half an hour but 31–0 at half time. At full time the scoreboard told the true story: 76–0. The on-field antics had been bad enough, but to make matters worse, the match organisers had employed a group of guys whose job it was to provide the crowd (mostly Australian) with a show of press-ups to match every point scored. Midway through the second half the scoreboard had hit fifty, and the press-up gang began to hit the wall. One by one they shook and trembled then collapsed to the ground, much to the amusement of the Australian fans who laughed and jeered. For a little while I was actually glad because it was taking their attention away from us. The final twenty minutes provided the other twenty-six points and, to be fair to the macho press-up crew they did try to continue, but only managed to do so in the form of sit-ups and finally squats. However, the embarrassment was all ours.

It was England's biggest ever defeat. A very bad dream, one that millions of people shared. Right there and then I couldn't absorb it properly. I knew it was bad, I just couldn't get a handle on how bad. In the changing room afterwards, I managed to lift my head long enough to catch the eye of another player, my friend Tim Stimpson. We shared an ironic smile and both just shook our heads in total disbelief. I had never lost like that in my life – it didn't seem fair. After the year I'd had, and the work I'd put in, it didn't make any sense.

The assault on my senses continued in the post-match function as we listened to the five or six speakers perform their duty as well as they could while still trying not to sound patronising. A near-impossible task when reviewing that particular game. I struggled to make eye contact with anyone, afraid they would see the weakness in my expression. I felt totally empty because I had lost my 'self'. The only thing to do was to stare at the floor and wait for this personal nightmare to be over. But my focus was all wrong. It was all about me. I should have been concentrating on the team and what we could learn from this disaster. But at that stage in my career, I hadn't yet been through those Grand Slam fiascos and the understanding that they eventually brought to me.

Later that same night, having endured all the formalities, the TV repeats and every conceivable comment from the public, the confusion began to transform into despair. My heart was sinking deeper and deeper into my chest as my mind entered into self-destruct mode. I felt embarrassed, ashamed and totally worthless.

I finally found myself alone in the hotel room and realised I was even afraid to phone home because I thought that I'd let my family down. I figured they would be disappointed in me. But I forced myself to make the long-distance call and, looking back, I am glad I did.

The tears flowed as I opened up to my dad. I expressed my bitterness, my anger, my frustration and humiliation. I was surprised at how many times I heard the word 'failure' come out of my mouth. When I finally ran out of steam and concluded my furious rant I fell quiet and let my dad speak. I remember exactly what he said. He asked me:

'What do you want to do about it? What is your next move?'

In allowing myself to become so consumed in this 'personal

tragedy' I hadn't even considered that. When I did, a few things started falling into place. Slowly, I admit. But they did.

This 'outcome' was not a failure but a lesson, albeit in disguise, a fork in the road that lay ahead of me. I became aware of something my emotions were hiding from me – that we all have this power to decide our own futures, no matter what happens in our pasts. It is our own right, obligation even, to choose the direction we take at these crossroads.

Since the final whistle I had spent my time fighting with what had just happened, carrying the pain of the event with me everywhere I went. When I realised that I had done pretty much everything I could possibly do before and throughout every second of the match, I found a touch of peace for the first time. In this state I began saying 'yes' to it all instead of 'no'. I accepted it. Doing this helped me to rediscover – bit by bit I admit – my positivity.

I have strengthened this concept over the ten years since – results have sometimes demanded that I do – and in all my losses and my wins I now see only helpful signposts. That is not to say I do not get hugely emotional too. I can't help the fact that I care so much about the game but I am more adept at seeing the guiding hand which helps me find a better route forward. For me these insights are the reward for remaining true to my ambitions. They serve as more than just a shove in the back, they offer me a better way to achieve my goal and sometimes even a better goal to strive for altogether. This is how I believe we grow.

* * *

Blackie: Enjoy the journey

'Along with everything else, you need to have fun.'
Mike Krzyzewski

It has often been said that success is a journey not a destination. I don't know who said it first, but in my experience they were absolutely right. I've been asked many times which lasts longer: the thrill of victory or the agony of defeat? The answer is simple – the agony of defeat lasts much longer, at least until you win again and sometimes, with certain defeats, it stays with you forever. But if the thrill of victory doesn't last long, the rewards of the journey certainly do – the good times you experience with your team-mates, the satisfaction of putting in the effort and seeing the result. All these things endure longer than the final climax. So enjoy the journey day by day. All you have is now . . . so if not now, when?

One of the things I learned from that fateful night in Brisbane, from the eleven times that I found myself beneath our own posts, was that I wasn't ready yet. I had got ahead of myself and I needed to go back a few steps. I'd had an incredible start to my career but there were gaps I'd papered over which needed filling in properly if I was to reach my lofty ambitions.

> **I learned about the danger of buying totally into what the newspapers said and believing my own hype**

135

The Aussie boys put on a great show that evening and in their performance I realised what I lacked as a player. I had been given a clearer idea of where I saw myself going and how to get there, the skills I needed to work on. I learned about the danger of buying totally into what the newspapers said and believing my own hype. I was starting on the road of finding new peace which came from doing my best and knowing that is the most than you can ever do.

Nowadays, when people ask me about the 'Tour of Hell', 'Shame', 'Death', 'Destruction' and 'Disease' – whatever description it is given – I tell them without any hesitation that it rests high up among the best experiences of my life and that I'll always be grateful for it.

Mind you, at the time, under the sheer intensity of that experience and with the amount of pride I felt I had lost, I inevitably came a bit unstuck. But prompted by Dad, the result – definitely a beneficial one – gave me the opportunity to access and fully examine my deeper-rooted beliefs.

I saw a few problems in myself, but those first seeds of learning from setbacks had at least been planted. I also saw my lack of balance. I appear to naturally lean (quite heavily) towards my obsessive side. I am quick to dive in with both feet, it is the animal I become when the first whistle goes and even after it blows for the last time. I want to fight to the death; there are no questions or hesitations, but this is an unbalanced approach. I realised this after that tour, but I didn't have the mental skills to do anything about it then. So I pushed those ideas to the back, hid them away as they didn't fit naturally with my personal world order. For so long I survived without balance, even though I was receiving some helpful and pretty persuasive hints on and off the field.

This competitive side can't carry on without a give-and-take relationship to support it. To be at my best and get the most from life I now consider it very important that there be times when I fully involve my 'self' in the action, and times when I step back a little to find crucial perspective. Previously I pushed it as far as it would go, and then further. And what happened? I burnt out. I received numerous injuries and, although for a lot of the time I was still performing, I was no longer thriving. So now, taking my 'self' out of it for a while gives me a chance to replenish and refuel my competitive side. This enhances me rather than drains me and brings a more fresh, enjoyable approach to everything. This is a reward, the fun is the prize. Balance is everything, everyone needs a little time to take stock, re-evaluate and get a different view of things.

The key lesson I began to learn over that summer is how to look at the things that come along and seem, on the surface, to make you weaker. But just like those Grand Slam deciders we blew, you have to see them as steering you on a slightly different, not necessarily worse, path. And that applies even when the 'nudge' that has sent you on that new road comes in the form of physically stopping you from actually being able to take a step.

8

Injury Time

> *" As I was about to make contact, still unseen, he inexplicably stepped sideways slightly and I was the one caught off guard. 'Boom!' he went down, but I went down much harder. I knew immediately that I was in trouble "*

I have been fortunate enough to mix with many amazing people from all over the world. In some way or other they have all changed my life for the better. The benefits can be enormous. When you meet someone with an incredibly positive and selfless approach towards helping you, it is impossible not to feel like you're already winning. People like this can take you to a level you never knew was possible. Their positive energy can seem to seep into you. Or hit you like a huge, world-famous Samoan winger! They are true team players, but when these individuals are also capable of winning games on their own, they seem to be more akin to superheroes.

When I arrived at Kingston Park to join the Newcastle Falcons rugby team I was just eighteen years old. The first player I met was probably my most influential to date. He was an intimidating nineteen stone, strong, fast and immensely skilful. Inga Tuigamala was his name. He was an All Black and Samoan international and he is maybe the best player I have ever seen.

He possesses such a vibrancy that everything he touches has no option but to turn to gold. It is impossible to finish a conversation with him without feeling like a better person, in a better place.

He has a smile which makes everything seem OK and an infectious optimism which turns life into pure opportunity and excitement. When he was with the team I admired his inner balance. He had a Christian faith which seemed to motivate and energise his every action, and a wonderful family. He demonstrated a natural predisposition towards enjoying himself and a speciality for lighting up the rugby field.

He displayed a balance in everything he did. I watched him smash people during our games. These were hits which made me cringe with sympathy for our opponents. It was not rare to see the studded soles of opposition boots swinging towards the sky as he knocked them over. Immediately after, however, he would drop to one knee and help them back up, ensuring they were OK. The opposing players actually seemed to love chatting to Inga – once they recovered their breath of course!

* * *

Blackie: Touched by magic

'Surrounding yourself with good people certainly
increases your chances of a fulfilled life.'

Jim Rohn

There are so many special individuals that we meet throughout our lives and I believe we are all part of each other's destinies, interacting for reasons we may not yet be aware of. So having good, charismatic, inspirational people around you matters. They rub off on you and they can change the direction in which you are travelling. Take a look around in your life and note which individuals make you feel good; make you feel worthy; make you feel capable of achieving whatever it is that you wish to. Try to define what it is that makes them special and add whatever their key ingredient is to your individual recipe for success. We are all capable of being a positive influence on others, the catalyst that can bring the most remarkable rewards.

I remember one particular tackle a few years back which almost rocked the entire stadium. Inga was possibly the only man capable of camouflaging a nineteen-stone frame on a wide-open rugby field. He would silently drift out a little wider on his wing then accelerate in on an unsuspecting attacker from their blind side.

Just after the Six Nations finished in 2000, we were playing Bedford in Bedford and late into the second half their French

> **When you meet someone with an incredibly positive and selfless approach towards helping you, it is impossible not to feel like you're already winning**

number seven caught a wide pass in space. He may have thought he was in the clear, but the next moment I don't know what he was thinking. My guess is — not a lot! Inga being the man he is, probably tried to catch the poor bloke before he hit the deck, or at least to soften his fall, but to no avail. I mean, this tackle was big! The devastating potential of getting hit like that one day was almost enough to convince me to hang up my boots. I've not seen the like of it since. Their flanker was carried from the field and I think Inga was equally hurt.

When he had the ball in his hands, his eyes really lit up. As a fly-half, I am responsible for directing the game and making the calls. I found this tough at times with Inga because he wanted to attack from everywhere. I wish I'd actually surrendered more to his flamboyance and flair but I figured I ought to kick the ball once or twice a year if only to avoid getting beaten up by a bunch of very tired forwards. Inga could knock two players on to their backsides then goose step around a third one, who would be left trembling and wincing, just glad to still be in one piece. He was irresistibly quick and his passing was sublime. Overall I'd have to describe him as the guy who precipitated dreams or nightmares, depending upon whether he was on your team or not.

* * *

Blackie: Junk Yard Dog

'Commitment is what transforms a promise into reality.'
Abraham Lincoln

Some people are great orators and, make no mistake about it, words can be powerful, but other superb communicators are men of few words, preferring instead to let their actions speak for them. Scottish international scrum-half Gary Armstrong, the Jedda Knight, the Junk Yard Dog, personifies that perhaps more than anyone else I have ever met. His actions didn't just speak, they positively screamed! Because of his attitude – 'professional' before the sport was professional – he was probably the best signing the Newcastle Falcons made at the onset of the new rugby era. He inspired because he went out and did it – time and time again. Knowing you have someone like that in your team – and we all need someone like Gary – gives you such a lift, such a surge of positive energy. Words alone can rarely muster that. Just because certain individuals don't shout their worth from the rooftops, be sure not to discount their invaluable contribution. Charisma comes in all shapes and sizes.

I played alongside Inga in the centre during that first season, and it was a hell of an experience when we won the league. In the statutory celebration game versus the Rest of the World XV at Twickenham which concluded the season, I started in place of Rob

Andrew at number ten for the very first time. A few minutes in, I had my first touch. I took a pass from Gary Armstrong and, with not a lot on, I did what we have all done at some point in team sport and hurled the ball towards our best player. Inga was standing about twenty-five yards away so I let it rip, but I sent it a touch high. The rest took place in slow motion.

Inga jumped to take the pass comfortably, and while still in mid-air feigned one way with his head and his eyes but, as he was landing, managed to begin accelerating the other way. The French centre, who had been delegated the job of marking him, was fooled clean out of his boots as Inga struggled to keep his feet. The situation now looked like this: three of them and four of us, two of their defenders swooping in on him as he was stumbling. They lunged, he fell, and as both teams prepared for a ruck the ball came flying out of the back of Inga's right hand. It must have been a ten-yard pass thrown totally blind and yet it hit our outside centre right in the hands. The situation now was three of us and barely one of them. Try time! The whole thing was all over in less that six seconds but it will comfortably last me a lifetime. I shook my head on the field at the time and realised that I'd been standing in the same place for the entire period of play with my mouth wide open when I should have been following up in support.

Inga is a big personality for me because he draws out the very best from all those that come into contact with him and have the privilege of feeding from his energy and spirit. People like him are the catalysts for taking us towards what we thought was impossible. An incredible friend, team-mate, mentor and inspiration. He taught me about how to never give up; how to fight back when the worst seemed to be happening and my dreams seemed to be turning to dust. Or certainly flakes of bone or scar tissue.

* * *

'I've got you now,' I thought.

It was my first game back with Newcastle two weeks after the end of the Rugby World Cup 2003 final and I was fired up. I wanted to show my team-mates that in no uncertain terms was I stuck in the past.

Northampton had come to visit us in the North East; they had come to play – and they were doing a good job of it. At one point, they broke down the right-hand side with the ball, and it was two versus two but only because they hadn't seen me yet. I was covering across from the other side of the ruck and was out of eyesight. Exactly the way I like it. I had the advantage – a chance to make a big impact.

'Make him pass, Jackie,' I pleaded in my mind.

I needed Hall Charlton ('Wor' Jackie – we're up north remember) to leave me one versus one. If he tried to do too much and bought a dummy then the two versus one would become my problem. He forced the ball inside and with everyone's eyes on the pass, I saw my chance and, unspotted, I accelerated hard.

'Here we go.'

It was their number eight I think, but at the time it didn't matter – it never does when you are in the heat of action. I

> **I wanted to show my team-mates that in no uncertain terms was I stuck in the past**

had the element of surprise on my side. If I caught him moving upright then maybe I could rock him hard enough so his head, the centre of gravity, would shift back over his legs. I started to pump my legs harder, in shorter steps, as I prepared to fly. I bent from the knees, kept my head and eyes up and my back straight. I like to visualise a door jamb, a straight piece of wood travelling at speed. I focused on the area just above the waist and just below the ball. As I was about to make contact, still unseen, he inexplicably stepped sideways slightly and I was the one caught off guard. 'Boom!' he went down, but I went down much harder. I knew immediately that I was in trouble.

'I can't feel anything in my arm,' I repeated over and over again to the physio, Marty Brewer. A dormitory full of alarm bells rang in my head, partly because of the mild concussion and partly because of the fear and panic I was feeling. The number eight's hip bone (his hardest part) had collided with my cheek bone (not my hardest part) which resulted in my right ear being slammed against my right shoulder. The fourth and fifth vertebrae in my neck had been fiercely compressed together causing the bone to bite down hard into the nerves from my spinal cord to my arm. Even now, as I write, I grimace all over again.

The initial sensation was one of a white-hot poker being threaded down the length of my arm, then came the pins and needles all the way to the fingertips. The classic 'stinger' as it is known in the world of contact sport. I knew all about those. I had experienced my first when I was fifteen years old, and then probably had the pleasure of being reacquainted with the sensation almost once a game (and near enough weekly in training) after that. In the 2003 World Cup final I had two. I think my record was six of them in one game. Each 'stinger' would follow the same pattern and initially the shock and pain made me think of leaving the field and never playing again. But the body is a remarkable thing, and after a minute or two, or even less, the sensation ebbed away and I would feel completely ready to get on with it. Not this time though, after almost ten years of them I'd finally met my nemesis.

'The feeling should come back gradually over the next seven to ten days. We'll test your strength and see if you are ready to get back on the field.'

The advice was to wait for the body to heal itself. Nerves tend to recover at a rate of about one millimetre a day. Depending on the stretch of the nerve damaged it shouldn't be too long. More importantly though was how deep the damage was. If the central axion part of the nerve was affected, that was a different story. It may never recover at all. And after two weeks, the sensations that should have come back, hadn't.

'We all agreed then – we should get the operation.'

The England medical staff and the Newcastle medical staff had debated with my dad and me for a long while before we all met on the same page. It had been about four weeks since I walked from the field and I had hardly recognised any trace of movement in my right arm. The nerve at the centre of the problem was the one responsible for stimulating the deltoid muscle (used to lift the shoulder from the body), the biceps brachii muscle (used to lift the forearm from the elbow) and the infraspinatus (used to rotate the arm outwards). Without any movement these muscles were wasting away. I saw bone poking through the skin all over my arm.

'We're fairly confident that you will experience a full or close to full recovery but there is a chance this procedure will not work and the feeling may never come back.'

It didn't seem to be coming back on its own, so I thought, 'What the hell.' The scans showed a fracture in one of the vertebrae but it may have been an old injury from a previous stinger. The catalyst was a bony growth, called an osteophyte, pushing down hard on the nerve, preventing any recovery. The surgeon removed it with precision then sewed me back up again.

Later the same day that I returned home from Newcastle General Hospital, I sat down and dusted off the little black book in which I list all my goals. I looked at what was left, where I now stood and what I really wanted. How was I to set about achieving them? When I examined the dreams that had already come true, I saw those accomplishments as the result of hard work. I had earned them. The ones which still eluded me I seriously hadn't worked hard enough for. For me it was quite simple – if I wanted to get better and achieve more then I needed to work much harder. And being injured wasn't going to stop me. Inga, among others, had installed the belief in me that I could still attain the seemingly impossible.

Blackie: Uneven balancing act

'Play sport with a passion, but always maintain balance in your life . . . be it heavily weighed towards getting better at your chosen sport!' A delegate at a Chicago sports conference, 1991

In all my years in sport and coaching business people, the true achievers I've worked with do not live balanced lives. Everyone likes to say that there's more to life than rugby/football/ golf/promotions/degrees and so forth. It is said that the most important thing in their lives are their loved ones and that sport or their careers should be a distant second. These people claim to have wonderful family lives, have healthy hobbies, take regular holidays, read and go to church. Well, some of those things anyway.

I doubt it. In most cases in order to succeed it's just not possible to live a balanced life. The truth is, individuals at the height of their careers become obsessed with what they're doing and devote to it a disproportionate amount of their time. This has to be to the detriment of their loved ones, pets, stamp collection, other worthy hobbies, reading...

The question becomes: when is it appropriate, or indeed possible, to live a balanced life? If you ask me if I believe whether we *should* all live balanced lives then I'd say, within our chosen pursuit, it *is* probably best for our lives to be rounded with equal time devoted to our careers and our personal lives. But if you ask me do I think that our lives *will* be balanced, then the answer is probably not.

As a coach I feel I have a duty to communicate the possibility of life balance and the potential benefits that can be extracted from its stability. The rewards of benefiting from the joy of home life can enable us all to effectively implement our better selves in the work environment and arguably gain greater success.

However, it is a very fine line which must be walked. We risk moving from one extreme to the other, from our successes meaning everything, to our successes meaning nothing. If the latter happens, then we may in fact lose the very essence of our being. And that is not going to help you at home or in the office. I must admit that I personally struggle to put into practice my own advice on leading a balanced life. My work as a coach means I am obsessed with sharing ideas that can help with another person's journey in life. So I spend my time preaching about overcoming an obsession for success, while I stay habitually obsessed with helping those in my charge to do so. Catch 22.

The only advice I'd give in this light therefore is that you simply try to be the best you can be, whatever that is. Be it the best manager, the best player, the best coach, or indeed the best mother/father, the best wife/husband, son/daughter and so forth. I truly believe this is the only way that a 'balanced' life can ever be truly achieved.

Hard work has been the key factor in the goals I'd been able to tick off, so why change? My mentality was, 'If it ain't broke then don't try and fix it.' But in my mind, I needed to raise the bar in every area, I had to step it up big time. The energy fuelled my muscles and the adrenalin pumped through my veins as I set my new standards. Could we manage back-to-back World Cups? What about Lions tours? Stupidly, the day after my neck operation I was pounding away on an exercise bike with my neck brace on. All I could think of was coming back stronger. I had months, maybe years, of free time ahead of me with a challenge in mind. To a highly motivated person this was an exciting proposition. But I wasn't going about

> **" But I wasn't going about it in a very smart way. I wasn't listening to the world around me. Only the 'Jonny Wilkinson way' would do "**

Right: Five Nations;
England 35 Ireland 17,
4 April 1998

Below left:
Australia 76 England 0,
6 June 1998

Below right: Five Nations;
Wales 32 England 31,
11 April 1999

Bottom left: Six Nations;
Scotland 19 England 13,
2 April 2000

Bottom right: Six Nations;
Ireland 20 England 14,
20 October 2001

England 31
New Zealand 28,
9 November 2002

England 32
Australia 31,
16 November 2002

England 53
South Africa 3,
23 November 2002

Six Nations;
Ireland 6 England 42,
30 March 2003

Above: New Zealand 13 England 15, 14 June 2003

Right: Australia 14 England 25, 21 June 2003

Right: RWC 03; England 28 Wales 17, 9 November 2003

RWC 03; England 24 France 7, 16 November 2003

RWC 03;
England 20
Australia 17,
22 November 2003

Top left:
Zurich Premiership;
Newcastle Falcons 23
Northampton Saints 19,
28 December 2003

Top right:
Powergen Cup final;
Newcastle Falcons 37
Sales Sharks 33,
17 April 2004

Right:
Zurich Premiership;
Newcastle Falcons 30
Sale Sharks 29,
2 January 2005

Heineken Cup; Perpignan 33
Newcastle Falcons 12, 8 January 2005

Zurich Premiership; NEC Harlequins 39
Newcastle Falcons 23, 13 March 2005

Above left:
New Zealand 21
British and Irish Lions 3,
25 June 2005

Above right:
New Zealand 48
British and Irish Lions 18,
2 July 2005

Left:
Guinness Premiership;
Sales Sharks 26
Newcastle Falcons 25,
2 September 2005

Below:
Guinness Premiership;
Northampton Saints 25
Newcastle Falcons 23,
3 September 2006

RWC 07 training;
4 September 2007

Above: RWC 07; England 12
Australia 10, 6 October 2007

Right: Paris,
18 October 2007

Below: RWC 07; England 14 France 9,
13 October 2007

RWC 07; England 6
South Africa 15,
20 October 2007

Summer 2008

it in a very smart way. I wasn't listening to the world around me. Only the 'Jonny Wilkinson way' would do. But that wasn't what the mighty Inga was all about. He took in everything around him. Me, I had my tunnel-vision specs on, and a serious neck injury for God's sake.

'You're suffering from over-training syndrome.'

I'd been putting in eight-hour training shifts for two to three months. With no game on at the weekend to taper down and rest for, I was training nine to five, six and a half days a week. My schedule went something like this:

9.00–10.00	General arm/shoulder rehab
11.00–13.30	Kicking practice
14.30–15.30	Fitness and weights
16.00–17.00	Neck weights and or passing/handling skills

I also had to fit in physio sessions and lunch. I was eating six to eight meals a day, but the food was passing right through me. I could not satisfy my hunger. One day I ate thirteen chicken breasts, a kilo of natural yoghurt and two protein shakes, not including breakfast! When I think about it now I feel a little sick.

The big side effect of my training regime was felt at night time. I could not sleep. Four or five hours was a good amount during that spell. I was deathly tired but I could not drift off. It seemed like I was actually too tired to sleep.

The whole process was self-destructive, I know that now. When anyone, qualified to or not, told me to slow down and rest, I played dumb. I misled everyone, including Blackie, about how much I was doing. I needed to fill these days, I needed a purpose.

I didn't even know if I'd ever play again, I couldn't stop to think about it. I would go mad if I rested. The quality of my training was affected and general life was uncomfortable. It was not a good time for me or those around me.

9

Nervous Energy

"For me, the hardest part of playing rugby has undoubtedly been dealing with the pre-match anxiety. It is something I have never, in the past, been able to escape"

By April 2004 I had already been out of the game for five and a half months. I tried to keep in touch with it all by taking over parts of training sessions and doing a little coaching here and there. On match day I liked to help out the players by running water and messages on to the field. One of my jobs that season was to look after the sidelines during the Powergen Cup final, Newcastle versus Sale at Twickenham.

For perhaps the first time in many years I was not in the dressing room for the big day. Instead, I witnessed the whole build up from outside, in front of the stadium. As the crowd grew minute by minute, the volume of noise built and the atmosphere noticeably intensified. It was a pretty eye-opening experience.

Blackie: Superstitions

'To thine own self be true! If it works for you . . . use it!'
Steve Black

One of the greatest moments that I have been involved in during my professional sporting career was the Falcon's Powergen Cup win over Sale in 2004. Everything came together that day. Collectively we believed that victory would be ours and that we deserved it – because of the brand of rugby we were trying to play and the fact that all the players and coaches had bought into that ethos. It was very special. I'd even say it was worthy of losing my bottle of Holy Water! A friend, Jimmy Rule, who had previously played for us at Newcastle, had collected it for me from Lourdes during a European Cup game earlier in the season. I'd asked for it because I'd had an incredibly strong feeling that at some point in the not too distant future I was going to want to underwrite my support of the team with some spirituality – and the final proved to be the day. I remember putting the bottle against the posts at Twickenham during the warm-up, having it at my side during the half-time talk and at the end of the game in the post-match huddle. And then it disappeared. I only hope it has brought the person who took it the same comfort it brought me. Many people have superstitions they feel they need to go through before a match and these shouldn't be discouraged. At the very least, it is part of a player's mental preparation for the task ahead. I can't say whether they have any impact on what is to come, but I do know that I have my own personal beliefs and at very important times they have delivered for me.

Before every international game in which I have been involved at Twickenham (and at the 2007 World Cup final) it would take less than five minutes between arriving and entering the changing room in full travel gear and leaving fully kitted out, ready to warm up. At this fairly early stage, still an hour and a half before kick-off, the stands tend to be relatively empty. I guess people are either meeting up in the local pub or enjoying the corporate hospitality in the boxes or in the main car parks.

My thorough warm-up involves kicking twenty punts (of varying style and trajectory) with each foot and five drop goals with each foot. I would then be looking to hit a total of fifteen to twenty left-footed goal kicks from almost along the try line, both sides of the posts. This very acute angle helps to narrow down focus and increase accuracy and precision before I go out in front for a further four or five more to check that

> "When the action heated up it started quicker than I thought it would; it was too intense, too precise, just way too much for me to handle"

everything is in place. For my restarts, six little scoops chipped over the cross-bar from a position virtually underneath it give me an opportunity to get used to achieving maximum height within as short a distance as possible. Finally, I work on long and short passes with either hand and some testing catching practice, a few grubber kicks and chips.

The whole process lasts forty minutes. By this time the stands have filled up considerably but the noise and obvious buzz is not something I am really aware of until I break my concentration to run back into the changing area and sit down. The next time I would see the crowd is when I see them in their full glory. When it's my turn to break through the tunnel doors and on to the field, I look up but I can't even see close to the top of the facing East Stand. With not a spare seat in the house, the experience is sensational, awe-inspiring – it is the moment that lasts longest and remains most vivid in the memory. My heart always skips two or three beats. I don't ever remember breathing until I settle on the field some fifteen to twenty seconds later. I feel the enormous surge of energy and adrenalin through my veins and into my muscles – the experience totally clears my mind.

Waiting for my Newcastle team-mates to come out this time though was a completely different experience. I was in a totally separate frame of mind. I knew exactly what they must have been feeling and going through, but the nerves made me feel vulnerable, not at all excited. As the players emerged from the tunnel amidst the raucous applause and lined up for the kick-off, I recall feeling pleased that I had my tracksuit on, not my strip. Dreadful though it is to say, I was glad that I wasn't out there, relieved that I wouldn't be touching the ball that afternoon. It all seemed like too much pressure, too much responsibility. When the action heated up it started quicker than I thought it would; it was too intense, too precise, just way too much for me to handle.

I guess it's pretty ridiculous when you consider that only six months prior to that day I had taken the field and survived the 2003 Rugby World Cup final, easily the biggest game of my career. Still, sitting in the Twickenham Stadium that spring afternoon, I wondered how I had ever managed that. Why didn't we all just break down under the stress and strain of it all?

For me, the hardest part of playing rugby has undoubtedly been dealing with the pre-match anxiety. It is something I have never, in the past, been able to escape. The churning in my stomach feels relentless, it is like I am being surrounded by a dozen people who are screaming at me and prodding me in the gut. My mind makes me see panic everywhere I look. The panic tries to force me to feed it with the most negative thoughts. That seems to be its preferred diet. It could be dropped balls, missed tackles, poor decisions, and sometimes getting badly injured.

One day I plucked up the courage to open up to a team-mate. I was rooming with Mike Catt. We used to room together as an England squad back in the early days and I really enjoyed it. Catty was a special roomy, he was very easy to talk to, and with his extra experience I thought he would be the perfect candidate for my one-to-one chat. I spent about ten whole minutes explaining the deep pain and agony I was feeling before these matches. I told him about how I paced and paced, pulling my hair out. I described then some of the things I've tried to set out here in this book – how my kicking sessions (hitting the three-hour mark at that stage) and four hours of sleep a night were draining me of any enjoyment. He nodded and laughed a little in a comforting way. I saw superior wisdom in his expression and when I finished, I was excited at the thought of receiving some of it. This was going to change my life.

'Get used to it,' he said. 'It gets worse with age!'

I burst out laughing because I presumed he was joking. He wasn't.

'But I look at you, mate, and you always look relaxed.'

'I've just learned how to hide it better,' was his demoralising sign off.

That's when I realised I had to find my own way. The source of this 'out of control' behaviour was a very vulnerable type of insecurity. Every competitive sport is played in the realm of the unknown; it is what creates all the excitement. If only I had been just excited. I wasn't, I was too busy being frightened. On the field I absolutely adore the undetermined nature of every second. It is such a challenge and such an opportunity. In waiting to play, though, I couldn't work out whether I wanted time to speed up so it would all be over with sooner, or stop dead so I could turn my back and hide.

I couldn't handle the thoughts of regret. If it didn't go absolutely right, I feared that something was very, very wrong. I strongly believed you only got one chance because second time around would never be as perfect. I wanted to be able to look into the future, to know that I had done OK, that I hadn't let anyone down. I hated this part of my job, it was almost becoming enough to force me to give it all up.

Blackie: Just the right amount of cooking

'Consistently delivering the goods when the heat's on, on match day? That's what makes a great player.' Bobby Saxton

Professional sport is all about performing well on match day and getting the right result. So you need to prepare as well as you possibly can and do what needs to be done in order to reach kick-off in the best possible condition. But some players find that a problem – they find it hard to transfer an excellent level of training performance to actual game play. This is generally because they can't handle the pressure and/or the emotions associated with playing in a competitive game, especially in front of a large crowd. The same can apply in business – presentations and pitches go wrong no matter how well prepared and slick they were in practice. And our personal lives aren't exempt either. No matter how witty and charming you found yourself in front of the mirror . . . in practice that first date can still go horribly wrong.

Don Shula, the great Miami Dolphins American Football coach, used to say that the week's preparation should have dealt with all the technical aspects of the prospective performance, and come match day, the total emphasis should be on getting the players emotionally ready to take on the day's challenge. That's true. On game day, it is the manager/coach's job to do what is necessary to allow all the preparation and hard work to pay off. If each member of the team isn't in the best emotional state to play the forthcoming match at the optimal level, then you've got problems.

Each player is likely to have his own rituals – some can be quite bizarre – to prepare for the game. The coach has to recognise and accommodate this. It is no use believing that everyone has to be pumped up to bursting point. For many, such over-the-top emotions will only cloud essential clear thinking – leading to poor on-field decision-making.

The coach has to ensure that each player, by whatever

means, is bright, urgent and confidently assertive, ready to embrace whatever the game will throw at him. To do that, you can't be overcooked, and you also mustn't be undercooked, hoping that the adrenalin associated with the heat of competition will get you up to scratch. Unfortunately, the truth is that by the time you've got into your best psychological state, the game could already be lost.

It is all about balance. Tailoring needs to individuals, while still keeping the team's overall success as the goal. In dressing rooms before matches everybody gets caught up in the emotion and just before the players go out there's a rallying call. The individuals come together and there is no doubt that the team that gets on the emotional front foot will have a hell of a chance of winning the game. But always there must be individual considerations to go alongside the combined stimulus. Some players don't need to be treated a little differently, they need to be treated totally differently.

A couple of players spring to mind as examples. Garath Archer, probably one of the world's finest locks when at his best, had a pre-match routine that didn't fit into the image of the hard-nosed, dynamic warrior that he was once the whistle went. Garath would sit quietly either listening to music or just contemplating, in order to keep his emotions in check. Just as well as Garath is six foot six inches, and tipped the scales at eighteen-and-a-half stone at his formidable best which I would suggest would be a frightening prospect if out of control! Then, once the game started, Garath was certainly up for it, as any-one who ever played against him would testify. At Twickenham against our Welsh team in early 2000 he was quite simply magnificent; a super athlete who did his job extremely well and stopped the opposition from doing theirs.

An example of going 'over-the-top' would be my old pal Gazza, surely one of the most talented footballers of all time. Part of Paul's personality has always been to enthusiastically embrace whatever it is he is doing at any given moment. It's made him a larger-than-life character and the football field was a stage where the person that is Gazza could thrive and weave all manner of magic and mischief, nearly always to the delight of his adoring public. But once in a while, that natural exuberance could almost explode, especially on the big stage. His 1991 FA Cup final appearance against Notts Forest, and his wild tackle on Gary Charles, the Notts Forest and England defender, is an example. Paul that day was so far 'cooked' that he became like a time bomb ready to explode.

It is impossible to say whether Gazza could have been 'toned down' a bit before he took to the field in that final, but both examples do serve to illustrate the spectrum that a coach has to be aware of if he is to get the best out of his team members. For Garath, it suited him to be left alone before a game, perhaps with one or two words and a pat on the back in the dressing room as the game approached. Over-hyping Garath would have been totally counterproductive. For someone like Gazza, an approach could be to reiterate that each game was an opportunity to celebrate his extraordinary talents, bring out the best in his team-mates and excite the crowd. That was his role and perhaps it was all he needed to be reminded of in order to allow his talent to flourish.

The manager or coach just needs to find what approach

works for each person. Easy! It might take time, but it will be worth it.

When I looked back at the big events of my life, however they had turned out, I knew that it was all OK. There was no fear of them. Not like the fear that paralysed me when I looked forwards towards my next challenge. So what I did was start to imagine that someone had come back from a few hours further on, to tell me how it all went and to inform me that I had done fine. I asked my time-travelling buddy to take this pain away. My imaginary conversations kept me awake for hours as I convinced myself that I would of course succeed, that it would be 'my day' and that I would come through this all unhurt mentally and physically. My 'friend' and I would run through all my preparation in an attempt to persuade me that I didn't deserve to miss a last-gasp game clincher from the touchline – he didn't get everything right – or a big one-on-one tackle five yards out from our own try line if it came to that. It did, I suppose, boost my confidence a little and eased the discomfort marginally, but maybe it just helped me to pass that difficult time. There was something not right about it all though. This was nothing like the enjoyable career that I once dreamed of. There was me 'trying to get by' in a situation that I knew was gifted to only a privileged few and which I had

> **Let me be nervous, let me embrace the sensation that is readying one's self for battle so that I may front up with all I have**

162

worked really hard for. This is what I always wanted, I had it and I was wasting it.

With a sense of urgency now driving me, I began to realise something crucial. I knew I had to find a way to harness my intense passion and competitive instinct while liberating my enjoyment, and quickly. I needed to find a way to fulfil my dream of a career with no regrets.

> *If you won't be better tomorrow than you were today, then what do you need tomorrow for?*
>
> Rabbi Nahman of Bratslav

Even off the field now, I have started to see the gaps between certainties as the truly fabulous parts of being alive. In actual fact they are the only part I would consider to be real life. If there was no unknown then this living experience would be nothing more than an exercise, a read through with black and white, correct and incorrect answers. There would be no extremes, no growth and no room for personal taste, character or personality. We would all appear desperately similar, as would all our worlds.

That realisation helped me enormously. Simple as it may seem on the written page, it was a major breakthrough for me and was a long time coming. When faced with uncertainty now, I see potential, I see a blank page waiting for me to fill. I see a chance to decide what this world can be for me. I want to face something new and challenging every day. Let me be nervous, let me embrace the sensation that is readying one's self for battle so that I may front up with all I have. This is what makes what I do truly worthwhile.

Blackie: Upgrade yourself and find an edge

'The time you take to sharpen your saw will be time well spent.' Stephen Covey

If you want to achieve in life, then there's something you need to know and the earlier you learn it the better. It is a mindset that allows you to constantly upgrade 'you' as often as you can, without allowing it to interfere with your daily living.

There is never a time in your life when you cannot subscribe to this process. You are learning continually – the books you read, the radio you listen to, the conversations you have, the world you view around you, the life you're taking part in. All of this contributes to that never-ending learning.

The Japanese term 'Kaizen' has become synonymous with the philosophy of wanting to become better on an ongoing basis. It is based on the belief that life is a journey, not a destination. If you agree that it is possible, indeed desirable, to improve the motivation behind all your actions, your thinking, your subsequent behaviour, then you must embrace education in the widest sense of the word.

One very powerful habit I suggest you cultivate is to keep a personal journal of your life experiences. Write down the things that happen to you or that you've come across every day – the stuff you want to remember. Never trust your memory. Get into the habit of jotting things down; facts, observations, feelings, things that you can take with you which will help you to negotiate life's future challenges. For once, the benefits of hindsight can actually be enjoyed – record how you dealt with challenges you faced so that you have a strong starting position when similar circumstances come along. Allow yourself the opportunity to learn and draw strength from your 'mishaps'. I like the idea of noting your daily feelings, your daily mood. Ask yourself are you happy? Sad? Positive? Negative? Energetic? Enthusiastic? Lethargic? Tired? Bright? Alert? Dull? Or even non-responsive? The entries you make every day should be reviewed before bedtime and then on getting up. It won't take long but the effect can be massive in terms of ongoing learning and knowledge retention.

Another good idea is to discuss what you've learned with a colleague, friend, loved one daily. It hasn't always got to be the same person. You share your beliefs/knowledge/understandings with ten different people and they'll each hear it once, but the exciting thing is you'll hear it ten times! This is a great way to reinforce and streamline your knowledge. You will distinguish the key points of your tale while also gaining a fresh perspective.

You need to honestly answer the questions: Are you preparing to win? Are you investing time and money into your personal growth? I've advocated for many years that people should read good non-fiction source material. When you get up in the morning or before you go to bed at night, try to read for twenty to thirty minutes of concentrated time. Over a week, month, season, year, you'll be shocked how much you'll get through. Turn your car into an automobile university. As you drive or commute to and from work listen to learning CDs – business, motivational, language and so on. The opportunities are endless. If you show the discipline to do this each time you get in the car or the train, once again you'll be shocked how much extra you can get through every week.

Go to professional seminars to listen to other people's experiences and views. This is all part of your pledge to yourself to learn more and to become more. If you change, the whole world will change for you. Are you the same person you were ten years ago? I hope not. You'll have evolved, even without knowing it, changing with the times because that's what survivors and thrivers do.

All that you learn, try, try, try to apply. It might just give you the edge, even if it is tiny. In athletics how much do we need to win by in the hundred metres to be wearing a gold medal around our neck? Not very much, just a nose, a short head, a hundredth of a second? And how much more does the winner get rewarded when they win one of the Major golf tournaments over the second-placed player. A fortune! And the difference between the two golfers? It could be as small as one centimetre. The winner's putt dropped, the runner-up's hovered on the lip of the hole. So practise doing what works for you in your life. Go for it, it'll give you the edge.

As a manager or a coach, if you are aware of this idea of Kaizen then you will be significantly more effective in your role. When coaching a team, there are certain principles that have to apply to everyone in the team, and each member has to abide by them. They become the foundations of the team. In addition to this basic building block of team performance, the coach or manager should also have an understanding of the uniqueness of each player's strengths, and from there they should formulate a plan, utilising the idea behind Kaizen, to formulate and execute a programme which will lead to the continual improvement of the individual.

The decision actively to embrace the philosophy of continual improvement is a major one, and one that should be taken as soon as possible.

One way to think of this approach to life is that you are completing a jigsaw. Or more accurately, aiming to complete a jigsaw. It will never be one hundred per cent finished. That is fine. If it were completed, there would be nothing left to strive for. And what is the point then? Of course there are times when the jigsaw fails to produce the rewards it promises. It may be that we have to find an ever-growing number of pieces just to complete a little section of the overall puzzle. It is during these difficult moments that we must try to maintain our curiosity. We must let our minds wander into trying to guess what secret the jigsaw holds.

Curiosity is a great attribute to have. Keep looking for new and better ways to live your life, be it at work or at home, spending time with your loved ones. If you wholeheartedly embrace this concept then you will discover something that you didn't already know about yourself. Everybody does.

On this road of continual improvement, you will meet count-less people along the way. Some for a long time, some only briefly. The key thing to remember is that every person you meet can help you, and you can help them. The stronger the relation-ship becomes, then the better equipped you both will be at sharing your talents unselfishly and growing into better people.

Needless to say, a process of continual learning isn't always easy. But remember, each step doesn't have to be a giant leap.

A small step, a tick-tack-toe, is still an improvement. It doesn't need to be daunting, or tiring. I can assure you, it will be exhilarating. But yes, of course there will be times when the wrong step will be attractive, because it will be easier. Try to avoid these moments at all costs as you will only let yourself down. This will drain your self-esteem and your enthusiasm. You will move backwards. Focus your energies on using what you've got as well as you can. This is a major part of my understanding of how you achieve success.

Obsessive anxiety isn't an easy habit to break, because it can be a big self-defence mechanism. But it really doesn't help. It will only sap your energy and weaken your spirit. When I feel the rising dread of worrying about what is looming ahead of me, I still call up my imaginary friend to help me understand this. I no longer want answers from him. I simply ask that he remind me that, come what may, if I surrender to my positive best, everything will be fine. And he will be absolutely right.

This time round, though, it isn't all the preparation that I've done that makes him correct. He doesn't tell me that all that hard work means I don't deserve to fail. I see that's nonsense now. The preparation, the kicking, the weights, all that stuff, it's still there. No one can perform at their best without practice. But now I see that what all that is giving me is the chance to succeed. It's a framework from which my natural ability can flourish in the unknown circumstances that will unfold around me. Beyond that, what my friend is telling me is that if I chase my dreams with all my heart then there can be no regrets and I will never really lose.

10

Playing the Game

> *The 'game me' is the instinctive, ultra-competitive being – the part of myself which, when fired up, shoots first and then leaves it to the 'everyday me' to ask the necessary questions later*

The 'revelation' that comes from relishing an unknown future took me some time to discover. It was certainly a way off on that April afternoon in 2004 when I was sitting in the stand at Twickenham. Then, I was not in good shape mentally at all. But again, just like when I spoke to my dad after the 76–0 humiliation on the 'Tour of Hell', being forced to sit there did at least give me some time to search inside myself.

My understanding, gained from match experience, is that when you are in the thick of something the mind reacts and responds. It causes you to focus on what is going on immediately around you; you act, you survive and you thrive. When you are not in the thick of it, but on the edge, things become more difficult. Only the most practised and accomplished visualisers can truly place themselves in other people's shoes. I was trying to do just that inside the stadium, but without the adrenalin, the fear and aggression that comes with impending collisions, or the right preparation. Physically and mentally I was inhabiting an altogether different zone. It meant that what was inspiring those guys on the pitch to be their best was frightening me back into my shell.

Blackie: Make your own blueprint for success

'He who knows others is wise; He who knows himself is enlightened.' *Tao Te Ching*

A big problem we face in the development and execution of highly successful teams is the need for individuals to impose themselves on one another. We are constantly told how to do something a different way, a way that has worked for another highly successful individual. The messengers believe they are right to inform us of this 'better' way but are more often than not too rigid in their views and beliefs and, despite the best of intentions, they actually exert a negative influence over the interactions and workings of the team. You and your team will never achieve your true potential following a blueprint for success that has been designed for somebody else.

I'm not suggesting that you can't *learn* from successful people ... of course you can. You'll be able to pick up a lot of important pointers from them which can be applied and incorporated into your own plan. But bear in mind that these individuals will almost undoubtedly have their own habits and practices – you have to adapt them to your own behavioural patterns if they are truly to be of use to you.

It feels like there are two very different parts to me. In my make-up there is the 'game me' and then there is the 'everyday me'. When I'm set to play I need to be on the field more than anywhere else in the world, but when I'm in the other mode, that's the last place on earth I feel I am ready to be. What decides these states of mind is a choice based upon which challenges I know lie ahead, and being able to prepare myself for them.

A part of professional sport in which I have encountered difficulty is when I fall into the 'touch and go' bracket for the weekend's match. The unfortunate reality is, I have spent far too many weeks trying to make decisions upon whether I will or will not be fit by Saturday afternoon. As much as the physios can do nowadays, there is still no crystal ball available and mentally speaking it can leave a player in no-man's-land. Waiting for the outcome of a fitness test on a Saturday morning drives me insane. From a very early stage I realised that if I let myself, very deep down, begin to feel that I was unlikely to recover in time, then my body naturally started to shift into a more relaxed mode. In this state, the prospect of taking the field filled me with more fear than excitement. So, what I learned to do was fill myself with an overwhelmingly optimistic attitude, regardless of physical symptoms. It is a great way to live life, but occasionally because of it, I masked my injuries and ended up doing more harm than good to the team and myself.

Blackie: Sir Alex gets it right

'A wisdom earned.' Anon

Sir Alex Ferguson was once asked how many of his players had ever changed from being undisciplined, inconsistent performers to becoming consistently effective with role-model, professional standards. His answer was none. Not one. I think he wasn't far off the mark with his assessment that people don't fundamentally change. We are who we are, and the best predictor of our future performance is our past performance. If you've been a good performer all of your life, then the likelihood is that you'll continue to deliver in the future. But although the key elements that make you tick remain constant, this certainly doesn't mean you can't grow and develop. You'll be aware that you need to constantly adjust and adapt to your ever-changing work environment and you'll do that, because that's what good players, coaches and managers do. It's something that you've obviously done in the past and can use to continue to hone your effectiveness in your chosen field.

The 'everyday me' is the conservative, thoughtful person. It may be a little too reserved, and overly considerate at times but

it is the side of me which tries to absorb all the available information and then do the right thing. And I like that. It also plays
the role of provider for the
other part of myself – the 'game
me'.

The 'game me' is the
instinctive, ultra-competitive
being – the part of myself
which, when fired up, shoots
first and then leaves it to the
'everyday me' to ask the
necessary questions later. It is
more animal than human; in
this state I go by what I sense
and I do what I have to do.

> " *I have come to accept
> that this instinctive side of
> me will step forward when
> the whistle blows; the
> competitive being will emerge
> from the shadows when it
> sees something important
> is at stake* "

I reckon we all have a 'game me' inside of us and in my
experience it is a creative beast. It is capable of showing you things
about yourself that you never knew existed, when deep habits and
subconscious learnings are unlocked by the right attitude and the
urgent push of pressure and need for action. This creative side
tends to surface when there is no time for thought, when there is
a small window, only big enough to allow for a split-second scan,
a quick once-over, before acting. Of course, when in this mode, we
will all make some mistakes and with hindsight we may all wish
we had done things differently. These mistakes though – and boy
have I been through enough to know – are the main influence in
improving the 'game me' in all of us.

Now when I am preparing for a match, I have learned to
surrender more to a belief in my 'game me' and fuel him with
excitement and enthusiasm. I have come to accept that this

instinctive side of me will step forward when the whistle blows; the competitive being will emerge from the shadows when it sees something important is at stake. The nerves I feel before the big event are just signs of my body feeding the 'game me' and vice versa. Nerves are sensations to be welcomed and actually enjoyed because they are the only fuel which can make our best parts that much better. They make us more alert and more aware of the opportunities around us, inspiring us to use and exploit them. The fear that still sometimes creeps in is the 'everyday me' trying to prepare for something in which he will never actually feature.

In everyday mode, when I do try to understand what it's like on the field, or try, like I did that day at the Powergen Cup final, to put myself out there, of course I feel unprepared and incapable. I feel fear and panic kick in. I remember another time sitting among the French supporters along with the rest of the non-playing England squad as we watched the team in Marseille. It was supposed to be a 'friendly' warm-up fixture ahead of both teams' departure for Australia and the 2003 Rugby World Cup. The French team were up to their usual tricks, running wild attacking lines and offloading miracle balls from just about everywhere on the field. The atmosphere was absolutely electric and it got to me – the 'game me' kicked in. I couldn't sit down, I wanted so desperately to be playing. I was in game mode, picturing myself running full steam and launching into a French attacker, completely wiping him out, turning the stadium deathly quiet all of a sudden. My adrenalin pumping around my body, I was a completely different person. I felt like I was going to explode. I remember thinking to myself that if I was in the gym on the bench press at that moment, I could double my personal best. (If I did, then maybe I wouldn't have to keep lying about it!)

Of course the idea of the 'game me' and 'everyday me' modes that I have tried to set out here isn't all that is required for successful sporting performance. What is also needed is a mixture of big picture outlook and small picture focus.

The big picture, the longer-term plan and perhaps the ultimate outcome, is especially important to keep in mind for a decision-maker on the field. It is imperative that you remain composed enough to keep every little event in context. It is crucial that you do not get carried away or over-emotional because it can lead to loss of focus and the danger of deviating too far from the team and the game plan.

I totally agree with the concept that top professionals in sport, operating under intense pressure, need to maintain a 'bodies on fire; heads in fridge' mentality. But I also know that sometimes it really helps if the mind catches alight every now and again. One whole game of rugby is comprised of lots of miniature battles strung together over the eighty or so minutes. Many of these battles are mental, but there are also a great number of them which rely purely upon physicality. This is where the smaller picture comes into play – the short-term, get stuck in and get it done stuff. Pace, collisions, agility, quick skill are all small picture facets involving only the few players around you and what you have inside. It mostly comes down to instinctive reactions and

> **As a number ten I take to the field with the complete version of the game plan tucked away, word for word, in my memory bank, but I know that almost all of it will go straight out of the window as soon as the whistle blows**

going with your gut feeling. We respond to switches in direction, back moves, different alignments, and the decisions of our team-mates. It is all about the little one- or two-metre square box around you, and you simply do the very best you can at that time before the chance has passed you by.

As a spectator or a substitute on the sidelines, the smaller picture is almost impossible to grasp. You have to be in there, experiencing it. Watching the one-on-one match ups, the huge hits, the clever kicks and the incredibly fast individual decision-making from outside the bubble is very unnerving. It makes the game look desperately difficult and complex, as well as lightning fast and bone-crunchingly tough. When you're out there though, these same events are moments you will hardly recall after the game. I've tried to remember when I'm watching a match that I too can cope with all the things I am witnessing on the pitch. The smaller picture is the 'game me's' bread and butter and with him at the helm dictating things, it is all just another day at the office. I try to have as much confidence as I can in him and what he does, for he has never really let me down.

In a similar way the balance is at work before the game too. Being selected to represent your country is a very proud moment and when I have been asked to do so I have wanted to satisfy the expectations of every English person. I don't believe it's healthy to play it all with that mindset however; I do try to accept these feelings and store them as fuel, but my main motivation comes from the smaller picture. I play for my team-mates, the whole squad and for those whom I call family. That has to be it; any more and it becomes too much pressure, too complicated and, as such, a distraction.

As a number ten I take to the field with the complete version of the game plan tucked away, word for word, in my memory bank, but I know that almost all of it will go straight out of the window as soon as the whistle blows. At the front of my mind I keep just a handful of key pointers that will guide my actions and keep me on track when the pressure mounts. There is not enough time while under fire to mull over two sides of A4 crammed full of notes. There is barely enough to conjure up one phrase and play according to it. During a longer break in play I may revisit the plan though, look to see where we stand, what we can do to improve, see what's working and what's not. I might even ask some of the forwards about it.

But then again maybe not . . .

11

Fighting to Recover

<blockquote>
"I was frustrated, becoming more and more irritated each time I was made to look foolish. All I could do was keep trying and then wait for someone to engage me head on. When they did I saw my opportunity to get my own back, to even up the scores"
</blockquote>

It was August 2004. On the field it felt like beginning all over again. With the exception of a few muscles, I was in the best condition of my life, faster, leaner, more eager and definitely fresh! My exceptionally long off-season had afforded me plenty of time to devote to all the aspects of conditioning for rugby, well almost all of them. I needed match practice and lots of it. It's the part that leaves you first and comes back last. Making decisions and executing them precisely under pressure is mostly a 'feel' thing for me, requiring confidence and self-assurance. Self-belief like that can only be fully achieved by putting yourself out there and seeing yourself do it over and over again. If you want to get better, you have to get involved. The 'game me' needs to be fed with evidence. The acquisition of skill comes from the experience of facing real-speed game questions and letting instinct answer for you. You need to play in order to learn and learn in order to play well. Catch 22 – for the first few games at least.

Every move I had made throughout the rehabilitation process following my injury in the Northampton game back in the previous December was reported, intensely scrutinised and pulled apart by the media – real news was obviously slow. I didn't understand it at all. I wish I hadn't even tried to. I should have left it well alone. The more experienced people around me and my closest supporters urged me to take my time, but unfortunately easing into anything has never been one of my strengths. I had done very little else but think of this moment for nine months. I was very aware of the speculative doubts raised over my future. I had spent many hours fine-tuning my new goals, and I was in a rush to start achieving them. I could not afford to start slowly and the newspapers obviously felt the same. I refused to accept that it would take a while to find my form. Basically, in my worldview I had a lot to prove to everyone. Once again I convinced myself that every second counted and they were ticking by fast.

Although I was making too many simple mistakes, and these were lingering long in my mind, on the whole I felt I was beginning to thrive again on the field of play. My arm was back to

> *If you want to get better, you have to get involved*

a healthy enough eighty per cent of its original strength but in certain planes of movement I was still very weak. When I attempted side-on tackles, or when I reached out instinctively to try and grab a shirt and slow an attacker down, my right arm was being batted away easily. There was nothing there, no force, no explosion, no resistance. I'd always hated that feeling of missing tackles and being handed-off, and now I was being made to feel it too often. I detested the 'Oohs' and 'Aahs' from the crowd and the immediate difficulties it caused my team as the opposition flooded through. I had never felt so passive in defence. At times I wanted the ground to swallow me up.

I was frustrated, becoming more and more irritated each time I was made to look foolish. All I could do was keep trying and then wait for someone to engage me head on. When they did I saw my opportunity to get my own back, to even up the scores and to change the game in an instant. I was in a more aggressive mood than I'd ever been, launching my body into every hit, but with little regard to where my head ended up.

Blackie: Stress your own strengths

'Play to your strengths. They are the area of your greatest potential gain.' Marcus Buckingham

Life is all about challenges and opportunities and whichever it is you encounter, you will inevitably experience varying degrees of what is commonly referred to as 'stress'. As more and more of us become 'victims' of the high-pressured and fast-paced life in which we all now exist, we must learn effective methods in which, not only to cope with stress, but also effectively to use this anxiety as a catalyst for exceptional performance. It is an integral part of stretching us to see just how far we can go in any given situation.

But just how can this be achieved? The most effective approach is similar to how we can begin the positive-thinking, energy-creating process. Essentially, I suggest that you practise visualisation techniques. Picture yourself successfully doing whatever it is you've been challenged with, the thing you've been worrying about. See yourself performing well and being rewarded for it. Use this to build your confidence so that you can not only manage those daily difficulties, but actually begin to use them to your advantage.

Does this seem too easy? I'm sure it does, but I really believe that this is how you deal with stress. Don't go and talk about it – you're simply giving undue attention to it by doing that, and what you give attention to is drawn towards you, whether you want it or not. So suddenly you are inviting negative thoughts into your world, and not only that, but you will also waste precious time feeling bad, feeling a failure, or even feeling like a coward. 'I'm too frightened to take this on. It is too much for me. I can't do it.' With thoughts such as those, you stand no chance. But if you recognise that we all experience these feelings and mentally focus your mind on your strengths and visualise doing the thing that is stressing you out, you will propel yourself to the next level.

Once you've accepted that stress will always be a guest at whatever party you throw – you've got to start catering for him. If you do, he'll add to the atmosphere on the night. If you don't, he'll ruin your party. It's your choice.

Opposition elbows, hips and knees – all the pointy bits – were digging straight into the bone of my upper arm. I had a constant dead arm, purple-yellow in colour and tender as hell. What I didn't realise (but was about to find out) was that blood when it resides in one place long enough, can become confused as to what it is supposed to be doing. The blood in my bicep around the humerus began depositing calcium – little fragments of bone – into the muscle, thinking it was repairing a break of some sort. This was causing the pain; sharp pieces of deposited bone were piercing my bicep from the inside every time I took a hit. More bleeding resulted and more trouble.

I met with the physio each morning to try to find a way to pad the area. I needed something which would allow me to play to a full one hundred per cent but which would also stop the bruising and let the arm settle. Nothing seemed to be working. The usual foam padding was not strong enough to block the collisions and more rubberised, heavier stuff was too hard to soak up the contact. I remember in an October training session we used a bit of creativity. I bubble-wrapped my arm. At the first relatively gentle tackle, however, the air-filled cavities had the effect of concentrating the force of the collision, increasing it at least two-fold. The compacted padding then sent the entire energy of the hit directly into the worst-affected part of my muscle. I rate it as being in the top five most painful experiences of my career. I immediately collapsed into a pile, much to the confusion of my team-mates.

With practically a week's full rest under my belt after the gift-

"The skull is a very, very thick thing – especially a forward's skull!"

wrapping experiment went wrong, I felt good enough to give the weekend's match a go. I lasted a solid hour but then the inevitable happened. Hugh Vyvian, the Saracens' number eight and an ex-team-mate of mine, picked the ball up from the base of a solid scrum. Their pack had manufactured enough of a wheel to propel him wide of our open-side flanker and directly at me. All forwards worth their salt like to run at smaller inside backs. Numbers nine, ten and twelve are decision-makers, prime targets. Making them tackle hurts them, keeps them on the floor away from the game and tires them out. Personally I have always rejected the stereotype of smaller fly-halves necessarily being weak defenders. I find it a challenge and have tried to prove my ability by making a stand whenever I have had the chance. I love to attack the tackle with speed and aggression but Vyv knew this and did a great job of getting his own body angle low. My big effort connected with nothing but the top of his skull. The skull is a very, very thick thing – especially a forward's skull!

To be honest, I squealed on impact. There is no other word to describe it. The noise was so high-pitched it would have better suited a dolphin. I felt myself recoil immediately as if I had been electrocuted. The pain was so deep and strong. Inside my top four this time! It made me feel sick. I wanted to lie down and curl up into a little ball until it subsided. I grabbed hold of the back of Hugh's shirt with my left hand and tried to hold him back. It was like trying to stop the family dog from running away on the lead. All I could do was hang on until help arrived and try to avoid any further knocks.

Deep into injury time I did something which I'd never done before. We were on the attack and with the clock already showing the eighty minutes were up, I made a conscious decision to go for the draw. I didn't feel like we had a fabulous platform to launch a last-gasp bid for victory, and with the league's bonus point system in operation I consolidated my options and elected for the drop goal. What did this say about me, my ambitions, my maturity? A story for another day maybe.

The Wednesday of the following week I was sitting with Rob Andrew – our coach and England's greatest kicking specialist. We discussed my decision at the end of the game and I think he agreed with my display of pragmatism. I know in a way he was pleased with the two points we earned from

> *" I felt myself recoil immediately as if I had been electrocuted. The pain was so deep and strong "*

the fixture. Like all of us he would have preferred four but would have been very disappointed with just the one for finishing within seven points. This was now a competition in which a point either way could bring glory, European qualification or relegation.

The bigger topic on the table, though, was my injury. The result had been and gone, the pain in my arm had unfortunately not. I hadn't really trained before the past two games and it was getting worse. Rob brought up the subject of rest and I listened. I wasn't aware that the doctors had suggested a period of at least eight weeks. Two whole months, encompassing the autumn internationals and finishing just short of the Six Nations. He was right though. He spoke common sense, but I had to make the final call. I have always considered a worthy career to be one in which you can strive to get better every day. This included better physical attributes, skills, health, confidence and well-being. Scraping by each week was not what I was about. I was not being true to myself, the team or my performances. If it meant being unavailable for England selection, even though I'd recently been appointed captain, in the name of undergoing a full and proper recovery, then there was no real argument.

'Rest' would turn out to be nine weeks of urine tests, blood tests, scans, injections and a few courses of drugs. It would also mean two months of solid kicking, speed and fitness training; upper-body weights were off the menu. But in my quiet moments, at home or in the gym, I still entertained the bitterness. Clearly, at that stage I hadn't properly learned the lesson that overcoming obstacles can make you stronger and can set you on a new path to success. Perhaps, deep down, the reason I refused to countenance such positive thoughts was that a fair degree of my resentment was directed at myself. My injury, after all, wasn't entirely an unfortunate fluke. My own stubbornness had played a part. Not that I allowed such thoughts any room to surface then. My view was that the world was against me. I'd already served my time, surely? I didn't remember doing anything wrong to anyone. Why was I being punished? I watched and heard stories of the team winning and playing hard together, the stuff I loved, the stuff I was born to do and it just made me feel even more let down.

For all that 'why me?' anger simmering away inside me, perhaps the toughest part about recovering was that despite the severity of my injury, it ultimately remained my own decision not to be playing. I knew that I could barely train and if I did so I would make it worse but it still frustrated the hell out of me to know I alone had made this choice and that I could be out there if I really wanted to be.

After nine weeks the scans showed that the bony deposits had cooled enough and smoothed out in shape to a level which permitted me to return safely to full duty. Rob Andrew, perhaps sensing my impatience, introduced me back into the league campaign relatively slowly. I got on for the second half against Leeds at the end of December and played the full eighty minutes of our next match, against Sale – a game in which I scored an injury-time try. Thank God it was under the posts because we needed the conversion to snatch a 30–29 victory.

So, I had begun my comeback in good shape, especially when it came to running with the ball in hand. I was starting to see all that speed and agility training I had been doing while recovering was bearing fruit in the offloads I was passing beyond the tackle. It had been two months' rehab time well spent. Any opportunity to push decent weights had been ruled out because the activity in the arm would undoubtedly cause too much blood flow and more bony deposits in that area. Instead, I had asked Blackie to help me

> *My view was that the world was against me. I'd already served my time, surely? I didn't remember doing anything wrong to anyone. Why was I being punished?*

focus purely on improving my ability to change direction (by pushing off either or both feet) and accelerate away. I worked hard on this, in conjunction with extending my peripheral vision. I wanted to be able to step and move while the ball was still on its way to me, so I could catch defenders flat-footed.

* * *

Blackie: Rebuild better than before

> 'We have the technology to rebuild this man.'
> *The Six Million Dollar Man*

Depending on its severity, it is certainly possible to emerge from an injury not just rehabilitated, but even stronger and more effective. Of course, a serious injury can cut short, or end, a career. In sport, that is unfortunately the equivalent of an 'industrial hazard' and is obviously devastating for the individual involved. But short of that degree of damage being done, players can ensure, with the right support, that they return to their chosen field of play well rested and suitably trained to become a better player.

Time out due to injury can be reinvested in the player's base conditioning programme (for instance, strength and power) but a sizeable proportion of time should also be spent going over and refining their role within the blueprint for success: how they play their part in driving the performance of the team so that all members can achieve the desired success.

If the injury makes the player more hesitant about physical commitment, in most cases they'll probably lose the very essence of how they play. If players become too concerned with trying to avoid injuries then their commitment will undoubtedly waver and they will begin to leak points, by missing tackles and so forth. The fear of going through what they have been through again becomes too much and unfortunately this can ruin the spark that makes a good player great.

Each time a player returns, they should consolidate, if not build upon, their standing in the game. That's the 'power-of-the-mind' effect. It is imperative that a player's self-esteem doesn't take a battering during the term of injury or in the preparation for a return. Players must stay part of the team. They must feel they are continuing to make a difference. Their presence and their views must still be sought and respected. And as soon as possible, the team ethos of hard graft must be applied. They can't be seen to be having an easy ride – for their sake and for the sake of the other members of the team. Coasting is divisive within any team environment. So, when out of rehab, they should be held accountable during training for their levels of fitness and performance.

We must, however, remember that being ready to play doesn't just mean being physically capable of doing so. The player in question must also be confident enough and in a positive state of mind so that they believe they *can* play well and that they *will* be recognised and rewarded for doing so. They need to have mentally lost the fear of doing too much work in case it sets the recovery back. It is critical that they feel confident in their physical condition so that their mind stays firmly on their game plan rather than on the worries about whether they are truly fit to play or are about to fall victim to another injury.

So, the final part of the rehab process entails making the player feel valued. Ensure that everyone welcomes that individual back into the playing environment with open arms, giving them the support they'll undoubtedly need as they regain their match readiness. There's a physical, psychological and emotional side to treating and recovering from an injury. All must be addressed if we are to give the player the best chance of a successful return.

The next fixture was a European Cup pool match against top French side Perpignan. I love playing in France, especially in the hotter regions in the south. The weather – even in January – is always nice enough to make it a major change from home (which is not necessarily too difficult when you live in Newcastle!). This time was no exception. We were given a 4.15–5.30 p.m. training slot to acclimatise ourselves with the match field and it was T-shirts and shorts all round.

Our thirty-minute team run-through ended up taking forty-five. It was then up to everyone how they used the rest of the allotted hour. I knew thirty minutes was never going to be enough for me so I pulled the ace from my sleeve and enlisted my brother's help. Sparks is a brilliant kicker of the ball – so much so that it often annoys me. He can pretty much land the ball on a handkerchief from seventy metres. When I kick with him I have the security of knowing that, with his accuracy and with only one or two balls to practise with, I will be able to work through a full routine with speed and effectiveness. I ran around furiously trying to get my final place kicks done as the remainder of the light dissolved into darkness and the mood of the groundsmen followed suit. Eventually they kicked us both off the pitch, much to the delight of the rest of the team sitting waiting on the coach. But at least I had got a good, solid look at all the angles albeit I probably ruined Sparks' experience with my inexcusably angry swearing at the light and abusive self-criticisms.

Blackie: He ain't heavy . . .

'A brother shares childhood memories and
grown-up dreams.' Author unknown

I've always maintained that Jonny would reach his best around thirty-two to thirty-three years old and I've seen nothing from him to suggest otherwise. The ongoing work we are doing alongside his brother Sparks will help continue to keep him at the top of his game. That brotherly bond is special and I feel proud to have experienced seeing them both in action through the years. Sparks has given, and continues to give, Jonny unconditional support. This has been extremely beneficial for Jonny, not least because Sparks is a highly skilled and very knowledgeable rugby person. In the world of rugby conditioning, this is significant – Sparks' combination of sport science and real experience of how to play the game is very powerful. In addition, Sparks definitely possesses the X-factor – that innate ability to have people enjoy their work on a daily basis while not compromising the effectiveness of the programme in any fashion. This will serve him, and those under his management, well.

Match day arrives quickly in France and what an experience it is. It never fails to impress me. As a team we arrive one hour thirty minutes before the start time. At this stage the stands are completely empty, not a soul in sight. It is so quiet I can almost relax. Even at the end of the team warm-up ten minutes before the kick-off, the atmosphere still seems subdued, like the match doesn't matter. Then, when you run out to play you are treated to a response from a 12,000-strong capacity crowd, who seem to have appeared from nowhere, ready to party. When their team emerges from the tunnel, the ovation stands everyone's hair on end.

It is a unique feeling inside the away team's changing room before a game in France. It is so tense, so full of energy, so nervy. The guys are always a little quieter for some reason, maybe because they know that, of all the teams in the world, the French sides are the best at scoring from anywhere and in any situation. They are the leaders in creating momentum and their crowds are the leaders in increasing it. The French teams can really turn on the physical too. They play at a pace which burns the back of your throat when you try to keep up, begging for a break in play to catch your breath. The buzz is infectious; it doesn't surprise me that so many English teams manufacture big results over in France because, if you get it right, you can feed from this energy in a very positive way and it can drive every team member to a new level.

On this occasion the big event was not letting anyone down. The action was frenetic. They were flying around the field and we were doing the same just to stop them scoring. The boys had given me four penalty goals to hit but we needed a five-pointer to stay in touch. Fifteen minutes into the second half and I spotted half a mismatch in front of me. I was being defended by a bigger forward. In a small area the mismatch would have been to his advantage, but there was enough room to give me the upper hand.

I tried to take him on the outside. I pushed hard off my right foot then arced and accelerated away. Just as I was beginning to sense daylight between us I felt a wrench on the collar of my shirt. I was pulled down to the ground by a heavy arm with significant weight behind it. The studs of my right boot, however, stayed where they were, lodged in the turf. The ankle or the knee, one of those joints was going to have to give. It turned out to be the latter. I heard a series of grinding noises as the inside of the knee stretched well beyond it's normal range of motion and then finally a nasty, guttural, popping sound.

As I lay on the ground I knew something was wrong but the pain was not horrendous. Had I been lucky and escaped a major blow? With help I rose to my feet and tried a gentle walk. It felt a little unstable but maybe I was imagining it. I tried a slow jog and I felt like Bambi on ice; it seemed like there was nothing binding my upper and lower leg together. The bones felt like they were just balanced on top of one another.

I was about to collapse so I signalled to the physio that my time was up. I knew in my heart of hearts that while I might,

> *I am not too proud to admit that I shed a fair few tears there and then in the dug out. I allowed myself to venture again down the 'why me?' route*

just, be able to jog tentatively around the field for a bit, there was no chance I could sprint. As for kicking, forget it. Could I imagine being smashed low at knee level by a fired-up French forward? I would never get up again! Ever. No decision to make really.

I sat on the sideline with a substitute's jacket draped over my leg which was already caked in ice and raised above my heart to help reduce swelling. I am not too proud to admit that I shed a fair few tears there and then in the dug out. I allowed myself to venture again down the 'why me?' route. A medial ligament tear (anything from four to twelve weeks) or an anterior cruciate ligament tear (a knee reconstruction and anything from six months to over a year) was the likely prognosis. The immediate cause of the injury – a twist and side bend – suggested I should begin preparing for the worst. I needed to know, so much so that I began to panic. The more time I spent on the sidelines watching Perpignan pull away, the more I convinced myself that my comeback season was already over, after only about five or six games. In the changing room after the match, the medics mistook my tears of frustration for those of pain and told Andy Buist – another player who had left the field with a seemingly less painful knee injury – that he should vacate the physio bed so that I could get comfortable.

After the game, at about 10.30 p.m. a kind French doctor opened up a nearby medical scanning facility and had me checked out. The scan showed up a big medial tear, but no anterior cruciate ligament damage, which suggested about two months' more rehab. After the paranoia and worry, this was a blessing. My mood immediately regained its positivity. I could still have plenty of rugby ahead of me that same season, and although the Six Nations was definitely out, the summer's Lions tour might still be on. Amazing what a different perspective can do for you. Speaking of which, Buisty's injury turned out to need a complete knee reconstruction and twelve months to repair itself. 'Don't judge a book by its cover,' seems an appropriate expression. Not exactly my most compassionate moment. Boy, did I feel bad about that one.

12

Grappling with Fitness

> **" *Rugby is not, in my opinion, a game in which you can hold something back for later; not when there is always something more you can be doing to help your team* "**

Up until this point I had never had much of a problem with the lower half of my body. No serious injury, at least, only a few torn ligaments in my ankles. I had, to be honest, taken my knees for granted and wasn't exactly prepared for the impact being rendered immobile was about to have on my life.

I spent the first week of my rehab on crutches feeling pretty useless. By the end of that time I was more than a little bit frustrated. The skin covering the palms of my hands was raw and blistered, and my wrists were constantly aching from the many slips I had had, most of them caused by the shiny floor of my kitchen. When I came off the crutches I fell straight into a monster knee brace. The device was hot, claustrophobic and sweaty but I couldn't complain because the brace was performing an important role.

I had torn the medial ligament on the inside of the right knee. Its normal function is to stabilise the joint and stop the knee from collapsing inwards. The brace was giving my knee much-needed back-up. There is nothing worse when you are suffering from a medial tear than to catch your foot and feel the knee over-bending horribly in the wrong direction. I was flinching awake at night after snagging my toe on the duvet. Being the clumsy fool I often am, I was catching it during the daytime too. Even with the brace I was hobbling around in pain, not able to do much, not able to be myself and becoming moodier and moodier.

I am one of those people who feels I need to be active to be happy. My brother and I grew up playing outdoors, only stopping when the sunlight faded, so it is a deep rooted habit. Saying that though, I also love to sit down and chill out, but only if I feel I have deserved it. I love my big meals and lazy evenings, especially when I'm on holiday, but these will always follow sweat-covered mornings or afternoons spent running until I can hardly breathe, or lifting weights until I can no longer feel my legs and arms. Being injured and able only to do relatively little to earn my rest, I really struggled to relax. I wouldn't allow myself to. Instead I chose to be uptight and, believe me, I sulked a lot!

When I am in my routine of training hard, I eat hard too. I have to stock up on energy and protein to ensure I reap the benefits of my work-outs. When I stop training, it takes a bit of time for this insatiable appetite to die down and align itself with my new lifestyle. There is therefore an interim period when I am doing nothing and still eating everything in sight. I really don't enjoy this time.

I like to try and keep my body in good shape. I think it is hugely important to do so. The body is our vehicle for experiencing life. The better our physical condition the more opportunities we open ourselves up to and I believe the better quality of experience we can have. I want to make the most of this gift of living. I want to see all that there is out there and be able to partake in it all too, if I so desire. To help to do that I reckon I'll need to be around for as long as is humanly possible.

I often forget the importance of the mind's role in this whole process of feeling great. My mind dictates my motivations. Every one of my desired outcomes and goals, big or small, is totally affected by my attitude. I am always jumping into things with both feet, so desperate to keep moving forward that I rarely stop to refuel mentally the way I do physically. I used to get firmly rooted in the habit of thinking that to sit still is to go backwards or be overtaken. I see it differently now. I know if I spend a little more time mentally putting my feet up, escaping from the chatter of constant thoughts and emotions, I can clear the stage for re-energising my drive, spirit and whole body.

I realise that we tire mentally too and when it happens to me the enjoyment drains from whatever it is I am doing. When I manage to find a little quiet and tranquillity inside my head I take the opportunity to feed my mind (like the way I feed my body); to replenish my zest and ambition. The right diet for me is one that alternates positive thought and peaceful quiet. When I think of exciting things in a strong, fulfilling way it really gives me a boost.

> *The body is our vehicle for experiencing life. The better our physical condition the more opportunities we open ourselves up to and I believe the better quality of experience we can have*

It lifts me up and I start to see the world in a better light, one in which nothing is too much, too hard or even a problem. In other words I feel ready to go again.

I try hard not to feed my mind with anger, worries and fears any more, because these are the equivalents of high-fat, processed foods. They are the ready-made, easy options which take away my energy and leave me feeling sick, in a worse place. I look more for a diet of compassion. I try to empathise with other people's points of view and modify my interpretations about world events, or the way things have been going for me. I even give myself a bit of a break once in a while, I tell myself that I'm human and that I'm doing the very best I can. Most of the time though I still tell myself that I can do better and to push for more.

With positive and effective motivation in place, it is astounding what can be achieved both as a team and individually. Situations which may seem impossible, wrong or difficult, can be turned around in an instant if we let them mean the right thing and in turn improve our actions to fit. The way we behave is dominated by our motivations, our motivations are dominated by our thoughts, and our thoughts by our attitudes. If you want to change your life, change your attitude – we can all do that.

When I can't train I feel like I change shape quickly – in a way that I don't like. I put on weight, probably never as much as I think, but I definitely become lethargic and slow. My mental outlook then starts to follow suit. Not surprising really. I believe the way we think inside manifests itself on the outside in the way we look and act. I also feel that it can work the other way too. When I feel good and inspired inside then I will radiate that energy in all that I do. My injuries were causing me to become frustrated physically, internally I became irritable, my thoughts upset and the cycle continued.

I needed to find a way to burn up this unrest. I wanted to get back to being me, working hard and asking searching questions of myself. I wanted that sensation I get when I know I'm pushing the boundaries physically, because internally it helps me to know that I am challenging the limits of how far I believe I can take my game.

I needed some kind of contraption which would help me get my heart rate up high and keep it there. Under normal circumstances I would have hopped on an exercise or spin-

> *I try hard not to feed my mind with anger, worries and fears any more, because these are the equivalents of high-fat, processed foods*

ning bike, maybe a treadmill. All I need is something on which I can move and simultaneously relate those movements to the images that I use of myself playing the game. It is so important to engage and train the mind as well as the body. It also makes it so much more fun. There is, I'm well aware, nothing more demoralising than watching the seconds slowly count down as you pedal away dreaming of where else you would rather be and what you might be missing out on. I know because I have been there and I am never going back. If I am on a rowing machine I can still close my eyes and simulate the changes in effort involved when accelerating or making a break, even taking and handing out big hits.

On a cross trainer it is not difficult to replicate the gut-wrenching pain which goes hand in hand with long periods of defending under pressure, sprinting across the field to make try-saving cover tackles, then having to get up and do it again. The more game-related the training though, the easier it is to put it into practice. This is why I spend lots of time out on the grass, changing my pace, sprinting, falling to the floor and getting back to my feet, jinking from side to side. That's all great in theory and practice when you are fit, but in early 2005 I was far from fit. With my leg out of action, I was going to require more clarity and precision in my mind than before, to make my visualisations work.

Blackie introduced me to an old friend from his gym at home: 'the hand bike'. It looks like a medieval torture device, but what a machine! Simple is often the best and it is impossible to be confused by this one. There is no digital readout, just a knob to turn one way for tougher, the other way for easier. There are two handles for gripping and two arm cranks for pushing – push and pull to make them go round and round. A real upper-body work-out.

When I visualised a big tackle, I turned the resistance up and punched the levers forward while conjuring up the image of me accelerating into the collision with bone-shaking impact. For a break in midfield Blackie would start me on heavy resistance, when I'm stepping, handing off defenders, driving through contact. He then lightened the resistance and let me power away, pumping my arms on the machine and my legs in my mind, as I fly through open field. After half an hour I could no longer tell if I still had any shoulders, and I didn't care. I was dripping with sweat, panting hard and back to feeling great again.

Then there was 'the grappler'. A thick loop of rope strung around two pulleys. You sit in front of it and 'climb' it, with varying levels of difficulty depending on how hard it is to pull the rope down and around the system. I thought it would hurt my hands but it didn't and I used the device to maintain a hard-working pace for as long a time as possible. Like the arm bike, it only took about two minutes before you felt you could bear no more. It is remarkable what the body is capable of when the mind and muscles are working together, because I was still feeling like I couldn't bear it forty minutes later. These machines really kept me going through this tough time and they helped me stay in shape for my return.

Through long training experience I have come to believe that to reap the rewards fully of our efforts we must enjoy what we are doing. Sometimes you may be able to see the big smile on my face. Sometimes this same smile is hidden underneath a grimace. In this case, the enjoyment is in the form of a contentment found in controlled aggression and pure fatigue. I feel awesome when I know I am stepping up to the challenge, attacking the demands and beating the voice in my head which says, 'Please, no more!' I really do love Babe Ruth's expression, 'There is just no beating the guy who never gives up.' I also love it when I become totally wrapped up in what I am doing, living in the moment. And then there is the major sense of achievement after the session, the feeling of tired satisfaction I get when I know I have moved forward and made the best of myself better – for that day at least.

* * *

Blackie: Tailoring for maximum performance

'A personal preparation evolution.' Steve Black

Jonny's training sessions are tailored to his on-field activities and requirements. But the general principles of training (body and mind) to withstand the rigours of whatever it is you do, without depleting your inherent talent, apply across the board, in sport, business and life. For Jonny we split his physical needs (upper body, arm and hand strength, muscle protection, leg power, recovery etc.) into components and train them individually to ensure they are progressing at a game-player optimal rate (that means enough to allow him to play the game at the level that's brought him such acclaim and success but not to interfere with his ability to move naturally and effectively). Ultimately, we need to be sure to develop the whole – so the individual sessions come together into a complete programme that tests all of Jonny's physical abilities. Throughout the entire process, we continually assess the quality of his decision-making – when he's fresh at the start of the session, right through until he's very tired. We look at the decisions he takes and how he goes on to implement them. Exhaustion, stress, distractions, pain even, can all infiltrate the mind and poor decisions or poor execution can easily result. It is possible, through hard graft and continual practice, to train yourself not to make such mistakes, whatever the circumstances.

I'm looking forward to seeing him play this year for club and country. He really is ready to step up to another level. Rob

Andrew and I have talked about the time in some players' careers when they begin to do and see things quicker than most others. They seem to find the space and wherewithal to choose and make good decisions at the right time. Kenny Dalglish talked about it happening to him at around twenty-eight years old. I'm sure it happens to many of the greats at around that age, when players start to peak. Jonny is entering that phase. His achievements so far have been outstanding; this next phase could see his performances become even more insightful, effective and, from his standpoint, more enjoyable.

Blackie has a gift for making something quite painful or distressing seem like a hell of a lot of fun. He also knows how to get the best from a player. His method involves really getting to know the person he is training. He understands what I mean when I say I'm feeling great or feeling tired. He knows my strengths, my weaknesses and what I might, one day, be capable of achieving. He then puts everything in place to help me realise that potential.

That's the great thing about working with him. I tell him what it is I want to accomplish, how I want to feel, how good I want to be, then I hand over my trust to him. I put the future of my career in his hands so that I can concentrate on the here and now, and the things I know how to do. This way I have less to worry about. There are plenty of pressures in this game already without trying to figure out what is best for me in a training environment, a facet of the game in which I am not yet informed enough. Blackie has broad shoulders and enjoys that responsibility.

He knows what he wants to achieve but appreciates that every individual is different and that one morning in every week or two, I may wake up feeling not quite right. These are the moments when injury occurs. I have never experienced any torn muscles or any damage while training with Blackie. All my problems have been a result of collisions on the field or repetitive kicking strains, which are only my fault.

When I'm lifting weights or doing aerobic training, Blackie does not tell me beforehand how many repetitions I will be doing unless a specific type of session requires him to. I think he realises that rugby is a game dominated by players and teams who take their one and only chance. So I get thoroughly warmed up, then I start at a hundred per cent until I am told to stop or until I fall down. It toughens me up mentally. When I don't know how many reps I will lift or shuttles I will run I cannot prepare for them in my head. Rugby is not, in my opinion, a game in which you can hold something back for later; not when there is always something more you can be doing to help your team. Rugby fitness is not about how beautifully you can sprint the hundred metres, nor is it about how long you can trot around for. It is about how hard you can push yourself, and then how quickly you can recover while the game breaks for scrums, lineouts and injuries and get ready to go again.

There have been times when I have dropped dumbbells through sheer exhaustion only to be ordered by the big man, in no uncertain terms, to pick them straight back up and lift. I have collapsed on the training pitch believing that it must be the end, only to find myself collapsing again half an hour later when time is finally called. Blackie has definitely helped me to do things that I never would have thought possible, but he is also just as capable of stopping the session after ten or twenty minutes when I still feel like I have tons in reserve. He finds the right balance in his programmes. He uses up my energy, builds my muscles, then refills the tanks and refreshes my outlook. He leaves me desperate to get out there, itching to perform with all the armour in place to attack any situation I may encounter, the physical training feeding the mental side again.

Blackie: Getting to know you

'Relationships are everything.' Brian Tracy

Coaches need to be with their players individually and collectively; constantly watching, listening, teaching, shepherding and cheerleading. They need to be out on the training field, in the gym, having a coffee, or occasionally socialising outside of work, in order to get to know who the players are, what makes them tick in different environments. This allows the players to get to know the coach as well, which is another vital part of the jigsaw. It is also essential to convey effectively that the coach has the best interests of the players at heart. And this must actually be true. If the message is effectively communicated, with sincerity and genuine affection, then the players will be more likely to accept suggestions and prompting. And the advice the coach will be able to offer will be all the more relevant and effective because the player will have opened up by sharing his views and feelings. Not only that, but the coach may also see talents the player did not even realise existed. In that way coaches can be the catalyst that allows players to fulfil their potential.

It is a funny old thing, but players almost always absorb more from people they like and respect. Good advice can come from an unwelcome source but more often than not, it will fall on stony ground. The same advice can be re-conveyed some time later by a welcome source and be regarded as life-changing and groundbreaking, despite it being the exact same message they have, at an earlier time, rejected.

One of Blackie's trademark special moves is the 'character test'. He likes to get an idea of how hard players intend to push themselves, how able they are to operate outside of their comfort zone. Many a time I have been peddling hard, lined up beside some newer players, all on our exercise bikes. As usual, Blackie would be telling us when to change difficulty level, when to sprint, when to relax, what rpm to maintain, and when to stop. His ploy is then to ask us to sprint for a period of time on the toughest level, as fast as we can. But, when it starts to get painful, Blackie will turn his back on us and begin talking to someone else in the gym. With no further orders, and the lactate building up in the legs, the new boys start looking at each other, wondering what to do. They've heard of Blackie's reputation so they don't want to upset him, but you can see it in their expression; they're thinking, 'He's forgotten about us.' He always reappears just as the unfortunate one or two decide to take the session into their own hands. Their next fifteen minutes are never pretty to watch!

His other strength is his creative side. The best thing about having Blackie as a coach is that day to day I never know what I will be asked to do. It keeps things fresh, exciting and fun. I have found myself playing tennis against the stadium wall, running up the steps on Tynemouth beach and even boxing in the ring against former cruiserweight champion, Glen McCrory. Not long ago I was on a trampette sprint training in front of my Nintendo Wii.

Whenever we can we keep a ball in play somehow. Practising any skills is hugely beneficial but not as effective as practising them when you are physically exhausted, when your heart is pumping and your mind racing. For this is when it matters most on the field of play, under pressure and under all kinds of stress. At intervals during the most demanding sessions Blackie will set up technical drills requiring enormous precision. The question that's being asked of me is – can I stay focused, keep my mind on track when my body is crying out for attention? These challenges involve passing balls here, there and everywhere, or volleying a football against the wall without letting it drop in between.

> **" Practising any skills is hugely beneficial but not as effective as practising them when you are physically exhausted, when your heart is pumping and your mind racing "**

After about nine weeks' solid training and rigorous physio treatment I was back in my boots feeling fabulous, fresh and fully fit. This time Rob Andrew, with my input, decided that there was no need for a slow introduction back into the league. I was selected to start my first game back against Harlequins, on 13 March 2005, down at the Stoop, their home ground in Twickenham.

I was super excited, and I couldn't have been less concerned about my knee. We had actually played it safe and held back a week longer than I perhaps needed to – just to make sure.

Harlequins must have spotted a weakness in our short-side defence at more or less exactly the same time I did because when they broke through I was covering across, out of sight again. I was lurking in my favourite position, waiting to knock someone clean off their feet.

One of their forwards was supporting on the inside of the ball carrier, crying out for it. In front of him was nothing but clear field and the try line. I was over to his right. When he received the pass into his stomach I was right under his nose. It is a lovely feeling when you time a tackle sweetly, when an opponent bounces away from your shoulder and on to the floor before you can even lay a hand on them. This tackle was not far from one of those moments. I

> " *In the space of about ten seconds I had gone from being in my element, engrossed in the game I love, to being sat on the sideline deeply believing that I could be finished. Forever* "

know that because I barely felt it, even though he was a lot bigger than me. It also meant I was able to get back to my feet immediately and legally challenge for the ball on the floor before their nearest player arrived to clear me away.

When he did turn up a split second later I was crouched low and pulling on the ball. He did his job well. He dipped nice and low and drove up through my body under my head and arms. Unfortunately my knee was at an awkward angle. The popping sound was one I remembered from before, except this time it was louder. I lay helplessly at the bottom of the ruck as more players piled on top, trying not to panic. I was actually close enough to the touchline and our substitutes' bench to call out to our physio over the noise. I didn't want to be out there any more.

'Marty, my knee's gone again. Get me off!'

Whatever you think your reaction is going to be in these times, you still can never really know. Instead of the predictable tears and frustration, there was simply emptiness. I was in a daze, without even the inclination to explain the injury to the medics. All my energy had been drained from me the moment I heard that horrible sound. In the space of about ten seconds I had gone from being in my element, engrossed in the game I love, to being sat on the sideline deeply believing that I could be finished. Forever.

That was a dark, dark moment in my life, but, thankfully the damage wasn't as severe as I feared and I was back playing in just five weeks. And the circumstances of that next comeback match put things in perspective for me. Although I had been doing my damnedest to prove my fitness to Clive Woodward and the rest of the rugby world in advance of the Lions tour, I was only on the pitch because one of my team-mates was being rushed to hospital.

13

The Main Attraction

"When each member is ready to stand up for what the team embodies on and off the field, then the pressure of tight situations can be the catalyst for extraordinary things. It almost gives the team the feeling of having an additional player or two out there with them"

My comeback after the injury suffered at Quins came on 15 April 2005 against Northampton. And I was off the bench and on the pitch a lot earlier than expected because our winger, Michael Stephenson, broke his leg in an unfortunate incident just short of the try line.

It is never nice to see at first-hand the pain and suffering of a fellow player on the field. You feel totally useless to help. I have seen plenty of situations like this during games. I remember when Neil Back had his head split in one of our autumn internationals against South Africa. The cut was above his right eye and the flap of skin which was hanging from his face was so large and grotesque that it folded easily back on itself and completely covered his eye. It looked like a huge fleshy pink monocle, and he reminded me of a B-grade zombie from a low-budget horror movie. I managed to hold (one) eye contact with him just long enough to mention that perhaps he ought to consider getting it seen to, then I went down on my haunches and dry retched, very nearly losing my pre-game feed.

Quite recently I watched, from very close up, Mathew Tait take a shoulder to the jaw when running at full tilt. Involuntarily he performed a classic three hundred and sixty degree spin and half twist in mid-air, while remaining completely unconscious. Due to the fact that he didn't know where, or for that matter who, he was, he was unable to use his arms or legs to break the fall. He bore the brunt of the landing on his face. After reviewing it in slow motion a few times – yes, guys do like to watch such things, even Taity – we reckoned he had been lucky. Had he not been so spaced out he may not have survived at all!

Watching Michael being carried away on a stretcher, his lower leg clearly in more pieces than it should have been, was awful. Shocking, in fact. It was all too evident that this was serious. You feel deep down for your team-mate but you have to play on. It's a challenge just finding a way to do that, unaffected. How can you mentally block out the obvious possibility (Russian roulette springs to mind) of something similar or worse happening to you? The answer is I really don't know. I don't think anyone can. I understand it may happen to me and on a number of occasions it could have been my turn. The training we undergo, the technical practice and awareness, the adrenalin and the on-field application of all these are, I guess, preventative measures. Maybe this is why I don't see the odds of it happening getting any worse, even though guys are getting bigger, stronger, fitter and more powerful. That is true, but our training and education are keeping pace. Physios are raising the bar in pre/during/post-game care too. It is all staying in proportion – just. What I do know is that if something as serious as that did happen to me, I would try to deal with it and, after treatment, intervention and rehabilitation, hope to come back stronger.

By observing and experiencing injuries I have become aware of how much damage can be inflicted by malice, lazy or poor technique and illegal methods or acts.

When I tackle a player hard, I want to cause an impact, that is true. I aim to make a dent in the opposing team's spirit while boosting our own. If I can force opposition players to feel like

> **" Training every day – especially kicking – had unfortunately become less of a personal choice and more like an addiction. In fact it was exactly like a drug "**

they need to be aware of my whereabouts on the field and distract their attention or game focus slightly, then that is a bonus and all part of sportsmanship. What I never want to do is inflict harm or injury. There are few worse feelings than when I have (always unintentionally) hurt another player. Finishing a game with a feeling of having been knocked about, with plenty of bumps, scrapes and bruises to show for it, is extremely satisfying. It signals that I've truly earned my crust, gotten stuck in and given a great deal to the cause. But if I am sitting in the medical room nursing a concussion, a split face, broken ribs or the like from cheap punches and knee drops, it is a different story altogether. The overriding feeling is one more akin to anger, bitterness and pure disappointment.

Not all injuries, of course, are inflicted by match-day collisions or incidents. Some are self-inflicted. I can vouch for that. Or more accurately, my obsessive kicking can.

I have found strength in good solid training routines and the results have reinforced my desire to lock on to these very habits which have empowered me. The sessions have become rather like daily rituals. The only point at which I've ever really felt like I was losing everything was when I got caught holding on too tight to the rigid repetition of the routines, the 'must-do' element that in my world was necessary to protect me from failure.

Training every day – especially kicking – had unfortunately become less of a personal choice and more like an addiction. In fact it was exactly like a drug. Its effect was to appease my fears and to create a widespread sense of inner strength, confidence and calm, allowing me at night to switch my brain off and the TV on – providing it went well of course. Without my daily fix there would be huge conflict in my mind between my desire to let go and a voice which told me I wasn't ready yet or that I should be doing more. When circumstances or other commitments dictated that there was not enough time, or maybe not even the facilities in which to practise, then I made up my own rules and my innovative side came out.

When I was very much younger, I used to kick cardboard toilet rolls over a set of paper posts in our living room at home. When I was older, and please understand unfortunately a lot older (playing professionally for Newcastle) I put my mattress up against the bedroom wall and smashed balls into it. Anything to get my daily portion of preparation.

I have been kicked off tennis courts on holiday for punting balls over the net, and put in detention a few times at school for kicking when I should have been learning. I have stood shivering in swimming pools with my eyes closed for hours, visualising imaginary sessions, I have broken football goals and I have destroyed the hedges at the bottom of my garden with kicking balls about.

The most challenging sessions have taken place on the mornings before matches. I love these because of the brief feeling I get from real contact with the ball. The problem is, however, when we play away from home, we never quite know where we will be staying the night before. I have always managed to find some way and some where to fit in a crucial forty-five minutes. Usually I will kick on some grass in the hotel grounds or I can often be seen in the car park, normally fishing a ball or two out of the bushes or from under a car. I have kicked in farmers' fields surrounded by cow pats and dog mess, on golf fairways too, but my favourite session may have been spent with Dave Alred before the 2001 Six Nations game against Wales in Cardiff. We spent twenty minutes trying to climb up to a nursery school playground and another half an hour kicking balls over the swings. My worst idea was kicking balls over the top of a hotel in North London. Needless to say that was a short session.

These moments have been great, and I keep in mind that, without a doubt, many of them will have contributed hugely in determining a good performance later that day. I continue to kick all the time, especially on Saturday mornings, because I enjoy doing it and I know it helps. But whereas, in the past, I have often wondered what on earth I was doing in my car on the motorway heading for the club at 7.00 a.m., with balls on the back seat and boots on the passenger side, now I try to be a little more flexible.

The issue with me was that I was always reluctant to give in, even when it was blatantly obvious I should. In my mind there was some logic in all that obsessive practice – after all why break a habit that seemed to work? 'If it ain't broken . . . ' You get the picture. Even today, the success that has come my way has made me very protective of this habit. It is going against my nature to let what has become an old friend – who has seen me through thick and thin – go. The problem was, I never questioned whether my so-called friend was actually the cause of this thick and thin.

My body is talking to me all the time. It offers me some great advice through aches and pains, gut instincts and feelings. I have, however, never been that good at listening to what it has to say. I become especially selective in my hearing when I am told to back off from training and call it quits for a day.

These signals are not just random thoughts, they really mean something – I know that now. They are not always right but they are there for good reason. I have really only fairly recently begun to take heed of these warnings and foresights and it is really helping me to enjoy my life. I am also finding that listening has made it possible to avoid more stumbling blocks along the way. I passionately believe that our experiences are our gifts and if we don't learn from them first time around then they will continue to appear in our lives until we get the message we are meant to receive. As Pat Lam, the ex-All Black, Samoan and Newcastle Falcons captain, used to say, 'It isn't a mistake until you do it twice!' I learned that one the hard way, about a dozen times.

* * *

So, unlike poor Michael Stephenson, I made it through the game against Northampton, running hard and kicking three penalties and a conversion (we lost by a point but I'll skate over that), and went on a couple of weeks later to play a full match against London Irish. With every passing minute my confidence, my concentration and my belief grew. But I couldn't tell whether it would be enough to book me a place on the Lions trip to New Zealand in the summer. And I wanted to be on that plane very much.

My chief worry regarding the forthcoming Lions tour was whether I'd run out of time to prove my match fitness, so when I saw Clive Woodward's number flashing up on my mobile phone I felt a shiver down my spine. I knew what I hoped he was going to say, but in reality I figured he was after an opinion on some other players I'd either played with or against. It turned out the hopeful butterflies in my stomach were well placed as he told me he wanted me on the trip. With only what turned out to be the final game of our season, against Gloucester, still to come, I had only played two full eighty-minute matches since damaging my knee on 8 January. But it appeared that Clive had his vision and I had done enough to be part of it. Suddenly, after what at times had been a hard four months, things were starting to look brighter.

Lions tours are wonderful experiences. For me they thrive on the unpredictable parts of life and the most positive parts of everyone's ambition – the bits that you can't put your finger on. With a team and squad concocted from four different nations, managed and coached by a mixture of the same groups, there is not really time for extensive preparation or for generating huge momentum. It is a case of building chemistry, finding the X-factors and the catalysts that will link everyone together and unlock the super talents of the best of Britain and Ireland. When you get it right the effect is mesmeric. When you miss the mark the team starts to look, and play, like four separate ones.

Blackie: The building blocks of success

'What really matters is how well they play together.'
Red Holzman

For as long as I can remember, there has been a fierce debate over what it is that makes a good team. I believe that it is the collective unity of effective managers, coaches, back-room staff and players gelling together in their quest to achieve a shared, common goal. You may think this is common sense and that surely, everyone must know this already. But my sporting life suggests otherwise.

Everybody is different and for the team to work to its full capabilities, this should be recognised. We are all motivated by different things which is as it should be. Sometimes we possess completely different skills which complement each other beautifully. But there has to be, without question, one major common factor and that is that we should all want to win, regularly. I think we probably don't take that point quite seriously enough.

The team itself should have an unquenchable passion and thirst for success. There is no use in building a team full of great talent but with different objectives, as the constant battle and conflicts between the individuals over the final destination will diminish the gains to be had. I'd even go so far as to suggest that a united vision is the most important factor in any team's success. Without it, the team will simply not be able to perform to its true potential.

The winning team performance-mix is made up of so many variables. Some of these I have touched on previously but they are so important, I think they are worth setting out again here. You need a head coach or manager who is ambitious, competent and has unquestionable integrity. They should consistently do what they resolve to do. They must be seen to be masters in their chosen field, displaying an overt passion for success while genuinely caring for the team that is going to deliver their vision. Alongside their professional appreciation of the game, these masters should have good management and people skills to positively influence and mould the individual relationships between the members of their team.

A lot of emphasis must be placed here on recruitment. The leader must ensure that they unite a group of people with complementary skill-sets to guarantee the success that the team craves. Each member of the team should want to be in the team. Sounds obvious, but it isn't always so. And if it isn't, then you will have a problem. They should have the drive and enthusiasm to get whatever the job is done, and they should be able to pull others along with them. Each member must have the requisite skill-sets to perform whatever their function is in the team – but there also has to be room for flexibility and growth.

Crucially, the team members must be chosen for who they are now – not for what you might hope they will become. And by that, I don't mean that people can't learn and get better at what they do, can't improve. Of course they can. They have to, in order to grow and add increasing value to the team. I am talking about their core values; whether they are an enthusiast, or a moaner, a schemer, a prima donna or a winner who wants to win with the team. Those aspects of a person don't change. And if you hope they will; if someone you know to be a 'trouble-maker' in terms of team moral and effectiveness has been recruited because you hope that they will change, then you are in trouble. So it is essential that each member should play to their strengths and should want and allow others to do the same. The manager's duty is to create an environment in which all individuals can flourish to their potential.

If the right person has been recruited to manage the team, then they should be left alone to do the job. If they don't succeed with the players they have available then they have to be moved on. Generally the directors who recruit senior coaches and managers have built their expertise in vastly different areas from professional sport. Because someone has the power of position, or money (or both!) doesn't automatically make them an expert in every aspect of strategy, tactics and coaching concerning the game in question. I'm sure that in the cool light of day they would realise this, but when passion mixes with monetary investment then, in many cases, a potently distasteful cocktail emerges.

It is a fact that some people are better team players than others. They naturally care and support those around them and understand that for the team to perform well, and maybe for them to get the kudos associated with success, their team-mates will have to excel. They know this and behave accordingly.

Wow! What a great description of the ultimate team person, supporting all of his or her team-mates to achieve their highest standards. The great thing about helping others to the top of the mountain is that more often than not you end up there too. Sometimes this course of action is your best chance of fulfilling *your* potential.

There are players who make a significant contribution to the team's performance all the time, but actually are not very good team people. They are selfish, living and performing for their own personal gain without giving so much as a damn whether the team, or the other players, do well or not. They want to be recognised for playing well and rewarded accordingly. The sad fact of the matter is that the management of a team and the fellow players sometimes decide to keep this poor team-man on for the individual playing contribution he or she makes. They are prepared to accept the negative idiosyncrasies for the haul of points, tries or goals that that player provides with the view that in turn, the entire team will benefit from that individual glory.

I don't buy it. I honestly believe that you can only truly thrive in today's society if your interpersonal skills allow you to release your own and other people's talents in order to achieve an accepted common goal. You can't do it on your own, no matter how talented you think you are. Everyone needs others. They depend on you, you depend on them. The team that's the most together, the most in tune with each other will win, all things being equal . . . or almost equal!

It is the role of the team leader, in sporting terms that of the coach, to open up the team's eyes to the possibility of achievement and to induce a mindset which uses the probability of success as the underlying factor behind a relentless drive for victory. This sounds manic and given the wrong mix of people, it undoubtedly is. In my experience, it's very rare that you find the right mix. I'm not being pessimistic; I'm simply stating the facts. The group of people with the greatest experiences, holding the genuine belief that they can and will achieve, will be the most successful.

Ideally there would be a forum, or better again, it would be part of the team culture, to share ideas and information from which everyone can benefit. I believe at the senior professional clubs there should be a new position created for a knowledge/ ideas coach; someone who accesses information and inspirational stories from a wide variety of outlets – other clubs, in other countries, other sports, business, academia, conferences etc. The list of sources is endless. And each seed gathered has the potential to add something new and exciting to the team. The better the knowledge of the team then the better the foundations on which the team can achieve great success.

Managers, coaches and players must take full responsibility for their own actions at the very least. But to be effective, they should also, as a member of the team, accept mutual accountability for the team's results. In reality, that can be more difficult to buy into when the input from so many people determines that result – but if the right people have been brought together, then the potential is there for that one hundred per cent mutual accountability.

When you're playing a South African, Australian or New Zealand national team often at the peak of their form, riding on the crest of an energy wave created by playing together consistently as a squad, then

" Suddenly, after what at times had been a hard four months, things were starting to look brighter "

you'd better start big and get moving fast. There is no such thing as an easy rugby game in the Southern Hemisphere. I get the distinct impression that everyone is pretty keen to put one over on us too.

What we encountered in New Zealand in that summer of 2005 was something extraordinary. Over there the public, the fans and the players (of all levels) live and breathe rugby. They know the game inside out. The media also are always totally supportive and positively encourage their national team. It has a devastatingly powerful effect. Add to that heady mix a team full of superstars and you start to get the picture of what we were facing on our six-and-a-half-week trip.

In the early games we were forced to fight tooth and nail for scraps of victory and for a while we struggled for fluency in our play. But by the time the Test series began to take centre stage, we had developed a strong belief and confidence ... even if it did feel like we were taking on a lot more than just fifteen players.

* * *

Blackie: Wooden principles

'Probably the best coach in competitive sports history.'
Bill Russell

It is an absolute myth that the best team have all the best athletes and all the most skilled players. One of the reason teams become successful, above almost all others, is that they are mentally more focused and intrinsically they enjoy the preparation process that allows victory.

For those who don't know the legend of the man, John Wooden is perhaps the greatest sporting coach of all time. He coached basketball at UCLA in the US in the 1950s, 1960s and 1970s. Over an incredibly successful twelve years they won ten championships, including nine in a row, and amassed an astounding eighty-eight wins out of ninety-two in that period. What makes the man even more special is that each year with a university side, you lose the vast majority of your team as they graduate. Imagine how difficult it would be to win the Premiership nine years in a row with a largely new team each year! How did he do it? The foundations set by Wooden in terms of how everybody within the team and within the team's environment behaved towards each other were rock solid. He promoted the idea that there are few things more important to teamwork than consideration of others. So at its heart, managing team chemistry is all about engendering consideration of others into each team member. This is rooted in serving the team in two main ways.

First, the team's cause will ultimately be best served by

each individual solely concentrating on being the best performer he or she can be. This excludes the 'competition' from team-mates for positions within the team; namely the timeless team spirit 'cancer' that grows from people being after other people's jobs. It is an integral principle; don't have any self-interest in other team members performing badly to make you look good, simply be the best *you* can be.

Secondly, being the best you can be is not something that relies on a huge ego. Don't be concerned about other great performers out-performing you – especially if they're on your team! Doing your best has never been mutually exclusive to helping other team members as much as you can, and celebrating their successes rather than envying them. Great teams adhere to both of these Wooden-inspired principles.

Successful teams, which foster this selflessness and great chemistry proposed by John Wooden, don't win regularly over a period of time by believing they are not capable of it, feeling that they can't, or by thinking that they aren't worthy recipients of ongoing success. In other words, no one attracts victory into their lives if they are consumed with a pessimistic, negative mindset.

New Zealand were a fabulous example of a great team and a perfect illustration of what happens when you get it right. There is an invincibility about a team firmly tuned into the same wavelength because the effect of the individual contributions is multiplied by exceptional team play and vice versa. Their team sheet read like a who's who of world rugby: key talismans and leaders, game breakers and then youngsters coming through with awesome reputations and almost mythical stories preceding them.

They were surrounded with an aura of brilliance and were a team you would never write off. Their ability and professionalism was a direct reflection of the ambition, integrity and selfless honesty of each individual. There was no weak link in the circuit, the power generated by each member of the group could not leak away any-where. It was all kept within the team, and used in cleverly con-structed game plans ready to be unleashed on the opposition – us.

It wasn't wild, untamed energy either. Precision underpinned the whole team ethos, which meant they were controlled and able to launch any number of threats from the awesome armoury of players they could field. They were truly a formidable unit. And what made it worse was that they were all nice guys when you met them afterwards, not a sign of arrogance, instead just a commitment to the values of the rugby way of life. Fight hard on the pitch, friends off of it, underpinned by respect.

> **Their ability and pro-fessionalism was a direct reflection of the ambition, integrity and selfless honesty of each individual**

When each member is ready to stand up for what the team embodies on and off the field, then the pressure of tight situations can be the catalyst for extraordinary things. It almost gives the team the feeling of having an additional player or two out there with them. Pressure, as I see it, looks for fault lines in understanding. It searches for weakness in preparation, hiding under the stones we don't turn over. It preys on papered-over cracks in the mind's conviction, because in these it can unleash its potentially negative and debilitating effects.

For me, it felt like the speed and accuracy of the All Black play pressured us into making decisions as individuals, not as a team. Without a history of togetherness, we were forced into uncharacteristic errors and at times we fell apart.

The best way I have found to deal with pressure – How many will be watching? What do people expect from me? What if it all comes down to me? – is to turn it around and make it a friendly influence. This is where it becomes the extra team-mate. I see pressure as one huge opportunity, offering a unique and majestic stage on which to perform, enjoy and embrace. Situations of high pressure have undoubtedly been the most exciting experiences of my life. If I can get it right I know I can use the extra energy it provides to drive even greater enthusiasm and performance. As for the negative interpretations that pressure invokes, I suggest you don't give these an inch of daylight. Try to starve them. If you invite these sorts of considerations in through your front door then believe me they'll soon be taking over the whole house. I fill my mind with evidence I need to support my convictions and thus give me the strength to fight back against the darker side of pressure. I know I have prepared thoroughly enough two or three times over to feel secure that I have a pretty fair shot at succeeding with any goal kick and any piece of skill the game throws at me. It doesn't mean it will always go right but I have been through too many matches on the field and in my head to be frightened by any situations when I am out there on a Saturday afternoon.

Boy do I get nervous though. My match shirts (even the really heavy ones of ten years ago) have always shaken with the accelerated beat of my heart when I am preparing for a shot at the posts. The pressure has the power to propel me, destroy me or drive me crazy. What determines which of these paths I take is the strength of my mind, the belief, the preparation and most importantly the quality of the thoughts I allow to run through it. If you plant seeds of doubt then very quickly you will have negativity sprouting up all over place. Practising breathing, relaxation and concentration techniques has helped me maintain my focus, vision and self-confidence. My desire to succeed and take on the challenge has helped bring results.

When I lose my place in the present moment, I am dragged from 'the zone'. And that's where I need to be if I am to analyse and plan while still performing. I've got to be able to take in all that has just happened, assess what it means in terms of the immediate play in front of me (Is someone out of position because they had to make a covering tackle? Is someone now too fired up or too tired to make and execute good decisions?), project into the future by a minute or so to visualise what the knock-out blow might be, work out when exactly to deliver it, and all at the same time making sure I don't drop the ball or forget to carry out my role in the play.

> " *If you are going to worry, don't do it. If you do it, don't worry* "
>
> Anon

This sort of thing happens constantly throughout the game, and has to if you are to beat the best teams. But undertaking that same process negatively is like pressing the self-destruct button. Living in the past – delving into the mistakes you've made, what they might have cost the team and ruminating over the 'what ifs' of a crucial goal, kick or pass, before you've even attempted it – is totally limiting. It wastes vital energy and creates extra stress and negativity which only hurts you and your team.

Instead I ask myself, 'Did worrying about anything beforehand ever help me succeed?' This approach helped me put a tough one through the posts after the end-of-match buzzer against Argentina, to earn a draw in the pre-tour warm-match, but trying to keep everything simple just got confusing from then on.

I wasn't used to the sensation I was experiencing. I felt helpless. All efforts seemed futile in nature. We had just lost the first Test to New Zealand in the blitzing rain by a convincing twenty-one points to three. It should have been more – a lot more. We couldn't find the flow or cohesion we needed. The harder we tried, the more disjointed we became. After the game in the dressing room, soaked to the bone, it felt like everyone was wondering what else they could possibly do to help our situation. That's where I got confused – I didn't like the fact that I was feeling it too. And didn't have any answers.

> " *I did manage to break the game up, but only for the two minutes that the physio dealt with my on-field concussion and painful neck injury* "

Sunnier, friendlier climates awaited the final two Tests. They would be ideal for speeding up the game and keeping the ball in hand; ideal for a team on top form; ideal for a team playing with momentum after securing a big win under their belts. You might see where I'm going with this. It wasn't ideal for us. But to be honest, it wasn't something that bothered us. Sitting in the dressing room after the first Test we might not have had the answer to how we could challenge the All

Blacks, but the reason for that wasn't because we were the clear underdogs. I've never minded being in that position. And we didn't let it affect us at all. We knew all we could do was prepare well and build up confidence and a head of steam, ready to throw everything into causing a shock defeat.

Unfortunately, it never materialised, not in either of the two Tests. We'd already lost our inspirational captain, Brian O'Driscoll, in the first minute of the first Test. He was replaced by Gareth 'Alfie' Thomas who led brilliantly. Alfie is a great character and got us off to a brilliant start in the second Test with a great try. It was all too much to ask of us though. Later in that game my frustration got the better of me. I went searching to break open the game and, seeing as we were defending all the time anyway, I thought a big tackle might just do it. I flew into collision areas which demanded more of a controlled and precise approach. I did manage to break the game up, but only for the two minutes that the physio dealt with my on-field concussion and painful neck injury. That event put pay to any further involvement of mine on the tour.

The Lions tour capped off a tough season and the All Black's performances gave me some new food for thought as I recovered from this latest set-back. I'd read somewhere that the subconscious mind is one million times more powerful than the conscious mind. The subconscious mind is where we store everything – perceptions, habits, experiences. It forms, in my eyes, a lot of who we are and our gut feelings and intuition. Compared to our louder and more recognisable conscious mind, which seems to deal with the surface matters of organising day-to-day life, the subconscious is largely silent. But it is very, very important.

I decided then that I wanted to make good use of that

subconscious mind. I want to fill it with pure positivity and inspiration. I want to store in it excellent skills on which I can rely. The way I try to do that today is by living the habit I want to create, whenever I possibly can, to 'be the change I want to see in the world', as Gandhi said. I try to entertain only the most positive thoughts, refraining from the temptation to whinge and moan or cower in the corner. I try not to judge others but actually to encourage instead. After enough time training these behaviours, the subconscious can look after the rest.

Just thinking and imagining is not enough. You have to practise what you think in order to form solid, effective intuitive responses. I need to see it in action. Supporting evidence, if you like. To prove to myself it is not just a flight of fancy. I need to experience the deliberate contact of the ball on my foot and see it travelling through the middle of the posts many times a week to nail down the belief that I am a good kicker. I need to see the boys doing superb things and improving on the field daily to really add weight to the conviction that we are a great team capable of winning things. This means driving your own and everyone else's standards each and every time you cross the white line, giving the brain the proof it needs to turn hopes and dreams into being second-nature. Inspired, ambitious thought and precise action combined gets the job done.

There's no cheat's way out of this. Telling yourself that you're going to do well when there's nothing to back it up is, to me, fairly futile. It is a chancer's choice. If you need to do that then there's something wrong already. The best teams and most consistent individuals – because of the work they've done and the way they spend their time, the people they spend it with, and the powerful messages that run through their minds – *know* they are going to be great and they expect to win. If those sentiments are being churned out one million times more by the silent over the conscious mind, it's no wonder great teams seem invincible. They exhibit intrinsic brilliance which translates to seemingly effortless displays of greatness on the pitch.

As a rugby player I had been in the relative wilderness for a long, long time. Whereas once I had managed six straight seasons full of evidence to support my aspirations, now it was a different situation altogether. I had to get back into the mix again. I needed to start living the change I wanted to see in my career, every day and every weekend. I needed to string together some serious performances on the field to match my beliefs, if they were ever to be given the chance to flourish as I hoped.

But before any of that could happen, there was still plenty I needed to take on board.

14

Ringing Changes

“ *I had done too much kicking. I didn't have the right balance in my life or my training or my understanding. And so I had finally learned my lesson, just about* ”

I was kicking on the main field at the club one afternoon in November 2005. It was business as usual. An empty stadium, myself and a bag of rugby balls. In my mind I was probably replaying a few fresh, raw, missed opportunities or imagining what challenges lay in store the next weekend. I remember I had been struggling with a stiff and sore groin for about two weeks but it seemed to ease once I got warmed up and stuck into my session. So I took the easy option and chose to ignore it.

This particular day, after a good few laps of the field, I took the first ball out of the bag and thumped a right foot punt down the touchline. When my foot made contact with the ball a shock of pain ran through my groin and up all around my hip. I crouched down on to one knee, and rode out the unpleasant sensation until it faded to an ache. Then I did exactly what any serious professional sportsman should never do. I stood up, waved away the agony and immediately hit another ball. After five exact recurrences of the same pain, it then started to ease off and I completed the session about one hour forty-five minutes later. I did at least have the common sense to pop in to the physio afterwards. I told him that I might come in and see him after the following game. I gave him a cheap reason, something like, 'I might have been a little bit tight.' It must have been a Thursday because I didn't want to explain the details to him just in case he pulled me out of the team for the weekend or, worse still, out of tomorrow's kicking session.

When the game had finished I knocked on the physio room door and poked my head round. I was in my suit already – trying to indicate that it wasn't all that important and that I didn't intend to hang around long. Which I didn't. But I wish I had.

The next morning I could barely get out of bed and I was struggling to walk. I managed to make it to the local hospital to meet the doctors in charge of the MRI scanner, with whom I am on first and middle name terms now.

It turned out I was off for a second operation in my right groin. This time there was more damage elsewhere to attend to. My adductor muscle was ruptured. It was decided that a 'tenotomy' was the best bet for a fuller recovery. This involved severing the muscle completely as it helps it heal quicker and more effectively. It was the most painful hospital visit I have had to date, but it was a success. Time once again to dust off the arm bike and start trying to get back on the field.

The following ten weeks went by slower than a lot of other periods in my life but I got through them with Blackie's ingenuity and innovation and a great deal of physio. Eventually I was back into full team training. I had already run all my movement patterns; swerving, sidestepping, bounding and spinning. At most, I had a week to go before my return. In a competitive game in training I took a short pass through a gap. The full-back stepped in towards me and instinctively I shuffled to the right to lead him away and tried to bounce back left. As I made the explosive part of the manoeuvre I felt like I had been shot in the crutch. I put the ball on the floor and hobbled straight from the pitch to the ice box. I packed a bag full and strapped it to my body. It was a very uncomfortable twenty minutes that followed but the ice did help reduce the swelling.

> **I was doing more or less the same thing each time and I was getting more or less the same results. I had to find out what I needed to change**

The same thing happened twice more; whenever I got close to playing again, I pulled the muscle at the last moment. I could not deal with sudden, dynamic movement. I was following all the instructions I was given, I even started taking the odd day off, but it was no use.

Looking back now it's no surprise. I was doing more or less the same thing each time and I was getting more or less the same results. I had to find out what I needed to change.

I like to see pretty much everything in my world as falling under the category of cause and effect. Every happening is the cumulative result of someone's choices or desires. That gives us accountability and responsibility while at the same time it helps us to understand that the world is a long chain of linked events. I needed to find the weakest link, the one which was causing it all to go wrong. The problem was, with the enormous level of emotion flying around inside me and my impatient desires to get back involved, I only ever seemed to be fixated on the last part of the chain. To make a long-term improvement, I had to look back further.

I had been having three herbal injections, three times a week and blood drained from a hole that had appeared in the muscle, every few days. It was calming down the symptoms but it was still not enough. I needed a specialist.

Blackie: Take a look in the mirror

'A competitive world has two possibilities for you. You can lose. Or, if you want to win, you can change.'

Lester Thurow

Change of any kind is a challenge. Jack Welch, legendary CEO of General Electric, said change shouldn't be an issue. It should be an integral part of the person, team and company's sub-culture and as such should become a part of everyday life. I couldn't agree more.

But the reality is that change is disconcerting for almost everybody. There are a number of people who work as 'change agents' pontificating daily that if you aren't changing, you're probably slowly going out of business. They sometimes claim that if the outside world is changing at a faster rate than you are internally, you are most likely to be in a lot of trouble.

Now I'm not saying that these are not both worthy points; they are very valid. However, when these 'change agents' themselves are subject to any form of change in their roles, they too become as stressed and unreasonable as everybody else. It is an inherent automatic reaction for human beings to negatively react to propositions of change to our individual lives and routines. In essence, change is OK until it affects us! Our habitual behaviour is an apparent comfort in itself and in a continually competitive and ever uncertain world this daily stability is regarded very highly. If our daily routine is working for us then this is great. The problem arises when it is not working in our best interests.

This truth explains why it takes so very long for us to actually decide to change, even when we know it'll be for the better. There are situations/people/moments when our destiny is decided. Something or someone finally gets the message across to us clearly and succinctly and we accept that we have got to change if we're going to survive and flourish. We recognise that if we don't, we will become resigned to a life of mediocrity.

Often change will be thrust on us. We may be made redundant from a job which we should have left a long time ago. At other times, change may not seem so obvious and we may fall behind, lazing in mediocrity. It is a true fact that many people never get the necessary epiphany moment and are never able to progress to the next level. Many others get the message but don't have the wherewithal or the courage to do anything about it there and then. Of course they want to change, but not immediately. They want time to think it through, to talk themselves out of it. This is often referred to as the 'Law of Diminishing Intent'. The stimulus behind the change incentive is at its strongest when you've just made the decision and the longer you leave the implementation then the weaker the attraction is to follow through with the action.

Not to implement change immediately suggests naivety at best and stupidity at worst. Do you want to stop smoking? Stop now! That's it, thank you! No more complicated than that. Don't wait until the start of next month, or when you've finished the cigarettes you have stockpiled at home, do it now. If you do, you've a greater chance of succeeding. If you don't, you've got just about no chance. So when you know you should change, change ... and get back on living your life to its fullest. Remember, you are in control of what you do, what you feel and where you are. It is common knowledge that we can't control what happens to us in the outside world. We can, however, control how we respond and this makes our individual decisions and personal ethos even more important.

The decision to persist with unchanging procedures will eventually be contaminated by compromise which suggests the bringing to the table of less than one's best. Unfortunately, most of life is driven by compromise because of fear of conflict and consequence. Most people want an easy life and by compromising they think they'll get that. We are told that 'perfect' doesn't exist, and although this might be true, why should we ever give up searching for it? I don't quite understand why we should accept something that we know is wrong in order to avoid the conflict of fighting to find something better.

The truth of compromise is that we get exactly the opposite of what we set out to achieve. Compromise does not lead to a life of fulfilment but rather leads to insecurity, frustration and heartache.

I love the idea of putting a full-length mirror on the back of the dressing-room door so that the last person each player sees as they leave to go to the field of play is themselves. Get them to look straight into their own eyes and make a pledge that their performance today will be representative of who and what they are, and they'd be more than happy to sign the film of their entire contribution to the game as a testimonial championing their capabilities. That person in the mirror is the person the whole world will see. Are you happy about that? Well, are you? Are you showing dependability, high intention and consistent performances commensurate with your position in the team and your profession? Too much pressure? Not if you've given it your best shot on the day. That's all you can ever ask of yourself and this should ensure you do that every game. You've nothing to fear therefore because you should have nothing to hide. If you do have something to hide, then I suggest you ask yourself why and it may lead to some startling revelations about who you are. Time for a change? Remember, we all have our own set of principles and ethics and so there are no rights and wrongs when it comes to this. If you have something to hide then it suggests that you are the one who is being let down and this can never be good. Look to make the necessary changes so that the face you see in the mirror smiles back at you proudly.

We found the specialist, a great one, working in Bergen in Norway. Far enough away to make a road trip out of it, too. I arrived with my brother and our physio with a tape of myself running topless. That was a new experience for me. I then spent the following hour-and-a-half session in my pants. That was filmed too. I hope the video is safe.

The guy was a genius, from the on-screen images and his assessments he helped to trace back to the root cause. The adductor was tearing because it was tiring itself out. It was tiring itself out because my lower back was a long way out of alignment. My spine was being pulled around because my right gluteal muscle was not firing. Instead my adductor was covering its workload – helping to speed up and slow down contractions of the leg during running and a lot of other movements. My backside was literally not working, as if someone had switched it off at the socket. My gluteal wasn't able to fire because I had learned a movement pattern which had taught it not to fire. And I hadn't balanced this out by building and training the antagonistically working muscles. I had also repeated this movement way too many times. So I arrived at the right link in the chain, the fork in the road where I had taken a slightly more painful and destructive path. I had also arrived back exactly where I started from.

I had done too much kicking. I didn't have the right balance in my life or my training or my understanding. And so I had finally learned my lesson, just about.

I don't really blame myself for not picking up the warning signs earlier because although it is important to listen to one's body, it is also vital to know one's body. I'd gotten pretty used to battling through my niggles, waving away physio treatment and scrubbing my name from the masseur's to do list. It all stood in the way of making 'real men's progress', the sort of improvements that are made when you sweat in the gym and excel on the field. I had had good results from playing the game this way so it was always going to take a lot of persuasion before I started amending my ways. Well, I'd eventually got just that.

We all change with time and we become wiser with every experience that doesn't kill us. This is life's way of giving us access to a better method of doing things, or in my case its way of finally forcing me to see a different (albeit only slightly!) method to achieve the same results – a way that better suits who I have become, and where I am in my life. Between the age of eighteen and twenty-four it was right for me to work myself to the bone every day, but the 2003 World Cup was a demarcation line and once crossed, my methods just didn't seem as appropriate.

> *I'd gotten pretty used to battling through my niggles, waving away physio treatment and scrubbing my name from the masseur's to do list*

If I could have watched this process from the outside I would have seen it quicker but that would have required me to take my 'self' out of the equation. To detach myself from my emotions. Easier said than done when you feel that it all means so much to you. Things either stopped working or more likely they started having too many unwanted side effects. To keep alive my dreams of fighting for what I want, the world was now offering me a way to change, to combine the unique things I had been through (which gives us our ultimate strength), with slightly less lengthy but more astute versions of the physical work. This new approach

> *The hardest part of following this path is that the thought of it makes me feel weak and more vulnerable*

to my practice regime and training would hopefully create the right balance for keeping pace with today's young whippersnappers. At the same time it would allow me to continue to improve myself while still feeling fresh and strong enough to play each weekend for a long, long time to come.

The hardest part of following this path is that the thought of it makes me feel underprepared and more vulnerable – there's a part of me that says I am giving away my best assets, and therefore my dreams, and that is the most convincing argument that my mind can come up with for continuing to encourage me to stand still while others move further ahead. Too much routine can sometimes create a reliance upon that routine for happiness. This is very tough to let slide.

Blackie: Be happy to change

'If you're not changing, you're probably slowly going out of business.' Zig Ziglar

Optimism is the friend of change. It expects change and actually provides the fuel to drive it forward. Pessimism, on the other hand, resists change as it fears the unknown territory of what lies ahead. It fears that the future may be worse than the past. Pessimistic people are drained during times of accelerated change whereas optimistic people thrive and gain a momentum that's hard to resist.

Change, however, does not have to be a bad thing! If implemented properly, it can be the only path to finding your best and then the only way of keeping you in touch with it. Change is whatever we want to make of it. I can affect change. I can still impress myself and my desires upon it. As long as I keep half an ear out for what it has to say, then I can work together with it. With this approach I can find the most helpful way of doing things, combine it with my strengths and turn that into easily the most successful and enjoyable way too.

Probably the key thing I learned from my trip to Bergen was that sometimes treating the problem by looking purely at the surface symptoms is like using a bucket to catch the drops from a leaking ceiling. It's like scrubbing or scratching away moss or mould from a rotting surface.

The bucket will eventually overflow and the mould will just grow back.

15

New Game Plan

> "*I had an opportunity to begin again and reinvent that normal life I used to know and loved so much*"

Sometimes when you think you've finally got a grip on things, when you really feel that you've worked it all out, something comes along to show you how wrong you are.

'Why is that the case?' I've often wondered. Maybe I was always expecting it to happen and I just wasn't aware of it. It can be unnerving to accept that life is actually going well. It's easier to be the victim, the underdog, the party with something to gripe about. I often used to like to imagine I was trapped in a corner with nothing to lose, but once I got into that mindset I found I had actually thought myself into that very situation; I made it my reality and thus discovered what it was like to face some tough circumstances.

It was approaching a few months short of the three-year

anniversary of the World Cup win. It was closer to two years from the day that I gleefully accepted the offer of England captaincy from Andy Robinson. My year-and-a-half reign had come to an end without my ever gracing the field. After a great summer off, physically and mentally, I believed I was in the right place. I had built a strong enough platform from which I could put all this madness behind me. I was ready to stop the rot, but I had to start looking at where that rot had actually set in. Even though my problems were manifesting themselves on the training field and in match situations, they lived and breathed in my mind.

> **This was my ninth injury setback since setting foot upon the ladder of top-class rugby. Was I flogging a dead horse by trying to come back again and again?**

I don't think I had much to do with the touch of irony which came to visit me in the North East at the start of the 2006 season. Eighteen months after I had indirectly and unintentionally bullied Andy Buist from the physio bed in Perpignan (despite his injury being unknowingly far worse than mine) he unwittingly returned the favour. We were playing Worcester Warriors in the second league game of the season. I had spilled the ball after being tackled and the whistle went. Buisty dropped on the loose ball and unfortunately on the outside of my left knee, which then also went loose.

The noise I heard, and the sense of disconnection I experienced around my knee joint, was now familiar enough almost to be an old friend; albeit the sort of friend who annoys you and in reality you hate. I was able to diagnose myself immediately. It was history repeating itself. It was another two-month medial rupture.

'You're past it! Time to retire!' These were not internal messages this time, born of experience, but comments which appeared to come from some of the opposition as I was carried from the field. At least they didn't come from my own team! At the time, while resigning myself to another two months in the gym and back on the 'grappler', I found the sentiments a little unsympathetic. Maybe they were just joking.

I'd be lying, though, if I said I didn't consider a few times if there was any truth in what they were saying. This was my ninth injury setback since setting foot upon the ladder of top-class rugby. Was I flogging a dead horse by trying to come back again and again? Was I supposed to pack up and head home? Was I missing the point? Was I rubbish? I

> **He who has a why to live can bear with almost any how**
>
> Nietzsche

had goals still to achieve and I intended to stick around to see them through. Setbacks – I'd seen them, done them, been there and for the sake of my dreams and what I really wanted from life, I was determined to overcome them again and again. I wouldn't complain, even when Blackie put me on the arm bike once more . . .

It doesn't take me long, even from the biggest setbacks, to return to my core belief in sport and in life too. If you want something enough and if it's worth enough to you, then you have to fight, fight, fight and then fight some more. I don't mean physically attacking other people, I mean smashing through challenges. I mean standing tall and believing in myself when others stop doing so. It entails getting up as soon as I physically can after I get knocked down and digging my heels in when it gets too tough for others. It is not time to call it a day until I decide I want to do so. That certainly wasn't now. Returning to Babe Ruth's saying, 'You just can't beat the person who never gives up', this is especially so if he is always looking for a better way.

Long before this moment I had already considered myself to be a seasoned pro in the art of injury rehabilitation. I was able confidently to distinguish between all the things which worked best for me and those which did not. All lessons in life, as I see them, are individually tailored for the person who experiences them. Even in a team sport environment there are many occasions when players need to be treated as the individuals they are, if they are to find their best. My recovery plan was, at this stage, certainly not based on the optimal method for the eighteen-year-old Jonny Wilkinson or even the Jonny Wilkinson of the previous year. It was specific to me (the person I was, not the person I had been) right then and there, structured to put me on the path to becoming stronger and more enthusiastic than ever before.

> **If you want something enough and if it's worth enough to you, then you have to fight, fight, fight and then fight some more**

As an eighteen-year-old, professional rugby absorbed all of my energy. I wanted to watch every minute of every game on television and boy could I talk a good game all night if I could find a willing/unwilling listener. With this latest injury though, I began to see that time away from playing the game was as big a motivational and preparational tool for the older, battle-scarred version of me. Previously, my greatest torture had been in that first week or two after receiving an injury when there's not much physically one can do to help it along except sit and rest. It was not something I have ever done well, especially not in the frustrated and often dejected frame of mind I would find myself in when watching the boys training and playing the way I wished I could be. This time round, I steered clear and put my feet up properly.

I was gradually getting a grip on the way forward for me. I was beginning to understand that, 'If you keep doing what you've always been doing then you'll keep getting what you've always got.' What had worked for me as a younger professional was now no longer bringing the same rewards. As a person and a player I had changed a lot, some of it through choice, some of it forced and now I needed to change a part of my rugby ways to bring them into line with the new me.

The other thing I really hoped to get a handle on was just how a split second of action can change the path of your life forever. I buy into the famous quote that, 'Life is what happens to us while we're busy making other plans.' For what seemed like a long time, these split seconds had brought only unwanted changes to my direction. And I had worked desperately to get back on the track I had paved carefully in my mind's eye.

Blackie: 'Give yourself time . . .

…there is always enough.' Steve Black

It is imperative that we use our time wisely. That's an obvious statement. But we are all guilty of wasting time and filling our days with meetings and chores that bring no benefit at all. But there are ways to avoid this, or at least temper it, so that you get more out of life and move forward. Jonny has been employing these basic principles for a while now and has benefited greatly.

ONE

The most important attitude to adopt when looking at what you do every day is very simple: do what works and do it well. Do what is effective and what will have a positive impact in your chosen environment.

TWO

Spend as much time as you can preparing to make good decisions. Review personal journals, watch others, study DVDs etc. Use whatever means appropriate to build tacit knowledge which can then be called on to make your decisions better.

THREE

Prioritise what you need to achieve in a day, in relation to the actual time you have at your disposal. Or, as Stephen Covey set out in the third of his *The Seven Habits of Highly Effective People*: 'Put First Things First'. We need to be disciplined to do what needs to be done. It's a constant challenge to keep doing that. The key is to develop the discipline as a habit. If you do that, it will become harder to slip into complacency. And complacency never brings happiness or success.

FOUR

Review whether the use of your time has been beneficial or not. Record the time spent on activities/meetings/ preparations etc and try to analyse why it differed (I'll bet it did) from the budgeted time. Look at how, or indeed whether, that time spent will influence your decisions in the future. Was it time well spent?

FIVE

Don't get bogged down. Points one to four allow you to free up time to focus on what you are good at. And the better you become at the things you are good at, the happier you will be. And the happier you are, the better you are at doing what you are good at. You get the picture. Jonny learned to say 'No' to things he didn't want to do. Previously, he would have said 'Yes' to almost everything, because he didn't want to appear to let people down. Being able to say 'No' gave him more time and relieved a significant degree of stress. So now he has more free time to focus on what he is good at, and the better he becomes at the things he is good at . . . and so we go again.

SIX

Delegate. Sometimes I am sure you want to do everything, especially if you have just joined a new team. You feel you want to make your mark. It is almost always the wrong thing to do. Try to fight the impulse. A key ingredient in helping to overcome this urge is to ensure you have the right team of people around you. People who are competent to carry out the tasks needed. If you don't trust, then you won't delegate. If you do, then there's a great chance you will.

SEVEN

But don't delegate the stuff that you're the best at doing. That does no one any good. It's foolish at best and downright lazy at worst. But if you are doing the things you are good at, the things at the top of your priority list, you must ensure that someone is doing the things that are also important, but which are placed second on your list. Delegate these tasks to others. This will not only release your time but it will very probably ensure that the less 'important tasks' will be done much better because they are being done by someone else who has those tasks as a focus. The tasks and works you delegate must be supported and monitored to ensure the outcome is as you expect. And ensure you are given and provide feedback.

EIGHT

Be effective in your use of time. 'What happens in Vegas stays in Vegas' is a well-known phrase. It is also true of many meetings unfortunately. What happens in meetings stays in meetings. In many cases there is absolutely no follow-up action taken, none. To ensure these meetings stay both necessary and productive, make them effective. Use an action list to follow up the meeting, with deadlines for each entry on the list.

NINE

Don't waste time just 'being there'. Success, contrary to popular belief, is not just turning up. If you're there and you're doing nothing, then you are a hindrance.

TEN

Don't overreact to victory/defeat. Having to rectify the damage is a waste of time. You are not the best in the world when you win ... and you are not the worst in history when you get beaten. Yet this is the mentality in ninety per cent of dressing rooms following a win or a loss. It is unprofessional and totally wrong but is the most difficult thing to eradicate. I think a general rule should apply whereby comments and feedback on a performance should be kept until after the immediate reaction to the success or failure. This helps filter out the over-the-top emotional response and gives those parties a chance to rationalise the experience and give realistic feedback of quality. You have to think objectively. A notepad throughout the performance/presentation/game is essential. A word or a phrase can encapsulate a moment. It helps you when you review, say, the game DVD to see if what you thought you saw coincided with what actually happened. What you need to avoid is the fire-fighting week-in, week-out, that goes with overreaction.

I now realise that in 'ignoring' the changes in direction that my life was pointing out to me, in favour of sticking to the path I had carefully mapped out for myself, all I was doing was jumping back on the treadmill. Working hard certainly. But going nowhere. And inevitably, I would end up just repeating what had gone before. I knew I had to change something inside me fundamentally or I was doomed to never move on. Initially it was taking a different approach to my rehabilitation. Actually putting my feet up as I have said. Not torturing myself by watching every minute of rugby that I possibly could. It was around this time that I really began to look at life differently. To enjoy life. Not to be in fear of failure. Failure isn't really failure if you use the experience that life is offering you positively. Sometimes it actually takes far more courage to let go of something close to you than it does to hang on through all the pain.

I slipped on the number ten jersey some eight weeks later as we prepared to face league leaders Bristol at the beginning of November. It was an excellent game and I think a great deal of wine-fuelled nostalgia in the match sponsor's box led to me being named Man of the Match. I received the customary bottle of champagne up on stage in front of the fans. It was great to be back but I gave the champagne to the up-and-coming local band who were playing behind me. I didn't feel much like drinking, although this was the sort of stepping stone I should have been celebrating. My insides felt like they were burning up.

> " *I knew I had to change something inside me fundamentally or I was doomed to never move on* "

During the game, shortly after half time, I had caught a high kick and had been cut in half by the Bristol full-back. We retained the ball and continued attacking as I crept on to the wing. I was trying not to reveal the pain I was in. I had to ensure that my body language kept the fact that I was hurting and struggling for breath a secret from everyone on the field. It soon passed and the next thirty minutes flew by as I went looking slightly cheekily to get my own back on their number fifteen. Perfectly legally of course!

After the game, as the adrenalin wore away, I began to feel the repercussions of running around with a bad stomach. I couldn't stand up straight at all. By the next day I resembled 'Old Man' Wilkinson, hobbling around my garden trying to help build the bonfire for some fireworks that the north east wind was going to render practically impossible anyway. The next day I just about made it to the physio room and from there I was sent straight for a CT scan.

I was told immediately afterwards in the imaging room that I had lacerated my kidney. I didn't even really know where my kidneys were, so I considered this quite an achievement. The impact of the tackle had driven my kidney on to one of my floating ribs at the back and sliced it open. The doctor also rather frighteningly remarked that had it cut a few millimetres deeper, the rib would have punctured the urinary tract, causing some really serious problems. If I had gone to hospital straight after the game then he said he would have kept me in for at least three days. I half wished I had done that. It would at least have saved me the hour in the wind and rain watching my dad and brother try to light a huge pile of wood with petrol and set off some fireworks. In one sense avoiding serious illness was a lucky escape; but it also meant three months away from normal life on the field. I say 'normal life on the field' but the truth was that playing rugby was becoming distinctly abnormal. So much so that I began to wonder if it actually qualified as my career any more.

The hole in my kidney represented a big hole in my season. The knee injury in the game against Worcester in September had again cut out the possibility of any autumn international involvement; I daren't even consider what this meant. I preferred to deal with the evidence of now. What did I know? I had to be careful and do this right. Dealing with important organs was a little different to ligaments. I needed my kidney to be working at a high efficiency rate so that I could keep on playing. No exercise whatsoever for four weeks was what they demanded. A complete lifestyle change was what I understood that to mean. When one door closes, another one opens. This time I was ready to go through it, all the way to Thailand, one of the most beautiful places I have ever been. There, by the pool, staring out over the sea every morning, I relaxed and I smiled. To be fair it was difficult not to. For the first time since the serious neck injury, which seemed to kick off this bizarre run of setbacks, I considered just how fragile my body (and the human body in general) was. It reinforced my growing understanding that our true strength and power must lie inside rather than in the muscles we build. Without a healthy vehicle though, I would not be able to express mine. I really had to start looking after myself better. It was such a wonderful experience being in Thailand that I even lasted three whole weeks before stupidly beginning running in the pool. My excuse is that I know my own body and it needed to work. The truth – I obviously hadn't quite tamed the obsessive beast within me.

> **In one sense avoiding serious illness was a lucky escape; but it also meant three months away from normal life on the field**

Against almost everyone's predictions I made the Six Nations the following February. I felt fresh and ready to go. My kidneys were doing equal shares of the work so I was back to being fully functional. I had an opportunity to begin again and reinvent that normal life I used to know and loved so much. Dealing with each stumbling block had not come easy to me. Tears of frustration, upset and too much self-pity had punctuated the journey. I was stronger for it in so many different ways than I could have ever considered before. I was not just a better player but a more balanced all-round person with an experience-filled perspective which allowed me to become more comfortable accepting and giving advice, more capable of understanding, empathising and finding middle ground. I'd also had my desire to continue to play rugby tested to the full, and I'd come through it, I felt more certain of where I was going than ever before.

It hadn't been until Brian Ashton had turned over the top sheet of the flip chart in front of the squad in February 2007, as we prepared to meet Scotland at Twickenham, that I knew the waiting was over. The last time I'd played for England had been in the Telstra Stadium on 22 November 2003. More than a thousand days previously. Throughout that period I had been waiting, hoping, dreaming of this moment for so long that I'd started to question whether it was worth it any more. I had been close to my breaking point. Sometimes, I guess, we don't realise that what we want may be simmering just below the surface – ready to break out. And we throw it all away.

How strange it was to see my name back on the team sheet. This time it was sandwiched between two new caps. At scrum-half was Harry Ellis, the young Leicester number nine, and at inside centre was rugby league legend Andy Farrell, a hero of mine. It must have been a big day for him too.

Much had changed since I was last there. That would be understandable I suppose but I also recognised that a lot of the discomfort I was feeling was down to the changes I had experienced inside me. On the outside the only difference was a few extra scars. On the inside I was a different person.

It took some getting used to. New coaches, new players and new tactics – I felt like the new boy again. The core components remained unchanged though and truer than ever – passion, enthusiasm, desire, precision, preparation, understanding, respect, confidence and being a team. I was a little concerned about the big event and what it was going to feel like. It had been a long time since I had been out there in front of thousands of expectant fans who somehow always managed to create an atmosphere worthy of a group ten times their size. I had already played fifty or so times for England, but I knew the eruption when we hit the field was going to be a shock.

I received a magical fax from Blackie on the morning of the match.

Blackie: Comeback fax

Hi Jonny,

Hope you've had a reasonable sleep/rest and are ready to embrace the day ahead – as only you can. The best way to approach this challenge is to accept and allow it as a marvellous opportunity you have to celebrate your outstanding talent.

Go with your intuitive flow. You've the belief and winning evidence to know that if you do the outcome will be inevitably the way you want it to be. Have enormous and unwavering faith that when the pressure is on in the heat of battle, you will revert to what you do and who you are, as you've done so many times in the past . . . and that's somebody who is driven from a superb source; somebody who makes hugely effective decisions that galvanise your team to a victorious performance. Someone who always finds the solution . . . always.

Jonny, remember the way we've explained the power and

effectiveness of your intuitive thought; those gut feelings that lead you to success. If prayer is us talking to God then a wonderful thought to consider is that our intuition and gut feeling might be God talking to us. Listen to those promptings today and bring to reality the thousands of rehearsals we've had during visualisations. The spirit underwriting your performance is so strong and well-meaning that your performance is guaranteed.

Believe this with all your heart and allow this effect to take place. All blocks to this thinking have been removed.

Have a great experience . . . one of your best.

God Bless,

Onwards and Upwards,

Blackie

I sat perched on the end of my hotel bed with the fax on my lap. To my side were all my notes from the week's meetings and my inspirations from training. I thought about all the mental preparation and I considered all of the hard, physical work. I was thankful for the strength my obsessive side gave me, but I had had enough of my mind. I was going mad trying to think about the game any more. I just wanted to be there in the stadium, I had to get moving. The time for talking was over. It was only the doing which mattered now.

For England it was a great afternoon, a good one for me too. The boys were awesome. Harry Ellis made his first cap a memorable one with a man-of-the-match performance. He flew around the field causing havoc and even managed to set me up for a dodgy try in the corner.

I didn't allow myself much time to celebrate in the aftermath of the event, as was my way, but a little later I did find some space to reflect. I realised something important.

For such a long time I had been physically confined to the gym, the physio's and the operating table. But mentally, I had remained on the field. In my mind, I had focused almost all my energy on one goal – to get back playing and playing my best. Whenever I thought about rugby I saw myself out there in the arena making good decisions. Whenever I watched rugby I put myself in the same situations as the players, always imagining what I would do if I were in their boots. Whenever I trained I made sure I pictured the scenes as I contributed to great plays. When I slept, I dreamt about my game. I heard the noises, felt the sensations and inhabited the incredible atmosphere. I had played this game thousands of times in my head, I had already experienced every moment and lived every outcome, I had made it my destiny.

By undertaking all this visualisation I began to believe I had already achieved my goals – specifically in this case once again playing for England. It was part of my life. Who is to say it wasn't? I definitely feel like I had in some way secured that experience personally, a little while before it ever actually happened.

> " *By thought the thing you want is brought to you. By action, you receive it* "
>
> Wallace D Wattles

In my eyes, the way I applied myself, the strength of the connection I formed with the event and the 'never-give-in' attitude made its arrival ever more certain. There are often a large number of people competing for the same prize, so the quality of every ounce of energy that can be focused on making sure it is you who succeeds becomes even more important. Visualising is part of it, certainly, but there is no escape from the fact that you also have to be prepared to work hard to make it happen.

I believe the power to make dreams come true is inside everyone. It is not a skill I have mastered in any way, far from it in fact. I wonder if maybe all the lessons we learn through our experiences are designed to teach us how to refine this talent, how to realise those dreams. It is a process I haven't allowed myself fully to relax and enjoy yet. When I do, I'll get better at it, I'm sure of that. But for a brief sparkling moment I did feel I got the hang of it on the day of my England comeback.

Something like thirteen or fourteen continuous setbacks separated my last England appearance with my February 2007 comeback, arriving, it seemed, always at the the times I needed them least, keeping me out of selection for every one of the thirty or so internationals over those three and a half years. How can that happen? These disruptions have sent me spiralling off in all directions, searching for the way back to what I envisaged was the plan all along. What has never changed though is that I have had to stay true to what I believe: it is a better life if you stay positive, making the most of every situation, and dedicate yourself to a worthy cause which always involves helping others. These are my two lines in the sand that I will never cross. There have been others that I have drawn over time. One encourages me to be open to learning and evolving. Oddly, this itself involves looking at my other lines, and learning to distinguish which ones I need to alter, bend and, every now and again, completely erase.

Blackie: 'Look forward to the best . . .

. . . it's on its way.'

At twenty-nine years of age there's a lot more to come from Jonny. If we thought he's been effective before, well we'd better watch out! His switch to living 'in the now' will ensure that he doesn't waste nervous energy as he continues on his quest for excellence. What's gone is gone. Every experience has shaped the person he is today. None of us have the ability to change the past. What we can do something about is the here and now. The best way to prepare for tomorrow after all is to be as good as you can be today, in the reality of your life now . . . and now . . . and now.

John Wooden spoke about each day being your masterpiece. Jonny talks about each day being a perfect day; a day when you've given all you've got, to do whatever has been required of you. It may, of course, be simply ensuring you get the necessary rest that your body is in desperate need of. If that's the appropriate and right way forward for you then do that to the best of your abilities. Make sure that you dedicate yourself that day to ensuring that your body can refuel itself with no physical chores eating into its already low energy tank.

Jonny didn't used to be like this, I must add. He sometimes used to do too much then forget to tell me! He needed to fill his days with effort, as a sacrifice, homage almost, to his perceived success. Nowadays, his thinking is clearer and he understands his intentions are always good. If the subsequent performance doesn't live up to expectations then he won't brood, dwelling on the moment. He'll simply switch his mind to planning how his next performance will live up to the standards he's set. In reality, he'll focus his mind to ensure that the next performance exceeds expectations. He now embraces the challenge and is excited about the opportunity.

As I have said before, I used to see life as a kind of way of earning a future reward. Suffering the pain of disappointment, injury and criticism was my sacrifice for something better to come. Not any more. Now I understand that what happens to us is all part of a continuous interlocking process. Being aware of what each plus and minus, each setback and victory, may mean helps refine and sharpen my growth. I am not saying that I immediately recognise why 'X' has happened. I certainly don't. But I do believe that whatever X, Y and Z may be, they are all meaningful points, if you want to use them, along the road to the bigger prize: the enjoyment of life. The World Cup 2003 victory was the incredible effect of a lot of hard work. It perhaps also became part of the cause of a lot of heartache. Confusing isn't it?! Simplified, everything happens for a reason and understanding that is perhaps all the control I need. Live for and enjoy what you're doing right now. Make the present moment better and more fulfilling, never pass up one chance to improve you, and the future will follow suit. There is nothing else to it.

16

Relative Values

" But discounting the spirit, experience and desire of the individuals in this squad to win would have been a mistake. We all knew the commitment was there, but we had to find the way to get it all out in the open "

The Rugby World Cup 2007 was full of exceptions to the so-called rules. Some of these rules I myself created, convinced I already knew why teams win games and why teams lost them. The cup was yet another outstanding motivational tool for helping me maintain a greater flexibility in the way I see things.

I had always been a fairly black and white character. I enjoyed, I think, the definitive outlook it offered me, the tool by which I could judge what was good and what was bad. With these values steering me through life and team sport I had a strong sense of direction and something to fall back on when things got tough and frantic. That still holds true today. As I see it, having a kind of moral compass, a set of personal beliefs, is absolutely necessary for guidance and purpose. It also allows me to let people see into my character, so they can decide whether or not they can trust and rely on me. It's just that now, I have attached a less rigid approach to those values. Simply put, I have liberated myself, and life is better for it.

When I ventured out into the real world, shortly after I left school, I found it a big challenge. I realised quickly that some of my rigid parameters of right and wrong were actually having a more troublesome effect than I could ever have imagined. Not only were they confusing me but they were imprisoning me, making life harder, rather than setting me free.

The rugby world, the professional world and the outside world were all showing me that there is in fact a grey area where the unexpected does frequently happen. Things and people change and they don't always make a lot of sense. By stubbornly holding on to my inexperienced and naïve values I was limiting myself. Not only that, I was also isolating myself. It took me way too long to realise that what makes things easier and more fun, and what made me more successful, was exchanging my negative 'right-and-wrong' values for more flexible, helpful ones. That was the place I had arrived at as we embarked on the seven long weeks of the tournament, and what it gave me was the ability to hop on the back of the opportunities that the changes all around us were offering.

I will always respect and hold dear my baseline beliefs of what is acceptable (like good preparation, effort, empathising with others and unselfish behaviour), and what is not (like hurting others and taking away their dreams). These are immoveable, but with a new, more sympathetic and open view of people and life there always seems to be a happy solution to problems which may have once appeared insurmountable.

> " *By stubbornly holding on to my inexperienced and naïve values I was limiting myself* "

So the World Cup got underway, and with a bang too. Argentina went ahead and beat the hosts, France; a spanner in the works of the French campaign on the opening day. For Argentina, however, it was to be the first step along a glorious path, a path which shocked a lot of people.

For Ireland, who had shown such ruthless form in the Six Nations tournament leading up to the big event, it also highlighted what a hellish group they had been drawn into. Despite huge courage and effort they would unfortunately not make it through.

Wales would perform brilliantly for long periods, as they did four years previously, but the Australians as usual had arrived with their 'A' game fully intact and keen to make life hard for them. The killer blow for the Welsh team would come in the form of electric attacking play and a magical last-minute try from a Fijian team full of talent.

Scotland did well to qualify in a group ruled by New Zealand, who were scoring tries for fun and looking every bit like the world beaters which their 'favourites' tag suggested they were. At this stage no one was arguing either.

For us, it might have been 2003 all over again. South Africa,

Samoa and England together once more in the group stage. But it soon became clear that that was the only similarity. The results were quick to let us know that over the last four years much had changed.

Our pool was a perfect illustration of the story of the opening stages. It was to be the 'tale of the underdog'. The USA pushed us hard and we looked a little shaky, never really getting control of the game. Tonga were also inspired in their performances, beating Samoa and coming to within the bounce of a ball of winning their clash with South Africa. Elsewhere in the competition Georgia, Namibia and others all took huge bites out of big name opposition. They were showing the watching public that rugby, globally speaking, is in terrific shape. It was a nice thought for the future and another reminder that taking anything for granted nowadays might return to haunt you. From early on, spectators, players, betting shops and commentators alike ceased counting chickens, and the latter part of the World Cup continued to surprise.

Our own preparations had been fragmented. The four seasons leading up to the 2007 campaign bore very little resemblance to the corresponding period before the 2003 Rugby World Cup. We had struggled to build and maintain any real momentum because our results and performances had been inconsistent. The composition of the squad and starting line-up had been equally inconsistent.

* * *

Blackie: Flourish or fail on your own terms

'Ability is what you are capable of doing. Motivation determines what you do. Attitude is how well you do it.' Lou Holtz

The secret to coaching or managing (or indeed almost everything) is to be authentic. Be yourself. We all have a unique perspective on the world, so share it! Make a difference. If you follow this advice and you have chosen the right career path then you will flourish or fail based on who and what you are. If you compromise your principles, you'll survive or fail to survive (but very rarely will you thrive!) on who and what somebody else is.

There is so much evidence to suggest that the people at the top, in charge of a team, who get rid of a manager or coach for being themselves will also get rid of that same person even if they weakly try to tow the line. Either way, the manager/coach suffers but the first way at least allows them to retain their dignity and integrity, living to fight another day hopefully in a less oppressive environment.

Consistency is the name of the game in rugby. Being a great team or player is not about showing you have the ability to do it, it is about actually more or less doing it every time. I'm not talking about winning every time, that just doesn't happen. What I believe is that the best teams usually win most of their games and when they lose they lose by a small margin, because bad days are generally separated from the good by just a few points. For our pre-World Cup friendlies we faced Wales at Twickenham, a game we won well, and a home and away double-header against France, which we didn't. That's not to say we didn't show promise. We perhaps should have won the first although we were well beaten in the Marseille contest.

A few years ago I might have been heard to say something along the lines of, 'If you don't feel you can win the World Cup then what's the point in being there?' An example of some of the black and white in me showing through. I believe now there is a fabulous experience and learning opportunity on offer for every member of every team, whatever their motivation. That statement I might have made, however, wouldn't have been a million miles out of place if it had been directed at us. Things hadn't been perfect in preparation, I admit that. Not like four years ago anyway. But so what? Did that now mean we didn't stand a chance? I'd learned at times along those four years that the past doesn't have to matter if we don't want it to, if we

> **"Things hadn't been perfect in preparation, I admit that. Not like four years ago anyway. But so what? Did that now mean we didn't stand a chance?"**

choose to let it go. On our day we knew we could beat anyone. We would just need to find the right recipe for getting the best out of each other and make each match day, our day. This we all bought into wholeheartedly.

I remember being interviewed at the O2 Scrum in the Park celebration in London a few days before we left to cross the

Channel. After hearing me talk positively, the interviewer asked, almost with pity, and slightly patronisingly I felt, something like, 'Do you really, honestly think you have a chance with your recent results and your present world ranking of eighth?'

In other words, 'Come on, who are you kidding? Admit it, you are going to lose.' It was almost as though it was aimed at quashing our spirit with negativity.

We don't need a script for answering interviews like this one, although it is important not to get ensnared in little traps. I try to speak honestly, it does seem to be the best way, and I remember being disappointed at myself for taking slight offence, on behalf of the team, to the defeatist attitude. I tried to hide those hurt feelings.

'Of course we stand a chance. This is a great squad full of great players. At our best we can win any game. It is going to be tough and a real challenge because this is the Rugby World Cup and there are a lot of other teams who are believing the very same thing, and rightfully so. It is up to us now, we have to relish that challenge, prepare thoroughly and give absolutely everything we have, in training and in games. One day at a time. Anything less will not be enough.'

There is nothing wrong in my eyes with being optimistic and full of faith, seeing the positive and committing to your belief. I think I was asked the same sort of thing a dozen more times by different newspapers, radio and TV channels. It didn't bother me in the least, I had no problem churning out the same sort of response. Saying it over and over again acted as positive reinforcement, and it is, after all, an energising message for the team and the supporters, playing right into the hands of the Law of Attraction.

And I needed to hang on to that message. We hadn't been in

France twenty-four hours before my faith was put to the test.

We arrived in the afternoon and I thought it might be a good idea to make the most of a sunny September day by kicking a few balls, throwing a few passes and stretching out after the morning's travel. Arnaud, our French liaison officer, learned very quickly that he would be spending a lot of his time kicking balls back to me and he loved the idea. His positivity was infectious, a great guy. He also took a hell of an ear bashing, because I used him as a sounding board for practising my French.

It felt good to be out there, getting used to the new balls and focusing my concentration. If I had known that it was to be the only session I would perform fully fit, would I have enjoyed it even more? Probably.

The next day we had our first training session. Only seven days separated us from our first game, so there was no time to waste. We were working on defence again. Along with belief, defence is the foundation of any successful team. You cannot fake having a strong defence. When you do create one which you can rely on, it inspires unbelievable confidence; if no one can score against you then it is very tough to lose. We were running through our positional responsibilities, communication and game readings. The opposition in this case was the other half of the squad, but we weren't going full on, just a two-handed touch instead of tackling. We didn't want injuries!

Steve Borthwick ran with the ball at Phil Vickery's outside shoulder. I stepped in to help our captain make the touch after I realised Borthers wasn't going to pass. Vicks stretched and brought Steve to the ground. I saw it happen in front of me and hurdled the two of them to avoid studding any loose body parts. The inside of my right foot landed on what I thought would be the ground, but was actually Steve's shin. The outside of my boot was unsupported. I tried to push off it and my ankle hyper-extended, turning right over until it was flat against the floor. Then it sprang back round. It was agony; up there with the worst of any other recent injury I can recall.

It was all over so quickly, I don't think anyone really saw it. I looked across to the side urgently seeking some assistance. I saw Barney Kenny, one half of our enormously likeable physiotherapy duo. He was following play with his eyes. He hadn't seen me. I screamed, 'Barney! Barney! For sh . . . sake, someone help me!'

The rest of the time I was unbelievably calm. My feelings astonished me, and I can only really remember weighing up what I could control and what I definitely couldn't. What evidence was there of injury, what information did I have and what decisions could I make based on it all? I had become a little more skilful at steering myself away from past and future too. Live in the here and now. That is all you can do.

It amounted to this: I had hurt my ankle, it was heavily swollen and that was to be expected. Without the fear of the things I didn't know for sure – for example, the extent of the damage and what it might mean for the rest of my own World Cup experience – there was nothing to get stressed about. What could I actually do to help? Put my foot in ice, get it elevated, compress it and get to hospital. So that's what I did. I reacted calmly, peacefully even, to an event which, I have no doubt, a few years earlier may have given me a heart attack.

> "*I didn't understand why everyone was asking me how disappointed I was. I was on a different wavelength. It could have been so much worse*"

Relatively speaking it was good news. The ligaments were torn on the outside (and the inside but I wouldn't find that out until later) and Phil Pask, the other half of the physio pairing, and the doctor were talking about an aggressive rehab programme of two or three weeks for a fair recovery. I had my target date. I would miss a couple of games but I would be back. Brilliant news!

I didn't understand why everyone was asking me how disappointed I was. I was on a different wavelength. It could have been so much worse. My supposed bad luck of the past four years didn't matter to me; it was gone. The games I would miss were all they saw. This also meant little to me – I was in the now, and that meant icing my leg every three to four hours, waking up twice each night. I also had a special electrical machine which passed a current through the area. I carried that one around like a pet. I didn't see much of the boys during that period, which was a real shame, but I was using up my energy focusing on healing quickly and making my way back.

The scoreline 36–0 is a heavy defeat in anyone's book. A few years back I would have argued that it would have undoubtedly spelt the end of our World Cup. I know I used to believe if a team was capable of losing by that margin then it wasn't deserving of the title. But discounting the spirit, experience and desire of the individuals in this squad to win would have been a mistake. We all knew the commitment was there, but we had to find the way to get it all out in the open.

> **Determine that the thing can and shall be done, and then we shall find the way**
>
> Abraham Lincoln

We needed a few longer, more detailed meetings, full of honesty and proper communication. With the level of talent throughout the squad we should have been able to play in any style; we just needed to be thinking the same way. I have no doubt that the squad of coaches and players had done all the right things and said all the right stuff; we had just interpreted the meanings a little differently and this was pulling us in slightly separate directions. After an open discussion which more or less clarified absolutely everything, we were suddenly tuned in to the same channel. We had narrowed the game plan down to just one hymn sheet. Then it was up to us to start singing from it. OK, I know this is a trip to Metaphor City but I want you to get the point.

Blackie: Recipe for success

'Great ingredients! . . . The blend of which will determine the quality of the meal.' Marco Pierre White

Each of us is different, with a wide range of goals, but I believe there is significant common ground on which we can all meet to built the foundations for what we each regard as success. The guidelines I have set out below constitute what I see as the basis of that common ground.

ONE
Be positive and optimistic. You must have a strong inner belief that life has great things in store for you. The strength this brings will give you your best chance of success. We all know many people who automatically accept failure. They do this by maintaining that they don't really want the promotion they've applied for, or that they are just doing it for the sake of it.

Others, in exams, will repeatedly say that they are going to fail, that they haven't really revised just in case their marks aren't up to standard. By doing this though, these people have already admitted defeat. Just one lost fight after perhaps forty wins can completely shatter a boxer's confidence. Their ability and preparation will have been the same as in all their previous victories, but by losing one bout, they have lost the belief and strength that a positive and optimistic mindset brings. So you should actively try to cultivate a positive frame of mind and work hard to maintain it. If you think that you will win, it's almost a certainty that you will. This is arguably the biggest and most important step of all. I urge you to adopt this positive state of mind now.

TWO

Once you have adopted a positive mindset, you should then set yourself a 'ballpark destination'. You should know where it is that you are going. Without knowing where you are going, how do you know if your daily efforts are effective in pushing you forward into the right direction? So begin with the end in mind. Set out a plan, a map, with interim, momentum-inducing goals along the way. When achieved, these will let you know you are heading in the right direction. The overall destination must be both highly attractive and beneficial to your life when you get there. Ask yourself:

Where am I now?

Where do I want to go?

How do I get there?

THREE

On your journey to your ballpark destination you may find that your 'sat nav' sometimes directs you off course. Strong challenges can divert you down the wrong road. To combat this we must always try to ensure that our daily work is effective. Don't waste time devoting valuable energy to lost causes. Do your first things first and don't procrastinate. Often, we lose valuable amounts of time pontificating over a possible journey or goal. While we reassure ourselves that we are doing the right thing, the race has already begun and we are lagging behind. Always maintain a sense of urgency and work every day to move a little bit further towards your destination.

FOUR

A very important part of laying down the groundwork for success is deciding to like people, especially those in your life! Everybody should win from a relationship if it is to be effective. Try to seek common ground with the other person in order to build a lasting and worthwhile bond. Imagine you were in that other party's position and try to see through the other person's eyes, hear through their ears and be prepared to walk in their shoes. Stephen Covey encapsulated this perfectly in the fifth of his *The Seven Habits of Highly Effective People*: 'Seek first to understand then to be understood.'

FIVE

Learn. Continually.

SIX

Practise doing your thing. A motto of mine is 'Apply and try'. Give it your all. There's no real use learning for learning's sake. You've got to apply that knowledge productively. If paramedics know the principles of life-saving techniques but don't apply them . . . well, the outcome won't be very rosy.

SEVEN

Once you have set your ballpark destination and have cultivated rewarding and fruitful relationships then ensure that you see things through to the end. If you have made the decision to do something then you should stay with it. As they say on *Mastermind*, 'I've started so I'll finish.'

EIGHT

I strongly believe that you'll get so much more out of life if you care about your family, friends, work colleagues, environment and society in general. Care enough and you'll achieve astonishing results. This links in with liking people. If we like people and effectively show we care about them and the achievement of their personal goals then they will undoubtedly want to do more for us.

NINE

Strive to understand what is expected from you (what you have to do, to what level, for how long) and where that fits into your team, company, industry as a whole. Ask for 'Indian Talking Stick' understanding. This is a communication tool explained by Stephen Covey. Articulate your message then have the recipient repeat back their understanding of what has been said. If there are any misunderstandings, this is the opportunity to clear them up. Then make sure the amended message is repeated. Once the communication is aligned then your recipient can 'take' the Talking Stick and add its message to their knowledge bank. They can then pass on that information to third parties in the way they see fit – provided the Indian Talking Stick procedure is followed. This way everyone understands what's expected, what needs to be done and there is a commitment to enthusiastically embrace the programme. Once we've all bought in then let's go!

TEN

Be a plus to everyone associated with you. Be recognised as a person who will consistently and dynamically make a significant contribution to anywhere you are. Living that change is very contagious – go out and infect people with it.

ELEVEN

Be interested in your friends; both prospective and existing. The quality of your relationships will determine your flexibility and your ability to be ready and able to deal with any surprises life throws your way. Be ready to adjust, adapt and respond positively and effectively. In other words, evolve to cope then adapt to thrive. You don't need adverse reactions; you need positive responses.

TWELVE

Have the discipline to do what needs to be done, when it needs to be done at a quality that meets or exceeds all requirements and expectations.

THIRTEEN

If you want things to change in your life then you must change. If you want more, you must become more. Change your behaviour and you will become the person that behaviour creates. I said earlier when talking about the make-up of a team, that you shouldn't hope or rely on others to change. That is true. If someone isn't open to it, then it is very difficult. No matter what you do. Such people remain constant to their core beliefs. If their behaviour isn't bringing results they probably haven't found the environment that will allow their personal strengths and talents to flourish and make a meaningful contribution, thus no matter how hard you try, neither party will be able to facilitate the change you both want at that time, in that place. But if you are the sort of person who wants to change and is open to it, then you are the type of person who will initiate change in your life. If it's in an area of strength then the change will most likely be seen as growth; if it's in an area where you are not particulalry talented you may get slightly better but you'll never scale the heights associated with your strengths. It is a personal thing. You can't assume it of others. You can train a donkey eight hours a day, love it, feed it well, give it the most up to date training methods, but it'll never win the Derby.

FOURTEEN

You need to have the right people around you. People playing to their strengths as you will to yours. In a balanced team there are complementary skills across all bases. Be in the company of highly motivated, well-intentioned, skilled, ambitious people because it rubs off. Everyone must be allowed to contribute to feel significant.

FIFTEEN
Finally, recognise that you are the right person for the job, and that you are empowered to do it.

There were many obstacles in our path towards success and two huge ones (physically) took the form of Samoa and Tonga. These two giants of the game were playing fabulous rugby. I have enormous respect for the Pacific Islands teams and the way they go about their business, with ambition, innovation, physicality and very little fear. Perhaps that's what makes them so scary to play against. On their day they can beat anyone and they would both have a chance to put an end to our World Cup dreams.

At the pre-Samoa press conference I spoke honestly about what I believed, but I sensed a feeling of negativity and doubt surrounding our tournament prospects. No surprise I suppose. This wasn't the positive New Zealand press culture that I'd witnessed on the Lions tour two years earlier. 'How on earth are you possibly going to turn it around after such a drubbing against South Africa?' they all asked, in so many words.

> *There were many obstacles in our path towards success and two huge ones (physically) took the form of Samoa and Tonga*

My response: 'We haven't seen the best of ourselves yet. We have the desire, the positivity and the capability but we haven't been able to unlock them on the field. Our understanding collectively was not quite the same throughout. Now we've made a few little changes, we're all on the same wavelength. I believe the huge efforts we are making will now be more effective as we will be pulling in the same direction. Hopefully we can see the best of players like Paul Sackey and Josh Lewsey because they'll have space to operate and good ball to play with. Maybe now we can help to get the forwards in a position to use their strength and get us going, because they won't have to run into brick walls of defence.'

Some of it at the time was, I confess, a bit of blind optimism. But knowing this team, knowing what I'd seen of them in practice and in match play, I felt we could back it up. There was nothing else to do but take the plunge and get on with it.

We secured those two wins. At times we all saw the team back in their element. From my vantage point on the pitch, I began to see options all around me. I was in a privileged playing position, often able to select the best move from a long list, unlike Mike Catt against South Africa who was too regularly forced to take the only option available to him, be it good or bad. In fact, for me the decisions often made themselves. That is when I know a team is playing well around me. The guys were opening up the field for me and taking pressure away with their communication, unselfish work rates and moments of inspiration. It is ironic, but my perceived better performances, for which I have been praised, have always originated from situations when I don't feel I have had to do very much myself.

Gathering Momentum

> **"** *We resembled ourselves again. We started trying a few things. Why shouldn't we? This may be our last chance for God's sake* **"**

I n rugby terms the World Cup 2007 had been a complete mystery. From the start it had developed into a tight, tense affair with teams seeming to place greater emphasis on rushing up with strong defence and feeding from opposition errors than creating opportunities. It was Argentina's upset over France in the opening round which illustrated the need for precision, pragmatism and an all-engulfing defensive line. It also reminded us of the difficulty involved in handling a wet ball; a problem ever present in autumnal European night-time fixtures because of the inevitable covering of dew. It quickly became evident that the spotlight would be on the tactical kickers in the big games, with the need for field position even more crucial to turn pressure into points and to keep slip-ups and turnovers relatively safe.

The quarter-final against Australia was played out on a great stage. We were down in the beautiful south of France amid the stunning atmosphere of sport in Marseille. It was sunny, hot and still and with that we got our second and last opportunity to bend the early established tactical rules and throw the ball about a bit more. It was fun. I guess England winning might have come as a surprise to a few people too. We had belief as always but with public expectation perhaps lying with the boys in the other camp, the shackles were off. We resembled ourselves again. We started trying a few things. Why shouldn't we? This may be our last chance for God's sake.

Losing is a nasty feeling, but it was, I imagine, an especially tough one for two legends of the game who had chosen then to call time on their illustrious international careers. George Gregan and Stephen Larkham, the half-back pairing for Australia, had dominated the game in so many ways for so long. I started watching George Gregan when I was just a fifteen/sixteen-year-old schoolboy. I remember staring in amazement as he managed to dislodge the ball from All Black winger Jeff Wilson's grasp on the final whistle in arguably the most famous try-saving tackle in history. It was incredible.

I have been on the end of a good few serious defeats instigated by him and have nothing but admiration for the way that he has performed at such a world-class level with such consistency. His tactical ability, his competitive instinct and his super-fast skills have been second to none.

Stephen Larkham I never really got to know although I played against him many times. He entered the frame not long after Gregan and was still a relatively new kid on the block when I played my first full international down in Brisbane. He was at fly-half that day, which I think must have been a relatively new experience for him, as he was a more regular full-back then. Not that you would have known it, though. He was electric, scoring perhaps the most clinical try I've ever conceded on a rugby

> *We managed to protect a two-point lead through to the final whistle and suddenly it dawned on us that we wouldn't be going home just yet*

field. He showed me very early in my career what it was I really needed to work on in my game in order to compete at the highest level. In short, he demonstrated how far I was from where I needed to be. It was a lesson he repeated to me, and others too, several more times, But it was one for which I was very grateful. With pace, courage, precision, skill and leadership both he and George Gregan took Australia to a World Cup success and rugby to a new level. I got a chance to shake the hands of two of my biggest inspirations that sunny afternoon on the rugby field; hopefully it won't be the last time.

We pulled together fantastically well for the game. We smashed into tackles intent on going forward and cleaned out rucks with the force, enthusiasm and aggression of way more than just fifteen players. We managed to protect a two-point lead through to the final whistle and suddenly it dawned on us that we wouldn't be going home just yet.

My girlfriend and I were walking down the beach in Marseille later that evening trying to find somewhere quiet to eat, when all the cars started beeping their horns randomly. After ten or so seconds I realised that it was not some sort of Gaelic road rage but actually something related to the France versus New Zealand night-time quarter-final. We dashed inside the nearest bar to see what was going on. It turned out that they were celebrating because the French had just fought back to level pegging, 20–20, with twenty minutes to go. Unbelievable. It's not that I didn't have faith in France, I mean they'd just disposed of us twice in the summer. It's just that New Zealand were invincible, or so I thought.

I couldn't bear to watch any more and hid the rest of the game out in a busy creperie. When we left, a kind of fever had hit the streets of Marseille. There were people sitting on the backs of mopeds trailing the French flag. Others stood up through sun roofs screaming and singing. They had done the impossible and beaten the unbeatable. Now I realised that, as their next opponents, I might need to lay low all of a sudden. It was a tense fifteen minutes spent diving behind road signs and trees before we hit the Holiday Inn team hotel. And there I saw the New Zealand analysis videos, which we had anticipated pouring over every second of, were all gone. In their place was the recorded proof of our summer's French disappointments. Life had afforded us one special chance to put it all right again, even if we would have to take on a whole nation to do so.

When describing the 2003 World Cup to everyone I would tell them that the semi-final and especially the final were such big occasions that they kind of looked after themselves. It is always easier to speak retrospectively because now, facing the same stage four years later, I wasn't feeling so sure. The anxiety and the fear reappeared and, as is often the case, when they entered they left the door open, demanding that my enjoyment close it on its way out. It was of course my decision to make it that way. I couldn't help getting caught up thinking about just how close we were and how great it would be to make it to the final once again. These were positive ambitions. It was just when I started worrying about how painful it might be dealing with missing out, after all we'd been through, that I felt the cold grip of fear.

> " *Life had afforded us one special chance to put it all right again, even if we would have to take on a whole nation to do so* "

When I began to concern myself with irrelevant things well outside my control and mostly complete rubbish – such as how much responsibility was on me and what it would feel like to let everyone down – I fell back into my old habits. I had spent so long trying to convert stomach-churning feelings and mental panic into something positive, and yet here they were again, returned like long-lost friends. With my real mates, there is nothing more satisfying than picking up exactly where you last left off. With these two, I was going to have to use all I had learned to prevent that from happening. I needed to be mentally tough to counteract what was threatening to go on inside my head, and refrain from locking myself away in my hotel room. I thought I had left that behaviour well behind.

'To try to enjoy something' is a funny thought. Some would say you either do or you don't and leave it at that. I sympathise. You see, I love playing rugby and I love life. When I am performing with a true smile on my face I feel I'm pretty good at both, but when I am drawn into the consequences and outcomes rather than the experience, I am no longer playing the same game and the fun disappears.

Working really hard to enjoy something sounds like even more of a joke but that is what it took at times to keep myself in the 'now', to set the stage for allowing myself to forget about tomorrow and rediscover the freedom of the eight-year-old child inside me who still longs for the next chance to get out in the fresh air and compete with the ball. I dreamed at that age of playing for my country for only the simplest reasons. Because I loved the game.

Thursday night, two nights before the semi-final in Paris, and my young Newcastle team-mates, Mathew Tait and Toby Flood and I ventured out to a local Italian restaurant in Versailles for dinner. We were the only customers, which was absolutely perfect as far as we were concerned. It was the two-hour break we all needed. I remember constantly checking the clock wishing the minutes would slow down and take it as easy as I

" *I needed to be mentally tough to counteract what was threatening to go on inside my head, and refrain from locking myself away in my hotel room* "

was beginning to. Here was me enjoying the moment with such a massive game only forty-eight hours away. We ordered . . . then ordered again when we were told all our first choices were unavailable. That's when a gentleman walked into the restaurant on his own, past all the empty tables, and sat down at the only one positioned right beside us. Now this was awkward. I figured him to be a journalist who had maybe seen us enter. We tried not to let it affect the meal but you can never be too sure how far people will go to get a story. As it turned out, we're pretty sure he was just a customer who prefered to eat in the company of other diners, happy enough reading the newspaper. Something I had stopped doing a long time ago.

Around the hotel the media intrusion had suddenly become more intense, which is probably why I had been so aware of our fellow diner. The paparazzi were camping outside so we all had to find our favourite back and side exits and entrances to be used outside of training times. The powerful sphere of influence of the media is perhaps one of the most challenging aspects of a professional sporting life.

For me, a relationship with the media can be a strange thing. When I trust someone, when I can see what angle they are coming from, and I know that they understand what I am trying to say, then I can feel confident to open up. A good example of that occurred a week after my visit to the Versailles restaurant. It was a couple of days before the final – I know I'm jumping ahead a bit here and I'll come back to the French game – and I went out for a little snack with my friend, Owen Slot, from *The Times* newspaper to help me round off my weekend's column. Four years previously we had done something similar. Owen, a journalist, and photographer Marc Aspland had wanted to take me down to Manly Beach outside Sydney, just outside our hotel, for a 'nice little feature piece'. I agreed on two conditions:

1. That we found a quiet beach.

2. That we got in and out of there before anyone clocked me.

I didn't want a scene. We drove around from beach to beach in our hire car – me lying across the back seat – like getaways from a heist, desperate to find a safe zone. We did find a suitable location, where by chance Lawrence Dallaglio was strolling along unbothered with his family. As I sprinted past him towards a sheltered cove he had to take two or three glances before he realised it was me behind the hood and the beanie hat. Now it seems funny, but at the time I was honestly terrified. I can't believe we got away with it. Needless to say I forgot to enjoy it.

This time around, the new laid-back Jonny Wilkinson said, 'Sure thing,' to a visit to a classic French café with every intention of enjoying a nice chat and having a few pictures taken. I was happy just to see how it would unfold. Marc's inventive camera work from the pavement outside was drawing a crowd of curious onlookers. My obvious ease brought the conversation around to my new, more relaxed state of mind. I mentioned how my related reading has taken me to topics such as self-help, spirituality, autobiographies, philosophy, religion, Buddhism ... and then I noticed something.

It happens all the time in press conferences and interviews. A word or phrase comes out of your mouth and all the press start scribbling. Journalists' ears prick up and you can almost hear their minds buzzing as they start to formulate their headlines. My mention of Buddhist teaching triggered the same response. The newspaper liked the potential impact of the theme but I knew it would be problematic for me. We agreed and met somewhere in the middle. *The Times* ran a nice insightful story with me and

> **I want to inspire and not offend but I also want to relax and enjoy living a normal life**

my best intentions at the heart of it all the way through. With the guys who don't know you and you don't know them so well, it is not so easy. It is why I find it difficult in public arenas sometimes.

After our visit to the café I heard a shout behind me as I walked back to the hotel. It was someone calling my name. I turned around and faced a man with his hand outstretched. I shook it. He said he was from a daily tabloid newspaper.

'I just wanted to know what you thought about the number of supporters crossing the Channel to support you?' What did I think? I thought the people giving up their time to come and cheer us on were incredible. They were making the experience even more memorable for everyone. I saw them as part of the team and their impeccable behaviour as a big part of why we are so proud and honoured to represent them and our nation. We were a stronger team for them being there.

What in fact did I say to this man? Nothing. It's not that I didn't want my feelings known, quite the opposite in fact. But it's not that simple. I take every chance I can to let the supporters know how important they are and what they mean to us but in order to do that properly and honestly I need to know exactly what I'm dealing with. In this situation I couldn't be sure. It seems silly, I know, and perhaps particularly paranoid, but I had been stung a few times before. I was miles from home and living in a different world. I didn't know what might be going on, what might be being said, and I didn't want to be led or coaxed into joining a public disagreement or controversy of any sort. I told him I'd thank the fans my own way in my own column and said goodbye. He followed me back all the way to the hotel asking me more questions. I concentrated on being polite. It was another awkward moment. Now I was worried I'd ticked him off and he was going to report that I'd snubbed travelling fans, the very fans whose sheer enthusiasm was about to boost our attacks and strengthen our defence.

In public my guard goes up and I struggle to lower it. Being singled out from the team is embarrassing and in my mind not justified. My team-mates laugh about it and support me in ways that enable me to be myself and cope with it all. Sometimes they make distractions so I can maintain some privacy, they do things that go way beyond the call of duty.

In a public place, I do get very conscious of the way I act, what I say and even what I am wearing. The reason lies somewhere in my over-inflated pride and ego, I know, but also in the importance I attach to setting a good example, sending a strong message and being the person I want to be. I am all too aware of the fact that decent reputations in this world can take a lifetime to build yet in a matter of seconds they can be completely destroyed. I want to do justice to my family and friends. I want to inspire and not offend but I also want to relax and enjoy living a normal life. When everyone's looking at me it suddenly feels more crucial that I do the right thing and say the right thing. Or don't say the wrong thing. When you are in front of a crowd there are so many interpretations that can be drawn from something very simple.

Many times my friends have overheard, or even been directly involved in, conversations with people who have expressed their opinions of me, not realising who they are talking to. No one can see into my mind to understand why I make the choices I do. None of us really has that deeper intuitive ability. Getting close to someone might give you some insight into his or her character, but generally that's not the case when we express opinions about someone else. When I realised the damage that being judged on my every move was doing to me, I began giving everyone else a break. I try always to start by giving someone the benefit of the doubt. I'd rather choose to like someone first than to start off on the wrong foot each time.

Blackie: It's all about you

'The only place you can win a football game is on the field. The only place you can lose is in your heart.' Darrell Royal

Everyone has an ego. It is our character, our identity. And it is a major factor in setting, meeting and celebrating our goals. So in that respect, it is a good thing. But it can have a darker side as well – involving feelings of greed, exploitation and cheating. If those emotions and motivations take hold, they can detract you from the task at hand – that of achieving your dreams. So we have to work hard to nullify our ego's darker effects. But it is a fine line. If we allow our ego to diminish completely then it can weaken our confidence because our self-perception falls. This, in turn, can stop us from contributing for fear of rejection, or from helping for fear of being ridiculed.

More often than not, such problems originate from worrying about what others think of us. Such concerns can dampen our enjoyment as we become increasingly conscious of how much emotion we display in our daily lives. We don't want to be seen enjoying ourselves in case people don't think that we're being serious enough. So we tone down our social, happy, fun self, not only because we want to maintain our privacy, but also because we don't want our reputation to 'suffer' as a consequence of our public displays of enjoyment. What we fail to realise however is that by spending too much time focusing on what we perceive others would like us to be, we lose the essence of who we are, what makes us tick. And so the world ends up having a negative perception of us regardless. To conquer this vicious cycle all that is required is that we focus our energies on remaining true to our 'self'.

There was a day to go before our semi-final showdown with France and I returned to the hotel as early as possible after my kicking and the final team rehearsal. I intended to relax all afternoon. When I returned to the hotel, someone had left the *Sun* newspaper on the floor by the room door. On the front page was my ugly mug and next to it read, '*Aviez peur, aviez très peur!*' which translated reads, 'Be afraid, be very afraid!' What!!! There I was ready to relax . . . I'd done all the hard work. All that was left was to look at the DVD clippings of the individual French players and peruse a couple of their recent games after dinner. During the next six hours I had a few movies, some nice food and a lovely walk planned. Maybe I would talk non-rugby nonsense to a few people on the phone. Now, after seeing the headline, and gauging the possible reaction of the public back home to it, I felt like I needed every minute up until kick-off the next night just to give my heart rate a chance to settle. It was back to trying to enjoy life again, rather than actually enjoying it.

We obviously carried our momentum with us all the way from the south to the north of France, from quarter-final to semi-final and hit the Stade de France surface running. Moments before we left the changing room for the field, after we had broken from our final team huddle, during the frantic phase when everyone is wondering if they need more to drink or where their tracksuit tops have gone for the anthems, Mike Catt turned to me with a purposeful look in his eyes and said with a smile, 'This is your time, Wilko! You know what to do.' Thanks mate! I do actually mean that. We were inside game time now. You can't add pressure at this point. It no longer matters because it's no longer about thinking. It's about doing. It was crunch time and Catty's demand was a statement of confidence in me (I think!) and not extra responsibility. It was up to me to do him proud and try to do my bit.

As the game neared its end I found myself somewhere I knew I'd been before. As I set the ball up on the tee I could hear the thump of my pulse against my temples. As I stood in that ridiculous position at the back of my run-up I saw my shirt (my very tight shirt) shaking more aggressively than ever. The boys had earned us a penalty wide out on the left. What did I feel about it? It was a challenging kick. It would put us in front. And I wanted it very badly. It was all coming back to me.

Kicking balls has been one of those acts for me which just feels right. When I'm in the zone it becomes my escape. When I do it right I feel a strong connection between what I want to happen and what actually happens – literally between me, my goal and my fulfilment.

I picture the result I desire in my mind's eye and I see it taking place, already feeling the sensation of the ball on my foot before I even start to approach it. It's like all but completing the jigsaw puzzle. The image is almost clear apart from the final few pieces.

That's where my actions come in. All I can do to fit those final pieces is to allow my practice to take over and guide me. It will provide the couple of key points I need to help me concentrate and execute the skill. Once the ball has gone, it's gone. There's no point in wasting energy on what happens to

"We obviously carried our momentum with us all the way from the south to the north of France, from quarter-final to semi-final and hit the Stade de France surface running"

it in the air, whether the scoreboard changes or how the crowd reacts. It will all fall into line with the quality of your contribution, what you deserve or what you are meant to experience. Simple really!

That night, I knew the ball would draw slightly on the breeze so I traced my line up to a point just inside the top of the near post. I saw it, I felt it and I believed it enough to ram it deep into my subconscious.

I felt the final piece of the jigsaw click into place as my foot struck the ball. When I raise my head I saw exactly what I wanted to see. The picture looked just as good in real life this time. I realised then what the connection between my desire and the outcome actually means: I can do anything I want if I put my mind to it. Maybe this one was worth all those misses. I should have had more faith.

About fifteen minutes later I was cycling away on an exercise bike outside the changing room. That's the way I recover after a game. It helps keeps the soreness away over the next few days. I'd need all the help I could get because we'd done it, we'd reached the final, and it felt out of this world. I felt sad for the French team, great guys who had carried unbelievable expectation and done exhilarating things, but our defence had been solid enough to consolidate Josh Lewsey's early try. We took our chances when it mattered and once again, the supporters held us together.

Winding down after the game like this, it all starts to make sense. I realised what I'd been striving for. The peace of mind and fulfilment I was feeling was still being made possible only by the fact we had won. Why does it have to be that way? Playing well and losing brings a different sensation; sometimes even a greater peace. But there was simply no feeling to match this one. Two World Cup finals in a row. I could have stayed there in that stadium all night. I knew that as soon as I left, the feeling would fade as the tranquil energy would be needed in a different guise ... as part of our final push for complete success.

18

Final Progress

How strange is this? Thirty minutes to go in the World Cup final with the result looming in the balance and I'm stood watching TV with 80,000 people

The Rugby World Cup final in 2003 was an amazing experience. But I didn't enjoy it the way I know I could have done. I wasn't ready and I didn't allow myself to.

Professionally speaking, I spent a large part of the next four years in a state of flux and it made me feel insecure about a lot of things. I was on a journey, not that I always knew it at various stages along the way, to finding out a lot about who, or what, I actually was and what my potential could be. It was pretty hard going at times. I found myself dragged through some harsh realities which I've tried to explain here in the pages of this book.

But experiencing all those ups and downs was essential if I was to achieve a 'bigger picture' view of my life.

Before I reached that realisation I had been defining myself, my purpose and my direction in terms of rugby only. I was a 'big player'. My sport, and the values I associated with it, was almost my entire identity. So when injury took that away from me, there wasn't a lot left. The foundations of who I was disappeared and virtually everything came crumbling down leaving nothing behind to work with. It seems ridiculous when I talk about it now, but it certainly happened. I couldn't get out of bed in the mornings. I had lost my motivation and a great deal of my reason for being. When I did get up, I just wanted to head straight back. This made me angry. I'd become the embodiment of the sort of thing I once stood firmly against. I didn't want to be at training, in rehab sessions, out kicking or amongst my team-mates. I felt weak and useless. I didn't feel like I fitted in anywhere.

> **If all the hard work, the dreams and 'the success' amounted only to this numb feeling, I asked myself quite seriously, what was the point in trying any more?**

It all sounds a bit sensational I know – maybe hard to believe even – but as an obsessive person who had aligned their total worth and 'self' to what they do, then it was bound to happen sooner or later, especially with the enormous pride I took in it all.

When I was playing well and winning, I didn't worry about the lack of balance achieved. After all, it seemed to be the very thing that delivered the results I wanted. But injuries and speculation of retirement brought enormous instability. That opened the door to some dark thoughts which, when repeated thousands of times a day, created a pretty serious void in my life. The only thing I could find to fill it was rugby and professional sport. And if that wasn't there, what then? If all the hard work, the dreams and 'the success' amounted only to this numb feeling, I asked myself quite seriously, what was the point in trying any more?

" In 2003, we looked to our momentum and our winning history for the resilience we needed in our toughest times. In 2007, we were looking to our spirit, courage, togetherness and the fact that we were peaking at the right time to take us all the way "

But I got past that. It was hard and painful at times, but slowly I began to fit the pieces together. Tough times, disappointments, setbacks were all steering me towards embracing that missing sense of balance. I began to see the benefit of a more peaceful day-to-day existence, in which I could revel in a trip to the beach or an afternoon sat at the piano the same way I already did between two loud whistle blasts on a weekend.

And it all came together beautifully – the injuries, the lessons, the mental torment, the self-exploration and the hard work – to put me back on one of the most privileged sporting stages, a second World Cup final. Against all the odds. The decision of how I would play it this time (I mean that in more ways than one) was ultimately mine.

In the summer before the 2003 final, Australia were beaten by New Zealand who scored fifty points. I made a crass but helpful judgement at the time, that the experience made them less deserving than us because we hadn't lost for a year and for four years never really by more than one single score. I felt it made us stronger. It was flawed and illogical, unsympathetic too. I realise this now but I really bought into it then. Four years on, I was having to turn that interpretation 180° because we were about to face the team who had just destroyed us 36–0 a month earlier. By my own previous assessment, this should have meant we might as well stay on the bus.

In 2003, we looked to our momentum and our winning history for the resilience we needed in our toughest times. In 2007, we were looking to our spirit, courage, togetherness and the fact that we were peaking at the right time to take us all the way. Losing 36–0 was a crucial brick in building our strong foundation. Without it, we may well have crumbled like I had at times done personally. We had to draw inspiration from that tough time and use it to propel this one last effort.

Walking out on to the Stade de France pitch, where South Africa had drop kicked us out of the Rugby World Cup in 1999 and smashed us four weeks previously, was an unbelievable experience. The tuneful cheers of the loyal England fan-base made one hell of an atmosphere underneath the raucous fireworks. All that filled our minds at this point, however, were thoughts of our first involvements in the game, on top of a stack of self-confidence, collective belief and positivity.

The sight of Mathew Tait's heels is one I had experienced a couple of times in Newcastle training games. He has great side-stepping ability and fantastic pace – as well as horrible coloured boots! This time though, I was happy to see him accelerating away. He beat three defenders and just fell short of the try line after a blistering fifty-metre run. I headed left of the ruck screaming for the ball. We were about to walk in a try. South Africa quite cleverly, and quite illegally, slowed the ball down on the floor. When Andy Gomarsall got his hands on it, two green-shirted defenders had made it back onside. I batted on the pass to Mark Cueto under pressure and he dived in while being hit into the corner flag.

How strange is this? Thirty minutes to go in the World Cup final with the result looming in the balance and I'm stood watching TV with 80,000 people. On the big screen it looked good, then it looked bad, then it looked good, then I could no longer look any more. The decision went the other way. We fought hard after that, not willing to accept that perhaps our moment had gone. We never found the five-point score we needed and thought we had. South Africa had deservedly won the 2007 Rugby World Cup, by fifteen points to six.

I was totally distraught but you know what, I enjoyed this one – at least a little bit anyway! I still had a lot of work to do, I recognised that. When I left the hotel room before the game I was in tatters because of the nerves. When I returned to my hotel room much later that night I would also be in tatters but for very different reasons.

Blackie: 'A tale of two teams . . .

'. . . one meeting expectancy, the other overcoming adversity.'

Steve Black

The build up to the 2003 World Cup had been ordered, it had longevity and ensured that England had a tried and tested team in place to take on the world Down Under. They were well-practised and well-rehearsed as a group and that was probably the difference between them winning or losing. They believed in themselves and the country believed in them. There was a mass optimism associated with that campaign that would have swayed even the most hardened sceptic.

The following World Cup in 2007 was different. The build up from a couple of years beforehand was fragmented. Political overtures, ambitions and constraints were brought to bear on the national team's preparations. Sir Clive moved on to that different-shaped ball and Andy Robinson stepped up to the plate. Sir Clive was a difficult person to follow after the success he'd had and in any case, it was a different assignment that Andy faced – trying to rebuild an ageing squad of players, many of whom were probably just past their absolute best. The ongoing debate between club and country looked set to run and run and the ethos of innovation that had been introduced by Sir Clive seemed to slow in both research and application.

Andy's a good, decent man with a tremendous work ethic and a passionate love of the game but the team struggled and confidence fell away, not just in the players, but in Andy. The seemingly inevitable happened and Andy moved on.

Another promotion from within saw Brian Ashton step into the head coach's shoes. Brian has a wealth of experience and, in hindsight, that fact probably underwrote an unbelievable performance by an under-attack and under-pressure English team at the 2007 World Cup. Whatever the media and public want to take from the newspaper stories and players' memoirs in the aftermath of the World Cup, the fact is that group of coaches and players came within a whisker of retaining the World Cup.

Enormous credit is due to each of them for that. Had Mark Cueto managed to avoid just touching the line before grounding the ball following Mathew Tait's stunning break then the result could have been different. And let's be fair, a few years ago, before the advent of technology employed to determine one way or another the validity of a try, that score would have been given say eighty per cent of the time as the emotions and adrenaline soared. The reaction of the players would have clinched it. But it wasn't to be. Justice was done and South Africa went on to lift the trophy.

The great father of management science, Peter Drucker, said that he'd studied successful people and teams throughout the business world for sixty-five years and that just about every team/manager/leader did it differently. Some were extroverts, some almost reclusive; some dictatorial, some very democratic; some the traditional inspiring leaders, others so quiet you wouldn't know they were there! All very different but still successful.

We need to have an open mind and not just try to apply the same methods as someone else has when they were successful. If you do, chances are they won't work. Take the lessons learnt from others of course, that's a must, but apply them in your way; in the way that best suits your players and your staff.

Brian Ashton was so close...I know, I know, yet so far. But he could have won it, and by employing totally different methods from Sir Clive. Questions of who, and what methods, are better are in effect irrelevant. As with aesthetics in art, beauty is in the eyes of the beholder! The truth is Sir Clive won and Brian didn't but he made a heck of a fist of it. After the 36–0 South Africa defeat in the opening round of games, the players and coaches recognised that they were and are better than that performance and result. They grabbed the tournament by the scruff of the neck, pooled all the individual talents and desires and used the newly acquired underdog status to rally around themselves in what seemed to the outside world to be a lost cause.

The team's support gained momentum and with that momentum came enormous passion, and a belief in the team that started to fill the nation with optimism and expectancy. By the time they played South Africa again, in the final this time, England had turned it around so much that the team genuinely believed they'd win the game and retain their world title. Within the squad and management there was a togetherness and synergy building. It was almost irresistible . . . almost.

As for Jonny, the way he stepped forward from injury, playing through constant pain and discomfort, it almost became his finest hour. As so many of the players said during the tournament, his mere presence on the field energised and lifted the spirits of the entire camp and challenged the belief and resolve of the opposition. That's the true mark of greatness for a team player.

From Rob Andrew, who showed a restrained and dignified managerial presence throughout, to Brian, who allowed the team to gain momentum, in my experience, an incredibly difficult thing to do, to the effect of Phil Vickery's captaincy and associated senior players acting as cheerleaders to solicit a performance out of nowhere, there was so much for all of us to learn about pushing towards success in a team environment. And as for comparing the managerial styles of Sir Clive and Brian, there's much to learn from both, albeit that they were very different from each other.

A friend of mine, without time to change after his own rugby game for Southend RFC, hopped on a plane and made it out for kick-off. This put a lot into perspective for me. He joined my family, a few friends, my girlfriend and me after the game and we chatted about the whole journey, not just the final or the obvious disappointment. As we reminisced it became clear it had indeed been one hell of an effort not just from us (the England squad) but from everyone involved in supporting the team in France and back home. Society too often creates a massive gap between first and second place in such situations but it didn't mean we had to. I said before that no one likes to come second. That is true. I certainly don't. I had been on the winning side and experienced all the associated glory. But now it was my time to see it from a different angle. If that is what I had to do, then that is what I would do. I desperately

> *When I returned to my hotel room much later that night I would also be in tatters but for very different reasons*

wanted to win. But we didn't. I had to take that and try and use it. Trying to focus on this new angle became a bit tricky later on

307

though. Or, more precisely, it became a bit blurry.

Phil Vickery – Captain Marvellous – had stipulated that everyone was to stick together and join him at the private celebrations later that night. Fair enough, a good idea I thought. We began this journey together, let's end it together.

Stood at the bar with special people around me, who had supported me wholeheartedly, and me them, felt great. We had lost such a big game, the back-to-back World Cup goal possibly gone forever. So close and yet so far. But so what. We had been perfect in every way because there was nothing more we could have done. We needed every single little drop of inspiration and energy to get to where we did. I suddenly realised this chapter of my life and our lives had to be celebrated and stored in its rightful place. It had to be given the respect it deserved, but in hindsight we may have given it a bit too much that night! The photographs of us all a little worse for wear that we encountered in the papers the next day (courtesy of a digital camera) were a touch embarrassing, but in all honesty quite a liberating experience for me – especially when I saw the one of Mathew Tait with no shirt on wearing a pink cowboy hat.

When I woke later that Sunday to a knock at the room door, I came face-to-face with Owen Slot and Marc Aspland, ready to work on my column. All due respect to the boys, but they were the two people I probably wanted to see less than anyone at that moment, considering the state I was in. My piece that week was probably one of my best; the photo of me accompanying it undoubtedly my worst. It was however the perfect way to wave goodbye to a great period of my life, filed neatly under 'P' for progress.

19

In a Perfect World

> *"Searching for perfect, lasting results in a world of forever evolving and unforeseeable events has been a very expensive and unforgiving vocation at times"*

After years spent chasing dreams, trying to protect myself, searching for answers, losing my way then believing I had it again, believing I had found the balance – I found myself dropped from the England team. It was only five games after reaching the 2007 World Cup final.

And the future will hold more unpredictable ups and downs. I am wise enough to know now that there is no benefit to be gained from getting negative about it. I am not going to punish myself for the fact that it has happened. I am going to learn and I am going to come back stronger. Life, and especially professional sport, is a rollercoaster ride indeed. It is full of soaring highs and plunging lows.

Would a fairground attraction which continues to climb gently and never drops actually be a really enjoyable experience? Would there be a big queue? To fully appreciate the rises surely you need to have felt a big fall or two. The plummeting down should form part of the exhilarating experience of living. Is part of the excitement of life found in the liberating effect of losing a bit of what I used to feel was the be-all and end-all of existing? Is it the adrenalin rush that comes with having to react and survive amidst chaos? The accelerated learning experience offered by such perceived failure and disappointment is definitely part of it.

The big dips and the steep drops on rollercoasters are stretches of the journey which gather speed for you as well as excitement. They build up your momentum. They certainly provide me with the power and ultimately the motivation to attack and overcome the next stage and to draw the next fantastic experience towards myself. I try to embrace the low moments and harness all that power.

I was born a perfectionist. For as long as I can remember I have fought for an ideal world and my own flawless self image within it. I had a fairly detailed image in my mind of a perfect life, a perfect career and myself as a perfect person. It was all about being invincible, being successful, being the best and never putting a foot wrong. I looked around me, at the people, objects and experiences of my life as an indicator of how I was getting on. If it wasn't how I wanted it, then I could really get out of control.

I have left these beliefs firmly behind. Searching for perfect, lasting results in a world of forever evolving and unforeseeable events has been a very expensive and unforgiving vocation at times. Expecting such high standards of return from the often uncontrollable and the inexplicable has cost me a great deal.

If perfection is to be found in the objects and experiences in front of my eyes then it must, I now realise, also be constantly adapting and changing form. And if that is so, how then can we ever hold perfection in our hands? How can we make it count? When I used to try to grasp perfection, every moment became a pass or a fail. There was no liberating peace.

> *If I have thought, however, that perfection somehow lies purely in acquiring these targets, then I have been misguided*

When England won the Rugby World Cup in 2003, it was a perfect goal achieved. I expected time to stop, allowing me forever to celebrate and embrace the joy, to keep it fresh in my hands. It didn't. Sometimes I think time even sped up. It definitely moved on and left me falling dangerously behind. Before I knew it, in the passing of one night, my perfect moment had been and gone and I was suddenly aware of myself at breakfast that next morning wondering, 'Where the hell do I go next?' With that journey behind me, I felt I was without purpose and, by my own rules, more imperfect than I'd ever been.

I use tomorrow as a target to be better than I was today. I have set ambitions and goals of all kinds throughout my life and launching myself towards them undoubtedly adds a fantastic, worthy sense of purpose and fulfilment to the experience of being alive. If I have thought, however, that perfection somehow lies purely in acquiring these targets, then I have been misguided.

We all begin as perfection personified. We all want something different from our life's journey and there can be no set path to follow. If we look too far outside for answers then whatever our dream of the ideal existence is, and regardless of whether we achieve it or not, it will ultimately end in a degree of disappointment. It may never be enough.

There is a saying which I think sums this up, perfectly. 'Perfection is not held by the man who has everything he wants but thrives in him who gives everything he has.' I think it might have been me who made the saying up though.

There will always be bigger houses than yours, faster cars, sunnier climates, greater tacklers, faster runners, more accurate kickers and greener grass somewhere in the world or sometime in the future, and they can steal the perfect parts of your life away.

Blackie: Just a perfect day

'It's Groundhog Day!' Inspired by Bill Murray

The concept of perfection is an interesting one. In its widely understood form, perfection probably isn't attainable, certainly over any length of time. But in special moments, we can use the term as a superlative to highlight the quality of a particular point in time, or indeed the effect the moment has on the prevailing circumstances. This is probably the way we use the term 'perfection' in sport.

The perfect score of Nadia Comaneci, the sensational Romanian gymnast, who produced a string of, in the judge's eyes, perfect Olympian performances catapulted her to global fame. When those 'tens' are achieved at such a high level, it's an undoubtedly wonderful experience for the performer and observer alike.

But striving for those moments, day in and day out – that's impossible isn't it? Well yes, but a new take on perfection could be to focus on giving your very best, one day at a time. That is achievable, yet strangely, almost no one actually puts that idea into practice. Why? It is probably because until you've honed the new habit, the daily process, the process of consciously doing it is difficult. It's also just plain hard work.

An old saying states that many real opportunities in life pass us by because they are disguised as hard work. While the propensity to work hard has had perennial worth, maybe perfection can be viewed as applying ourselves as effectively as possible at any given time. That might mean resting when rest is the best option to take; going to the gym; following a scientific programme to the letter; practising passing/kicking/ tackling for an optimal length of time. In other words, it can be regarded as whatever the appropriate behaviour is at that time on any particular day.

Vince Lombardi's famous quote 'Winning is everything' has always been bastardised much to the detriment of its intention. The actual quote, which I heard years back but unfortunately can't remember the source, was, as far as I remember it, 'Winning isn't everything, it can't be – but trying to win undoubtedly is.' I suppose that's our message here, trying to win by giving all you've got on that particular day. Maybe that day comprises of hanging out with your friends, going to the movies, having a meal, glass of wine, and so forth. If it does, then that's what you've got to do! Perfection, in more ways than one. Of course too many days of that type of perfect behaviour may lead to an imperfect result . . . The point is, of course, to achieve your goal on that day, on your way to realising the bigger picture.

Sometimes athletes train too hard, too many days in a row, striving to be perfect, and then become jaded for the game. On review it's decided the player isn't fit enough so, guess what, they are trained harder the week after to get them fit! The accumulative fatigue takes its toll and a spiral of mediocrity ensues. Careers are lost in so many cases this way, when there's not a problem with talent or natural athletic ability. The problem is with the training programme. Players do too much, or have too much imposed on them and that's definitely not perfection.

Therefore, with this in mind I'd suggest that having the discipline to do the right thing daily while allowing yourself to do what needs to be done, whether that be hard or easy, physical or social, grants you lots of moments of excellence. So you can bask in wave after wave of perfection.

If I concentrate solely on what my own contribution is, including my intentions and my efforts, then I start to play by a different set of rules – a set through which perfection becomes a demanding yet eminently achievable, fulfilling and lasting constant: whether you are winning or losing in any area of life, never stop being the absolute best you can be at that single moment and always try to help others in their pursuit of their own perfection.

Comparisons to others will never be relevant in this scheme of things, and the outcome, whatever it is, will only serve to provide lessons and new paths to something even more perfect. My goals will be achieved because I will have been as good as I can be. The experiences and sensations will last because they will be connected as one long string of enjoyable moments – a celebration of something unique that is solely mine, that no one person or thing can ever take away from me.

So I still believe in the existence of perfection. It is offered to all of us every day in the shape of unbelievable potential in an interrelated world.

If two people give something their best shot yet only one 'succeeds', is one more perfect that the other? I don't believe so. For me, perfection is search-

> " *My goals will be achieved because I will have been as good as I can be* "

ing deep to find and unleash the unique talent in the best of ourselves while having the compassion not to miss the chance to help others do the same. So enjoy it, make the most of each opportunity, every second and then let it go. The rest, as I have learned through experience, is being taken care of, however hard that is to believe sometimes.

Bibliography/
Further Reading

Albom, M. (1997) *Tuesdays with Morrie*, Time Warner Books.

Alexander, G. (2005) *Tales from the Top*, Piatkus.

Allison, J. and Gedimen, D. (2007) *This I Believe*, Holt.

Adler, B. (2003) *Coaching Matters*, Brassey's Inc.

Austin, J. (2006) *What No One Ever Tells You About Leading for Results*, Kaplan Publishing.

Bronson, P. (2007) *Why Do I Love These People?* Vintage Books.

Buckingham, M. (2007) *Go Put Your Strengths to Work*, Simon and Schuster.

Bull, S. (2006) *The Game Plan*, Capstone.

Butler-Bowdon, T. (2003) *50 Self-help Classics*, Nicholas Brealey Publishing.

Butler-Bowdon, T. (2004) *50 Success Classics*, Nicholas Brealey Publishing.

Butler-Bowdon, T. (2005) *50 Spiritual Classics*, Nicholas Brealey Publishing.

Butler-Bowdon, T. (2007) *50 Psychology Classics*, Nicholas Brealey Publishing.

Butler-Bowdon, T. (2008) *50 Prosperity Classics*, Nicholas Brealey Publishing.

Byrne, R. (2006) *The Secret*, Simon and Schuster.

Canfield, J., Hansen, M.V. and Hewitt, L. (2000) *The Power of Focus*, Vermilion.

Canfield, J., Hansen, M.V., Carter, C.C., Palomares, S., Williams, L.K. and Winch, B.L. (2005) *Chicken Soup for the Soul: Stories for a Better World*, Health Communications Inc.

Charan, R. (2007) *Know-how*, Random House Business Books.

Chopra, D. (2003) *Spontaneous Fulfilment of Desire*, Harmony Publishing.

Coelho, P. (2004) *Life*, Harper Collins.

Coffman, C. and Gonzalez-Malina, G. (2004) *Follow this Path*, Random House Business Books.

Covey, S.R. (2004) *The 8th Habit*, Simon and Schuster.

Covey, S.R. (2006) *Everyday Greatness*, Rutledge Hill Press.

Covey, S.R. (2005) *The 7 Habits of Highly Effective People: Personal Workbook*, Simon and Schuster.

Drucker, P.F. (2006) *Classic Drucker*, Harvard Business School Press.

Dyer, W.W. (1998) *Wisdom of the Ages: 60 Days to Enlightenment*, Thorsons.

Dyer, W.W. (2007) *The Invisible Force*, Hay House.

Edwards, H. (2005) *You Play to Win the Game*, McGraw-Hill.

Gautier, F. (2008) *The Guru of Joy*, Hay House.

Goleman, D. (1996) *Emotional Intelligence*, Bloomsbury.

Goleman, D. (1998) *Working With Emotional Intelligence*, Bloomsbury.

Goleman, D., Boyatzis, R. E. and McKee, A. (2002) *The New Leaders*, Little Brown.

Goleman, D. (2006) *Social Intelligence*, Hutchinson.

Gostick, A. and Elton, C. (2005) *A Carrot a Day*, Wiley.

Hanh, T.N. (1995) *Living Buddha, Living Christ*, Riverhead Books.

Hay, L.L. (1996) *Gratitude*, Hay House.

Haynes, A. (2007) *Time, Money, Happiness*, Pier 9.

Hicks, E. and Hicks, J. (2007) *The Astonishing Power of Emotions*, Hay House.

Holtz, L. (1998) *Winning Every Day*, Harper Business.

Imai, M. (1986) *Kaizen*, McGraw-Hill.

Jacobs, A. (2005) *The Ocean of Wisdom*, O Books.

Jones, C. and Doren, K. (2000) *Be the Ball*, Andrews McMeel Publishing.

Jones, L.B. (1995) *Jesus, CEO*, Hyperion.

Kanter, R.M. (1997) *Rosabeth Moss Kanter on the Frontiers of Management*, Harvard Business School Press.

Kanter, R.M. (2004) *Confidence*, Crown Business.

Kasparov, G. (2007) *How Life Imitates Chess*, William Heinemann.

Katie, B. (2002) *Loving What Is*, Harmony Books.

Katzenbach, J.R. (ed) (1998) *The Work of Teams*, Harvard Business School Press.

Kline, N. (1999) *Time to Think*, Ward Lock.

Kotter, J.P. and Cohen, D.S. (2002) *The Heart of Change*, Harvard Business School Press.

Kyokai, B.D. *The Teaching of Buddha*, Bukkyo Dendo Kyokai.

Lama, D. (2003) *How to Practise*, Rider & Co.

Lama, D. and Cutler, H. (1999) *The Art of Happiness*, Hodder Mobius.

Lama, D. and Hopkins, J. (2007) *How to See Yourself as You Really Are*, Simon and Schuster Audio.

Leighton, A. (2007) *On Leadership*, Random House Business Books.

Lipton, B.H. (2005) *The Biology of Belief*, Hay House.

Lombardi, V. (2001) *What It Takes to Be Number 1*, McGraw-Hill.

MacKay, H. (1990) *Beware the Naked Man Who Offers You His Shirt*, Piatkus.

Maxwell, J.C. (1993) *Developing the Leader Within You*, Thomas Nelson.

Maxwell, J.C. (2001) *The 17 Indisputable Laws of Teamwork*, Thomas Nelson.

Maxwell, J.C. (2002) *Your Road Map for Success*, Thomas Nelson.

Maxwell, J.C. (2003) *Thinking for A Change*, Warner Business Books.

Maxwell, J.C. (2005) *The 360° Leader*, Thomas Nelson.

Maxwell, J.C. (2007) *Talent Is Never Enough*, Thomas Nelson.

Maxwell, J.C. (2007) *The 21 Irrefutable Laws of Leadership*, Thomas Nelson.

McTaggart, L. (2003) *The Field*, Harper Element Books.

Metcalfe, F. and Gallagher-Hateley, B.J. (2001) *What Would Buddha Do at Work?* Seastone.

Millman, D. (1993) *The Life You Were Born To Live*, HJ Kramer.

Millman, D. (2000) *Living on Purpose*, New World Library.

Millman, D. (2000) *The Way of the Peaceful Warrior*, HJ Kramer.

Mintzberg, H. (2004) *Managers Not MBAs*, FT: Prentice Hall.

Moawad, B. (2005) *Whatever It Takes*, Compendium Publishing and Communications.

Neuschel, R.P. (2005) *The Servant Leader*, Kogan Page.

Neill, M. (2006) *You Can Have What You Want*, Hay House.

Niven, D. (2002) *The 100 Simple Secrets of Successful People*, HarperCollins.

Niven, D. (2005) *The 100 Simple Secrets of Happy People*, HarperCollins.

Niven, D. (2006) *The 100 Simple Secrets of Great Relationships*, HarperCollins.

O'Connor, J. and Lages, A. (2007) *How Coaching Works*, A & C Black.

Osteen, J. (2007) *Starting Your Best Life Now*, FaithWords.

Pattakos, A. (2004, 2008) *Prisoners of Our Thoughts*, BK Publishing.

Posner, K. (2003) *Encouraging the Heart*, Jossey-Bass.

Rohn, J. (1994) *The Treasury of Quotes*, Health Communications.

Rubin, E. (2004) *Ambition*, Viking Canada.

Schembechler, B. (2007) *Bo's Lasting Lessons*, Grand Central Publishing.

Seaman, D. (ed) (2005) *The Real Meaning of Life*, New World Library.

Seligman, M.E.P. (2003) *Authentic Happiness*, Nicholas Brealey Publishing Ltd.

Sharma, R. (2004) *The Monk Who Sold His Ferrari*, Harper Element.

Sharma, R. (2006) *The Greatness Guide*, Harper Element.

Sharma, R. (2007) *The Greatness Guide: Book 2*, Harper Element.

Shinar, Y. (2007) *Think Like A Winner*, Vermilion.

Snair, S. (2005) *West Point Leadership Lessons*, Sourcebooks Inc.

Starr, J. (2008) *The Coaching Manual*, Prentice-Hall.

Taylor, C. (2005) *Walking the Talk*, Random House Business Books.

Taylor, D. (2007) *The Naked Coach*, Capstone.

Tichy, N.M. and Sherman, S. (1994) *Control Your Destiny or Someone Else Will*, HarperBusiness.

Tolle, E. (2001) *The Power of Now*, Hodder Mobius.

Tolle, E. (2005) *A New Earth*, Michael Joseph.

Tolle, E. (2006) *Through the Open Door*, Sounds True Inc.

Torre, J. and Dreher, H. (1999) *Joe Torre's Ground Rules for Winners*, Hyperion.

Tracy, B. (2001) *Focal Point*, Amacom.

Tracy, B. (2002) *Victory*, Amacom.

Tracy, B. (2003) *Change Your Thinking, Change Your Life*, Wiley.

Tracy, B. (2003) *Goals*, BK Publishing.

Tracy, B. (2004) *Time Power*, Amacom.

Tracy, B. (2005) *Turbo Coach*, Amacom.

Tracy, B. (2006) *Million Dollar Habits*, Entrepreneur Press.

Wattles, W.D. (2007) *The Science of Success*, Sterling.

Welch, J. and Welch, S. (2005) *Winning*, HarperCollins.

Woodward, C. (2004) *Winning*, Hodder & Stoughton.

Various, (1990) *Manage People, Not Personnel*, Harvard Business School Press.

Zander, B. and Zander, R.S. (2000) *The Art of Possibility*, Harvard Business School Press.

Ziglar, Z. (2001) *You Can Reach The Top*, River Oak Publishing.

Ziglar, Z. (2006) *Better than Good*, Integrity Publishers.

Picture Credits

Credits are listed according to the order the pictures appear on each page, left to right, top to bottom.

Page 1: Colorsport, Action Images, PA Photos, PA Photos, PA Photos

Page 2: PA Photos, PA Photos, Getty Images, PA Photos

Page 3: Action Images/Jason O'Brien, PA Photos, Offside/ L'Equipe, PA Photos

Page 4: Getty Images, Getty Images, PA Photos, Getty Images, PA Photos

Page 5: PA Photos, Getty Images, Getty Images, Offside/L'Equipe, PA Photos

Page 6: PA Photos, Getty Images, Getty Images, PA Photos

Page 7: Getty Images, PA Photos, Marc Aspland/NI Syndication, Getty Images

Page 8: PA Photos, Getty Images, Dave Rogers for Getty Images

"Wilkinson going for a drop goal. This could be their place in the final. And Wilkinson has done it!"

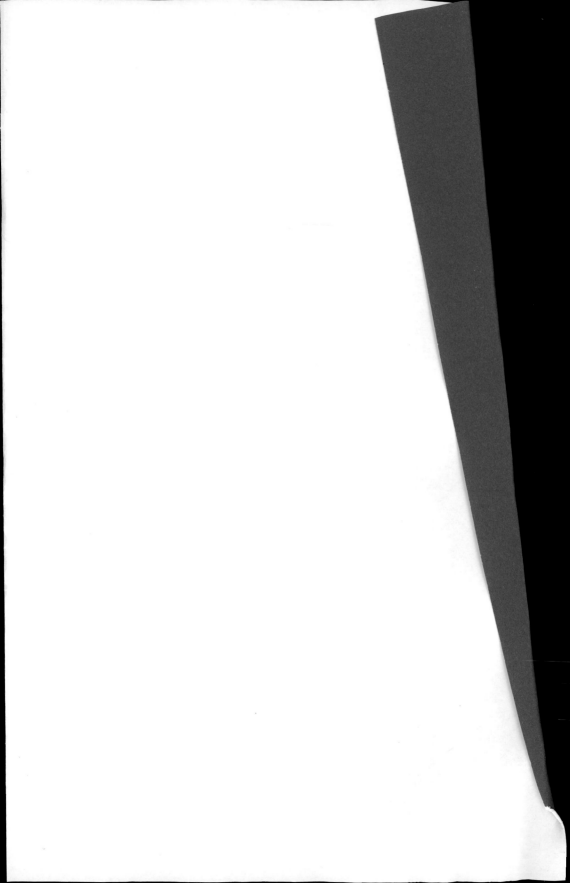